A Thousand Honey Creeks Later

MUSIC / CULTURE
A Series from Wesleyan University Press
Edited by George Lipsitz, Susan McClary, and Robert Walser

Published titles

My Music by Susan D. Crafts, Daniel Cavicchi, Charles Keil,
and the Music in Daily Life Project

*Running with the Devil: Power, Gender, and Madness in
Heavy Metal Music* by Robert Walser

Subcultural Sounds: Micromusics of the West by Mark Slobin

Upside Your Head! Rhythm and Blues on Central Avenue by Johnny Otis

Dissonant Identities: The Rock'n'Roll Scene in Austin, Texas by Barry Shank

Black Noise: Rap Music and Black Culture in Contemporary America by Tricia Rose

Club Cultures: Music, Media and Distinction by Sarah Thornton

Music, Society, Education by Christopher Small

Listening to Salsa: Gender, Latin Popular Music, and Puerto Rican Cultures
by Frances Aparicio

Any Sound You Can Imagine: Making Music/Consuming Technology by Paul Théberge

Voices of Bali: Energies and Perceptions in Vocal and Dance Theater by Edward Herbst

A Thousand Honey Creeks Later: My Life in Music from Basie to Motown—and Beyond
by Preston Love

PRESTON LOVE

✳

A Thousand Honey Creeks Later

MY LIFE IN MUSIC
FROM BASIE TO MOTOWN —
AND BEYOND

Introduction by George Lipsitz

✳

WESLEYAN UNIVERSITY PRESS

Published by University Press of New England

Hanover & London

WESLEYAN UNIVERSITY PRESS
Published by University Press of New England, Hanover, NH 03755
© 1997 by Preston Love
All rights reserved
Printed in the United States of America 5 4 3 2 1
CIP data appear at the end of the book

Contents

✳

Illustrations

＊

Foreword

Norman Love

Many of my dad's older musician friends have seemed reluctant to accept and realize his enormous contribution to first alto sax big-band playing since he first joined Count Basie on lead sax in 1943. Even more so, these friends and former colleagues underestimate Dad's rather newfound ability as an improvisational soloist. This is probably due to the fact that in his early career Dad's total focus and interest was in playing first alto sax in the reed section. Many consequently regarded him as *only* a lead player with little, if any, ability as a soloist, except for an occasional ballad melody.

Dad himself has always treated his solo improvisation very casually, but that image of his early career is no longer valid today, as he began to take improvisation more seriously in his late thirties and early forties. At one stage of his early career, Dad looked on solo improvisation with disdain. His "thing," his interest, was in playing parts or only taking an occasional ballad solo to highlight his pretty tone. Dad began to take interest in improvisation about thirty years ago and found that he had more talent for jazz and R&B improvisation than most ever dreamed. It is my feeling that Dad plays much better solos than many of his contemporaries who gained much more fame than him. Of course, many of them were overrated anyway.

I am in Omaha, Denver, and Los Angeles often, and musician friends of mine rave over Dad's "tasty" and "fitting" solos that are also surprisingly "modern" for his advanced age. He is the first to admit or protest that he will never be a Sonny Stitt, Lou Donaldson, or Cannonball Adderly, but on nights that Dad and I perform together, I am amazed at the solos that Dad gets off on certain tunes. After all, even though everyone can't be Charlie Parker, my Dad's solos have to be rated as world-class. On every European jazz festival at which Dad performed, he received rave reviews. At the Birmingham, England Jazz Festival, a reviewer said, "Preston Love played a memorable 'Take the A Train' on his tenor sax." At the Northern Festival in Holland, another reported that "Preston Love's solo on 'Harlem Nocturne' literally broke it up."

In 1985, I replaced Dad on alto sax in the Johnny Otis band when the band returned to the states from Europe. In Lake Tahoe, we members of the band hung out for several days with members of the Ray Charles band, which was also in town. Most of their talk was about how fantastic Preston Love sounded when Ray's band spent a night backstage listening to the Otis band at the North Sea (Holland) Festival. "Man, your Dad's alto really lit up that stage," one of them told me. "Norm, your Dad was my reason for standing backstage for Johnny's whole show on both nights. He sure is an underrated player," said another.

For all of the instruments that Dad plays, I think his improvisation is best on the flute, although I would have to rate him as one of the finer rhythm and blues tenor saxophone soloists, too. Whatever limitations he had on soloing when he was young have certainly been overcome later in life. Both my brother Ritchie and I enjoy popularity as saxophone players in the Omaha area, but we often call Dad in to play solos for recording dates in my brother's studio (located in Dad's basement). Many of the young singers and players even request Dad for their backup music. I don't think any book about Preston Love should neglect the musical aspect of his life, especially as seen through the eyes of younger musicians like myself and my contemporaries.

Preface

Johnny Otis

With all his intellectual sharpness and artistic ability, I sometimes wonder if the most amazing thing about Preston Love might not be his uncanny memory. As I read the manuscript for this book, I was bowled over by his ability to recall in sharp detail events of forty and fifty years ago. He deals with things that occurred a half century ago as though they happened yesterday. I was transported back to the time when we were two teenage musicians hoping to make a place for ourselves in the fascinating world of black show business while also trying to understand and deal with the crippling cruelties of a racist America. Time and time again, I would think to myself, "Damn! How does he remember all that early stuff so clearly?" At one point, I muttered aloud, and my wife awoke and asked, "What are you cussing about?" I said, "Phyllis, Preston is reliving our early times in his book with such accuracy, it's just amazing. He recalls names, dates, and details."

Moms Mabley used to explain that when you got old you'd only have one nerve left. When someone would upset her, she'd say "Listen, I've only got one nerve left, and you're getting on *it*." Having such a fuzzy recollection mechanism myself, I'd often wonder if I had even one functioning nerve synapse left to my name. Not to worry, Preston's reminiscences have brought the good old days (and the bad ones, too) back into sharp focus. My memory banks weren't erased after all, just sleeping, waiting for Preston to jog them back to the surface with this book.

Even as a kid, Preston was a dominant personality—highly opinionated, and very emotional about his ideas on music. Woe to the individual who voiced a negative thought about the Count Basie band. A sharp dressing down was the least he could expect. Most of us in the Lloyd Hunter and Nat Towles bands shared his enthusiasm for the Basie band, but Preston served as our philosophical spearhead. The young midwestern players of the 1940s were in awe of Preston's abilities on lead alto saxophone. At a time when most of the men and women on the instrument were marginal readers and possessed a flat, droning tone, Preston played with a bright "singing" tone à la the great Earle Warren, and he could read music with the best of the adult pros of the era.

Preston was known as a Young Turk who would not take any abuse from anyone, and that went for black or white, north or south. He had been a middleweight Golden Gloves contender, and that fact underscored the respect he received from his peers. Whenever we were in the South together, I used to hope that none of those peckerwood racists would start anything, because Preston would drop that devastating right hand on him and we'd all get killed down there! Fortunately, Preston was not with us when we did experience racist episodes in the deep South. I knew, just as most of us knew, that we couldn't win, so better to keep our cool and live to see another day.

I don't want to create the impression that Preston was a mean guy with a chip on his shoulder. He was, and still is, just the opposite—easygoing and fun loving. In this respect he is very much like his late mother, Mexie Love. She was a woman with a super sharp mind and a wonderful sense of humor. We were close friends and I cherish the memory of the many hours I spent listening to her spellbound as she recalled the times of her youth in the deep southern town of Minden, Louisiana. Mex lived to be 103, and Preston, it seems has inherited her longevity genes. He refuses to grow old. At age seventy-five, he is physically and mentally indefatigable. His work day and weekly schedules would be too much for most people years younger than him. His activities include working in the sales department of Omaha's African-American weekly, the *Omaha Star*, playing regularly at a local nightclub, lecturing and doing musical residency programs at midwestern universities, plus going fishing at every available opportunity.

Mexie Love and I were (and I still am) watermelon addicts. During my early years in Omaha, and later, when we both lived in Los Angeles, we would buy a big melon and kill it off all by ourselves. "Isn't it ridiculous," she would say, "somehow a silly stigma has developed about colored folks liking watermelon. What I want to know is, who in their right mind would *not* like watermelon!" We would laugh and keep on chompin'. I looked forward to those times because I knew I was possibly going to hear some fascinating things about the turn-of-the-century South. She could verbally reconstruct that racist era with a riveting delivery that would leave me wide-eyed. But she was just as apt to convey the sweet sense of being an impressionable young girl in the beautiful southland and do so with a poetic flair.

Preston and I share a penchant for fresh seafood. Whenever we happened to be in San Francisco or Boston at the same time, we would haunt the wharf eateries. I can still hear the cats in our bands going "Yeech!" as we gulped down live clams and oysters. During these meals, Preston would hold court, in the manner of his mother before him. We both have an understanding that the blues, jazz, R&B, and related forms are strictly African-American inventions. While whites had no part in creating them, they certainly have a right to interpret these alluring styles. What is so disgusting and disturbing to both Preston and me, however, is the tendency on the part of white society to elevate the usually lame "great white hopes" above the artistically superior black innovators. This results in fame and fortune for the white players and singers and a harder way to go for the blacks.

Preston Love has the ability to bring the past fifty years into sharp focus. So many of the musical brothers and sisters who lived through this time and had the ability to set down their memories in writing have passed on. If for no other reason, this is a valuable book.

Acknowledgments

✳

Certain individuals were most helpful and encouraging to me in my preparation of this manuscript. When I first conceived the idea of writing this book, Arleen Thompson was the most instrumental of all. She constantly reassured me that it wasn't presumptuous or self-deluding for me to take on such an ambitious task. Arleen had access to a first-rate typewriter at her job, so I would rush to her house every evening after I finished some pages, and she would faithfully return my "ravings" in neatly typed form the next day when she returned from work. Being a knowledgeable jazz devotee, Arleen often steered me back on course when she felt I was being excessive or even a bit off track. My wife Betty and I count Arleen as one of our most valued friends; she is a gem.

Stanley Dance came on board after my manuscript was mostly completed, but he offered and provided invaluable help and encouragement. As a prominent critic and jazz historian, Stanley gave me the impetus to keep trying when I was very discouraged and felt that my book might never be published. The thought that a man of his stature would be interested in my manuscript was very flattering to the kid who grew up amid the privations of the "Love Mansion" and whose bands traveled in "the Green Hornet" and the infamous flex buses.

Help from my friends Johnny Otis, Frank Driggs, Harold "Stemsie" Hunter, and Marcia Hunter came in the form of encouragement and reassurances that my book had merit and that I should remain confident. Toward the end of the time when I was seeking a publisher, the Hunters especially did their best to dispel my pessimism.

Thanks to Beverley French for being such a valued member of our family and to Joe Miloni and also the *Omaha Star* staff for being so supportive.

P.L.

Preston Love's Life in Jazz
The Significance of His Story

George Lipsitz

Who is Preston Love and why is his story significant? To many of his fellow musicians from the big-band era of the 1930s and 1940s, Love was one
of the truly great lead-alto saxophone players of all time, yet his artistry has
gone largely unacknowledged in popular and academic jazz histories. When
he worked as the leader of the West Coast Motown Band during the 1960s
and 1970s, Love shared the spotlight with some of the most popular performers in rhythm and blues including Stevie Wonder, the Temptations,
Smokey Robinson, and Martha and the Vandellas. Yet he also spent years
toiling in relative anonymity as a member of territory jazz bands, rhythm
and blues troupes, and as the leader of his own small orchestra during the
1940s and 1950s, playing a long string of engagements at military bases, private clubs, school auditoriums, and dance halls in cities and towns all across
the country. In Europe, Preston Love has been lauded and celebrated as a
distinguished artist many times, yet he has often been ignored by the musical establishment in his hometown of Omaha, Nebraska. Love has performed his music on television, in recording studios, and in prestigious
concert halls and nightclubs in North America, Europe, Central America,
and the Caribbean, yet he has also devoted his time and talent to serve as an
instructor and artist-in-residence at jazz camps and school music programs
in Iowa and Nebraska. He is one of the few people to have firsthand experience with both the genius of Count Basie and the commercial acumen of
Berry Gordy, to have the opportunity to play music behind both Billie Holiday and Diana Ross, to span the gamut of popular music from Jimmy
Rushing's "Good Morning Blues" to Marvin Gaye's "What's Goin' On."

   A Thousand Honey Creeks Later tells a dramatic and absorbing story,
replete with reversals, ironies, and surprises. Love relates how he trans-

formed himself from a child who listened to the radio in a dilapidated and unheated house in Omaha's Near North Side black ghetto, captivated by the music of the Count Basie Orchestra and its lead alto saxophonist Earle Warren, into the young man who, less than a decade later, took over Warren's chair in the Basie band, serving as a suitable replacement when health problems caused his idol to take a leave of absence. Love also tells about his encounters with Ray Charles—how he met the very young and undiscovered singer in a chance encounter outside a hotel in Cincinnati in the early 1950s, only to find himself fifteen years later employed as a member of the Ray Charles Orchestra, experiencing every night the awe and admiration that Charles's extraordinary talents provoked from his fellow musicians. In another episode, Love recalls his initial introduction to musician Maurice King backstage at a performance by the Lucky Millinder Orchestra in the 1940s, and his eventual long-term association with King when Love led the West Coast Motown Band and King served as conductor, director, and arranger for the stage shows featuring the rhythm and blues artists recording for Motown.

Yet what is most significant about Preston Love is not so much where he has been or who he has known, but rather the story he has to tell. Preston Love provides unprecedented and unparalleled insight into the life of a working musician, into all forms of African-American music, and into the role played by racism in denying black musicians their proper recognition and reward. But this is also a book that teaches younger generations what Love has learned from his life in jazz, that uses the knowledge acquired over a lifetime to teach us about aesthetics and economics, about creativity and commerce. Because of his exceptionally diverse experiences as a musician and his intimate exposure to so many different ways of making music, Preston Love has developed unique intellectual, analytic, and emotional understandings of a broad range of topics, from the achievements of Count Basie and his featured musicians to the deficiencies of formal jazz education, from the corruptions of commerce and the realities of race in popular music to the responsibilities of soloists and the importance of reliable and economical transportation to bandleaders.

One of the most significant accomplishments of *A Thousand Honey Creeks Later* is the challenge that it raises to established histories of jazz, which tend to focus on a select group of individual geniuses in only a few cities at the expense of the broad-based, collective, and geographically diffuse practices that gave this music its determinate contours. Preston Love's history of jazz pays proper tribute to the great jazz artists he encountered as a musician, including Jo Jones, Freddie Green, Walter Page, Lester Young, Duke Ellington, Dizzy Gillespie, and Dicky Wells, but he also insists on celebrating less well known music, like the solo technique and command of chord changes exhibited by George Salisbury at the College Inn in Boulder, Colorado, in 1941, the artistry displayed by seventeen-year-old Charles Thompson when he joined Warren Webb and His Spiders in the mid-1930s, the solo on alto saxophone by Frank Sleet on Jimmy Witherspoon's "'Tain't Nobody's Business" in the late 1940s, and Clifford Jordan's tenor-saxophone solo with the Cedar Walton Trio in the mid-1970s. His account reveals the hidden genealogy of contemporary music styles, as in the story of Buster Coates and his innovative playing of bass runs on acoustic guitar with the Ed Lippert Orchestra in St. Cloud, Minnesota in 1940, and then later Coates's performances as one of the first musicians to realize the jazz potential of the electric bass when he was performing in clubs in Amarillo, Texas, and in Artesia, Clovis, and Albuquerque, New Mexico in 1955.

While enlarging our understanding of the contributions made to jazz music by lesser known artists, Preston Love also reminds us that New Orleans, Kansas City, Chicago, and New York have not been the only significant sites in jazz history. To be sure, the radio broadcasts that he heard from these cities and others during his formative years played an important role in shaping Love's lifelong devotion to jazz, but his native Omaha was a rich source of inspiration and education about jazz all on its own. His older brothers Norm and Dude introduced him to music on records and on the radio, but also to the sounds emanating from the stage of Omaha's Orpheum Theater and from the bandstands of nightclubs like Jim Bell's Club Harlem. Dude Love played saxophone for Warren Webb and His Spiders and brought the group home with him for practices in the Love family living room. Preston Love played jazz with a group for the first time during one of those practices, keeping time for the group on drums using wire brushes when the regular drummer was not available, and he played his first job for pay with the same group in Honey Creek, Iowa, some months later. Territory bands led by the likes of Nat Towles and Lloyd Hunter brought musicians from other cities to Omaha; Buddy Tate and Jo Jones turned out to be particularly important in Preston Love's life. But the city's rich jazz culture produced its own musicians as well, including Wynonie Harris—who went on to an extraordinary career as a singer with the Lucky Millinder band during the 1940s and as a solo rhythm and blues artist in the 1950s—and George Miles, who played bass in the Preston Love Orchestra for many years and who was the father of Buddy Miles, best known for his work as a drummer in the 1960s and 1970s with the Electric Flag, Jimi Hendrix's Band of Gypsies, John McLaughlin, Carlos Santana, and his own Buddy Miles Express.

Omaha emerges as an important site in the generation of jazz in this book, but it is not alone in that respect. Preston Love's story reminds us that the music that we encounter in commercial culture through recordings, radio broadcasts, motion pictures, and television programs are just nodes in a network that extends to small cities and towns all across the country and all over the world. We have become accustomed to thinking about jazz music as something played at the Howard Theater in Washington or the Kiel Auditorium in St. Louis, as indigenous to nightclubs like Minton's in New York or Billy Berg's in Hollywood. But the musicians who play at these centers of the music industry have come from diverse and obscure places, including Butler's Chicken Shack in Minot, North Dakota, where Herb Whitfield's Swannee River Boys included Preston Love's brother, Dude. Preston Love tells his own stories about seemingly obscure places: about sitting in the Merchants' Hotel in St. Cloud, Minnesota, and dreaming of one day getting to perform at the Apollo Theater in Harlem or the Regal Theater in Chicago. Then, after realizing his dream through his brief stint with the Basie band during Earle Warren's absence, he found himself stranded in a remote farmhouse in Alma, Nebraska, when his band's bus broke down, listening to a radio broadcast of the very orchestra that he had been a participant in only a few weeks earlier. Most important, Love details the life of a working musician providing live music for grateful fans outside cosmopolitan centers of commercial culture in the Great Plains, Midwest, and West. He tells about playing for dances promoted by African-American entrepreneurs like Warner Barber in Guthrie, Oklahoma, and Walter Green in Big Spring, Texas. He highlights the importance of the military to musicians like himself through his accounts of the engagements available during the 1950s at military outposts such as Walker Air Force Base in Roswell, New Mexico. He traces the uneasy racial aspects of popular music that influenced him and his band as they performed at a panoply of school proms, country-club events, and summer recreation area dances in Minnesota, the Dakotas, Kansas, Nebraska, Iowa, Texas, Colorado, and New Mexico in the era after the big bands and before Motown.

Because he has been a working musician and bandleader, Love's memoir addresses the business in show business and offers a stark and unsentimental perspective on the relationship between commerce and art. His account reminds us that most people who try to make a living in music end up losing money and that the fabulous fortunes obtained by artists most visible to the public disguise the harsh realities of the music industry as they are experienced by most working musicians. Love's detailed descriptions of his band's buses and their repeated breakdowns and mechanical failures underscore the financial risks and difficulties that artists can encounter. His efforts to keep his band alive in the face of unexpected transportation expenses, unpredictable revenues, and constant surveillance and monitoring by the Internal Revenue Service reveal a powerful dedication and devotion to his artistic vision, but they also testify to the hard work, planning, and simple luck required for success in show business.

Love relates what he has learned over the years in direct and accessible prose, delineating the ways in which a fancy bus and flashy outfits can influence a band's reception, showing how even supremely successful bandleaders such as Count Basie and Johnny Otis found it hard to make ends meet during periods of slow sales. Love also recounts the logic of leaving the music business altogether, as he had to do in the early 1960s when he worked at Douglas Aircraft in Los Angeles.

Yet despite his detailed and sophisticated understanding of how the exigencies of economics must be attended to, Love remains a passionate and committed critic of commercialization. He decries the pressure on artists to produce hit records that can be conveniently and profitably marketed rather than music with integrity and artistry, and he laments the banality, superficiality, and gimmickry that he thinks results from those commercial pressures. He condemns a system that forces great musicians such as Jimmy Smith, Dicky Wells, and Ed Lewis to seek work outside of music simply to survive. But even beyond the issue of direct financial reward, Preston Love uses his platform in this book to attack the ways in which recording-industry executives, radio and television programmers, promoters, journalists, scholars, and entrepreneurs have used their wealth and power to deny recognition and reward to the true creators of jazz and to rob the public of exposure to one of the world's great forms of artistic expression.

A Thousand Honey Creeks Later comes along at a propitious moment. After years of neglect, jazz has begun to acquire a visibility and a respectability that has long been denied it. Prestigious cultural institutions such as New York's Lincoln Center now sponsor jazz concerts and workshops. Popular films including Francis Ford Coppola's *Cotton Club*, Clint Eastwood's *Bird*, and Robert Altman's *Kansas City* pay affectionate homage to significant moments in jazz history, even though they misrepresent the artists and the art that they depict. Even the U.S. Postal Service participated in the growing acknowledgment of jazz with the issuance of commemorative stamps in 1996 honoring leaders of big bands from the 1930s. Yet as Preston Love's book demonstrates so clearly, the contemporary celebration of jazz is contaminated by exactly the same pathologies, prejudices, and prevarications that have demeaned and distorted it in the past. Love argues that jazz is an African-American art form, a music that springs from the artistic practices, moral visions, and social conditions characteristic of black communities throughout the United States. He is not being exclusionary or essentialist in saying this; in fact, he argues over and over again that people of any race can play jazz properly under the right circumstances, and he reminds us that his own bands and his own personal friendships have never excluded white people. But he does insist on linking the practice of playing jazz to African-American aesthetics, to certain ideas about improvisation, ensemble playing, and expression. The question is not whether white people can play jazz, but rather what white individuals and what white-dominated institutions do with jazz when they confront it.

Cultural institutions that make museum pieces out of improvised jazz from the past or that lionize individual artists in isolation from the musical contexts in which they worked operate antithetically to jazz, not in appreciation of it. Any account of jazz that attempts to cordon it off from other forms of black music or deny its origins in the collective culture of African Americans collaborates in yet another act of cultural genocide. Films that turn jazz artists into tortured souls isolated from the communities that nurtured and sustained them graft a Romantic European notion of art and culture onto musical practices that proceed primarily from very different premises. As James Baldwin said about *Lady Sings the Blues*, "the film suggests nothing of the terrifying economics of a singer's life, and you will not learn from the film that Billie received no royalties for the records she was making then; you will not learn that the music industry is one of the areas of national life in which the blacks have been most persistently, successfully, and brutally ripped off." For that reason, Baldwin claimed that *Lady Sings the Blues* "is related to the black experience in about the same way, and to the same extent, that Princess Grace Kelly is related to the Irish potato famine: by courtesy."[1]

Today, the cultural institutions, filmmakers, and even the Postal Service selection committee continue to isolate black geniuses from their roots in black communities and to elevate undeserving white artists to the center of the stories, while marginalizing or erasing African Americans of much greater significance. The Postal Service series on big-band leaders is a clear case in point: its four stamps honor Jimmy and Tommy Dorsey, Benny Goodman, Glenn Miller, and Count Basie. Three of the four stamps and four out of the five individuals honored were white, while African-American bandleaders of undeniably greater artistic and

1. James Baldwin, *The Devil Finds Work* (New York: Dell, 1976), 129, 120.

historical significance (such as Jimmie Lunceford) were ignored. This kind of quota system has always been used by whites to gain undeserved advantages; it determined the disproportionate reward allocated to white artists in the 1930s and 1940s, it has played an important role in the unjust allocation of remuneration, recognition, and reward to black artists ever since. That individuals and institutions who purport to love "jazz" do not even try to correct these injustices—even in respect to rewards that are largely symbolic, honorary, and matters of the historical record—testifies to just how deeply the pathology of white supremacy remains embedded in our society.

The truths that Preston Love has to tell about the pervasive racism of the music industry, about the corruptions of commercial culture, and about the inseparability of jazz from the broader contours of African-American life may not be easy for everyone to hear. Readers often turn to books on popular music to have their prejudices reconfirmed, to have their consumer preferences and tastes validated, to use their attachments to music to fashion a fantasy world that allows them to escape from the world in which they live and from their responsibilities to change it. But while the things that Preston Love has to say may not be welcome truths, they are truths nonetheless. He has a story to tell and a message that we need to hear.

According to tradition, elders among the Yoruba people in West Africa teach younger generations how to make music, to dance, and to create visual art, because they believe that artistic activity teaches us how to recognize "significant communications."[2] Without this training, young people might be easily fooled, prizing as significant some communications that may ultimately have no value, while dismissing as insignificant the messages that may contain the greatest knowledge and importance. Those of us who live in societies saturated by commercial culture are confronted constantly with sounds and symbols, with images and ideas that sometimes seem significant because they are marketed to us by sophisticated and skilled individuals in control of the most powerful communications apparatuses the world has ever known. Our attentions are directed to people simply because they are celebrities, because they are famous, or rich, or both rich and famous. Yet the things that appear to be significant and essential to the marketing mechanisms of commercial culture can be quite transient, ephemeral, and insubstantial. At the same time, communications that might seem marginal, eccentric, or outside the mainstream can contain profound insight and understanding. Preston Love has known

2. Robert Farris Thompson, *Flash of the Spirit: African and Afro-American Art and Philosophy* (New York: Vintage, 1983), 19.

famous people and he has enjoyed the warm glow of public recognition and reward. But that is not why his communication is significant. He is a man who has struggled his whole life, who has used the tools available to him to make great dreams come true, to experience things that others might have considered beyond his grasp. But that is not why his communication is significant either. He is a writer who comes to us in the style of the Yoruba elders, as someone who has learned to discern the significance in the things that have happened to him, and who is willing to pass along his gift and his vision to the rest of us. His dramatic, humorous, and compelling story is significant because it uses the lessons of the past to prepare us for the struggles of the future. It is up to us to pay attention and to learn from his wisdom.

A Thousand Honey Creeks Later

CHAPTER ONE

The Love Mansion

✳

If this essay appears to be a subjective diatribe at times it is only because subjectivity is an inevitable human characteristic—especially among those "presumptuous" enough to offer their opinions and criticisms in the form of books or speeches. The very nature of making choices in our everyday life is the height of subjectivity, and on this score I consider myself very little different from any other individual. In expressing preferences and distastes, none are more subjective than the millions of music fans and show business consumers. Therefore, I feel compelled to remain true to my convictions while exercising the right to express my opinions according to my subjective taste. I will be rather unkind to certain individuals and to certain cherished institutions in these pages, but it is my sincere desire always to avoid being unjust or unnecessarily negative.

Some years ago I noticed that almost none of the manuscripts published about jazz and the lives and experiences of black performers were written by Afro-Americans or by the performers themselves, without a ghostwriter or amanuensis. Almost without exception, the ghostwriter or amanuensis was a white person and a pedant. No matter how concerted an effort the author and amanuensis make to avoid it, the composition always takes on a degree of the ghostwriter's personality, and the final product loses some of the character and flavor of the original storyteller's personality. The fact that many performers lack eloquence and articulation is no excuse for there not being more books completely self-written by the musicians and performers who lived the life. There have been oh-so-many monographs written by pedants and professional writers who have only chronicled the lives of jazz performers or described the personalities of individual musicians in the same terms that any outsider would describe a subject. Only an insider, a person who has lived the life, has that certain perception of the subject. I am realistic enough not to imagine myself a Somerset Maugham or an

Ernest Hemingway, but I have these things raging in my mind, and at least I will avoid this becoming another soap opera à la *The Benny Goodman Story, The Glenn Miller Story, Lady Sings the Blues,* and others.

When I conceived the idea of writing this book, I resolved to avoid the word "jazz," because this word has become an elastic term stretched in recent years to describe all kinds of often nonsensical music that has no resemblance whatever to jazz as it was originally conceived. Furthermore, when I first entered music professionally in 1940, the term "jazz" wasn't taken very seriously or regarded as a legitimate description of the music it alluded to, nor was the world so conscious of labeling or categorizing as it has become in the past twenty-five years or so. The word "jazz" was used predominantly to describe the creative improvisations of Afro-American instrumentalists, but nearly all the black musicians regarded the word with derision and generally used it only satirically. We regarded the word as a term of the "squares" and the "cornballs"; so most of us black musicians used the word jokingly as a "put on" of the squares in the audiences or of the many "Mickey Mouse" Guy Lombardo–style bands around the country in the thirties and forties. However, the critics and devotees of improvisational-innovative music needed a means of identifying the art form, so the word "jazz" became a more legitimate term and gradually became more and more acceptable even to musicians like myself who had derided it. It is only in recognition of this need for classification that many of us musicians have acceded and accepted the word "jazz" as a legitimate identification of the music to which it originally alluded.

In very recent years, however, the word "jazz" has become an even more elastic word—stretched by certain people and certain instrumentalists to cover any kind of musical garbage that couldn't be given any other musical label. The newest elasticity of the word has almost made it unacceptable to me all over again. I haven't become so much of an anachronism that I can't appreciate even the most far-out jazz if it is sincerely performed and has any real value. But I could never pretend to give my approbation to any of the charlatans who happen to become famous as "jazz" players simply because they happen to catch hit records or because they happen to receive more publicity and public attention than some of the true giants of jazz.

Our family, the Loves, was one of several large families in the black community that was located on Omaha's Near North Side. I was born at 1610 North Twenty-eighth Street in April of 1921, the youngest of nine children. At the time of my birth, my mother, Mexie Love, was a widow, forty-one years old. Mex, as my mother was known, was a gritty little Texan, and she set out valiantly to support her nine "stair-step" children by doing day work five days a week without the help or presence of a husband

Preston Love, ten years old in 1931, in front of "The Mansion" at 1610 North Twenty-eighth Street in Omaha.

or any other man. She was one of the first workers in the twenties and the Depression to accomplish a five-day work week, because nearly everyone, especially the poor, worked six days, with Sunday off. However, because she was a devout Seventh Day Adventist, Mex wouldn't work on Saturday under any circumstances, even though we were constantly no more than one step ahead of financial disaster.

As we grew up, our dilapidated house became known as the "Love Mansion." It became the gathering place for most of the neighborhood youths because each of us nine children had his or her circle of friends and playmates. Daytimes, with Mex away at work, the order of the household was entrusted to Sonny, the oldest child in the family, who was fourteen years my senior. Household chores were delegated to my sister Laura, who is ten years older than me.

The Love Mansion was a constant bedlam of activity that subsided only temporarily for the dinner break when all of the gang went home for their evening meal. With Mex home and dinner out of the way, the revelry at the Mansion resumed nearly every evening and night until bedtime. Mex enjoyed the festivities in spite of her tiredness from the day's labors because it kept her children at home and out of mischief and because she found the many youths to be interesting and entertaining.

Early in 1931, my brother, Dude (Tommy), went to work as a porter-houseman at Omaha's Paxton Hotel for the "fabulous" salary of $55 per month. Dude was the next-to-oldest member of our family and a most handsome and lovable extrovert. As a result of his employment, Mex received some part of the $27.50 Dude earned on the first and fifteenth of each month to supplement the $15 she earned every week to support the large Love clan. In November of that year, after Dude had been working at the Paxton for several months, we were all sitting around the kitchen table awaiting dinner when Dude arrived with a small case which we conjectured was some insignificant object. Warmth was always a problem in our drafty house on chilly or cold days but our kitchen was the warmest spot during mealtime because meals were cooked on an old-fashioned cook stove that was fueled with coal or logs of wood. This was one of the many times our electrical service had been discontinued because of our inability to pay the utilities bill, so a kerosene lamp glowed in the middle of the dinner table, with its plates, bowls, and utensils. In spite of the fact that he was always fatigued from the long hours of hard work at the hotel, Dude purposely presented a jovial and carefree facade when he made his "grand entrance" every evening. This night was no different, as he pushed several plates aside, and—with a magician's flourish—set the case on the dinner table, snapped its two latches, and lifted the top to reveal a beautiful and shiny object: a brand new Buescher alto saxophone.

None of us had the slightest suspicion that he intended to buy this marvelous and mysterious instrument. Later, we learned that Dude had become enamored of the saxophone through hearing Pluke Simmons play it with different Omaha bands at dances he had attended. Pluke Simmons was one of the finest alto saxophonists and clarinetists ever in the Omaha area. Although Dude's salary at the hotel was small and although he contributed all he could toward the support of the family, he still managed to purchase the horn on small monthly terms from one of Omaha's downtown music stores. Of course, the cost of a new horn then was about one tenth of current prices. On the night that Dude arrived with the horn, each of us took turns holding the exotic object and fingering it. Then Dude treated us to a rudimentary concert lasting well into the night. His command of the instrument was very limited, and his fingering was quite awkward, but he had been an excellent ukulele player since his early teens, so he was not without some semblance of musical sensibility. Mex and all the neighborhood kids were enthralled.

Within days after he acquired the alto sax, Dude was taking lessons from his friend, Pluke Simmons. All of the local musicians began to express awe at Dude Love's beautiful natural tone and sound on the alto. His tone was compared to a beautiful voice or a violin. Many of the black players of that era had a characteristic natural warmth to their sound, but they were more mindful of the "bluesy" or what is now called "jazz" sound, so they usually imitated the famous jazz names of the day. Dude's was more of a so-called "legitimate" sound, with very little of the jazz inflection. Within a very few weeks, as his lessons progressed, Dude set out to make musicians of nearly every boy or young man that frequented the Mansion. Each was assigned to some instrument or other; and although he knew only the saxophone, Dude patiently instructed every kid who arrived at the Mansion with a horn. His arrival from work every evening was like the arrival of the Pied Piper, as all the gang converged upon the Mansion to receive instruction. Dude would relay Pluke's instructions to his own students while offering encouragement and praise to each aspiring young player.

An old trumpet in fair condition was acquired from some charitable person in the neighborhood, and my brother Norman, eight years my senior, was assigned to it. A number of other boys shared the trumpet for lessons. I was at a stage where I seemed insincere about learning music, and Dude did not feel I had much, if any, musical aptitude. Nevertheless, he assigned me to the trumpet as well, even though very little time was spent instructing me. My brother Phillip, who is two and a half years older than me and whom we called Dodda, showed an apparent aptitude for the saxophone, so Dude began to spend a great deal of time diligently instructing him. Dude took two lessons per week from Pluke, and quickly relayed all newly acquired knowledge to Dodda and to a couple of others in the community who had acquired saxophones a few months after the "Dude Love Music Project" began. Next to Dude, Dodda showed the most progress in the project. My interest in the trumpet waned soon after I learned the C-scale and a portion of a few easy melodies.

Slightly more than a year after Dude had gotten his alto, somehow a tenor sax was acquired for Dodda. By that time he could play several

Preston's sister Phylis Love on the porch of the Mansion.

standard tunes in their entirety, and his reading had progressed to the point that he could play sixteenth notes if the tempo wasn't too speedy. Dodda's main difficulty came with syncopation. Most of the black instrumental students around Omaha who had reached the stage of development achieved by Dude and Dodda were by this time playing catchy chord changes and very nearly professional jazz solos, but ad-lib soloing and chord changes were not Dude's or Dodda's forte.

After the acquisition of the tenor, Dodda continued to study and practice sporadically at Dude's urging, but Dodda found the practicing very tedious. Furthermore, his interest had always been more in mechanical devices and experimenting with them. For this, Dodda had a natural aptitude. Mechanical genius finally began to emerge as his innate talent and his complete interest. He soon lost nearly all interest in the saxophone. Dude was somewhat dismayed, but accepted it philosophically, as was his nature. Although Dodda's saxophone lay untouched under the bed in Mama's room for weeks on end, he continued to keep the case stocked with the best reeds, mouthpieces, and other accessories "expropriated" from time to time from Schmoeller and Mueller, Omaha's biggest music store.

By 1933, Dude had become a proficient reader, and his beautiful tone was described as "lighting up a reed section," but it was his athletic prowess that brought him his escape from the demeaning houseman job at the Paxton and brought him his first professional traveling venture. At Omaha's Central High School, Dude had been an outstanding football star and basketball player, and throughout his early adult life he diligently kept himself in good physical condition by participating in sports years after he finished at Central, no matter how hard he was working at something else. In the early fall of 1933, Harry Crump, the owner of the black House of David basketball team based in Sioux City, Iowa, drove the one hundred miles from there to Omaha looking for a couple of good basketball players to travel with the team for the 1933–1934 season that was soon to begin. Dude was one of those recommended to Crump, and after some persuasion and a promise from Crump that a show and dance would eventually be incorporated into the House of David operation, Dude and another local basketball wizard—Jabbo Curry—agreed to leave with him.

On a beautiful Indian summer morning in mid-September of 1933, Dude liberated himself from the drudgery of the Paxton Hotel and loaded his horn and other belongings into Harry Crump's 1931 Model A Ford sedan for the trip to Sioux City and a week of workouts with the House of David before their tour of the Midwest would begin. For our mother, Sonny had been the first of her beloved young sons to leave home four years earlier when he drove to Los Angeles with some Omahans to seek his fortune. Now again, brave little Mexie had to bid good-bye to one who was "spreading his wings and taking to the sky."

Judging from Dude's letters, the venture with the House of David was exciting and rewarding for him, but the musical part of the package never materialized. Dude was able to get in quite a few hours of practice while sitting around the hotels in the small towns of the Dakotas, Iowa, Nebraska, and Minnesota. When the basketball season finally ended, Dude stopped in Sioux City to spend a few days before coming home to Omaha, but we were not to see him again until 1936. Well honed on his sax from the many hours of practice, Dude made a big impression on Sioux City's few black musicians upon his return there that spring of 1934, so much so that one of the local groups took him on with their four-piece combo. Dude remained in Sioux City for several months, and every week he promised himself to make the hundred-mile trip to visit Mex and his four kid brothers and three sisters still at home; but he considered it more important to play the six nights on their steady gig and rest the seventh, while sending a few dollars home each week to help the family survive the Depression.

Before Dude got around to visiting Omaha later in 1934, a group in Minot, North Dakota, called Herb Whitfield and his Swannee River Boys heard about Dude and sent to Sioux City for him to join them in Minot. Dude readily accepted because Herb's group was slightly larger than the Sioux City group and better organized. Dude spent nearly two years in Minot with Herb Whitfield, playing nightly at Butler's Chicken Shack, a small but popular nightclub there. On their night off at the club, the group played an occasional one-nighter in the area. As the spring of 1936 approached, Dude had grown very tired of Minot and longed to see his mother, the kid brothers and sisters, and his friends back in Omaha, so he made his preparations to leave Minot, giving Herb Whitfield a reasonable time to find a replacement for him.

During the last year or so that Dude was away, I shared a room with my brother Norman. By 1934, Norm was working full-time as a porter at the Omaha distributorship for MGM Pictures. That year, he paid one of the local jackleg carpenters to convert the rickety shed porch into a rather attractive bedroom. Norm's furniture was ornate by Mansion standards; his prize object was a studio couch that divided into two separate beds placed against opposite walls of the narrow part of the room. Radio was still quite a novelty and a status symbol in the impoverished black community of Omaha, but we had owned one at 1610 even before Dude left. Several years earlier, one of Norm's friends, the son of a wealthy bootlegger in the neighborhood, had given Norm a vintage secondhand Majestic radio. However, after the room renovation, Norm hungered for one of the sharp, new-style Zeniths. So in 1935, as soon as his account at Mayper's Department Store was paid down to the level to permit another purchase, he had one of the sharp Zenith consoles delivered to the Mansion.

The Zenith with all its gadgets and its complex tuning dial was placed at the far end of the bedroom between the two sections of the studio couch, facing the length of the room so that the heads of those sleeping on the two beds would be only a foot or so from the radio and its rich-sounding speakers. I showed such fascination with the radio and the new distant stations we could get that Norm allowed me to move in permanently and occupy the second half of the studio couch across from him. My enthusiasm and ravings over the radio pleased him. Besides, he enjoyed having someone in the room to discuss the programs with late at night. He and I developed a mutual appreciation for several programs, certain stations, and a number of the popular orchestras we would hear nightly. Some of our favorites were Hal Kemp, Kay Kyser, Isham Jones, Glenn Gray, and naturally such bands as Duke Ellington and Earl Hines. Hines used to come in loud and clear from the Grand Terrace in Chicago—Fatha Hines! Father Hines!

We kept very late hours at the Mansion for that era, and one summer night in 1935 at about eleven-thirty, a group of us young friends were sitting around listening to the Zenith. Norm was toying with the tuner looking for something interesting. Suddenly, as the tuning needle reached far up on the dial in the area of 1600 kilocycles, Norm increased the volume, put his head closer to the speaker, and signaled us to silence. There was quite a lot of static, but we could still clearly hear the orchestra's theme in the background and the announcer as he enunciated "Count Basie and his Orchestra from the Reno Club in Kansas City, Missouri, with vocalist Little Jimmy Rushing."

Norm commanded, "Be quiet now, you guys. This is the band Jo Jones just left here to join. That Count Basie was here on piano with Benny Moten, and that's the same singer Moten had with him. I used to see them up here all the time at the Dreamland. They always stayed at Mrs. Emmons' rooming house around from the Dreamland, and me and Little Bull delivered them some barbecue around there one night after they got off." Norm was very excited about hearing Basie and Rushing on the air now, after having had the slight association with them and having seen them perform. He was also anxious to hear Jo with the band. Judging from Norm's conversation, those appearances of the Moten band must have occurred two or three years earlier.

Most of the others in the gang lost all interest in the music, since they had to be quiet and perfectly attentive, so they scattered one by one to other parts of the house. But I remained with Norm, our ears glued to the radio to hear those lilting strains of Basie's music and the songs of Jimmy Rushing. Rush sang a blues, and "The Glory of Love," and I remember that he rolled his *r*'s. This radio station was a high-fidelity station, and it seemed there wasn't much depth to the sound, so I got the impression from the sound of his voice that Jimmy Rushing was a small man.

Basie's band of that moment could be described as the purest essence of the Kansas City sound and the Kansas City style. It was brand-new to me, and I remember vividly the driving rhythm of Walter Page's bass and the moaning or bluesy sound of the sax section that then was made up of three giants on the instrument: Jack Washington, Buster "Prof" Smith, and Lester Young. The solos were inspired and monumental, and most of the arrangements were unwritten or "head" arrangements of riffs and beautiful sustained notes by the various sections to back the soloists. I guess this is what the kids of today would call "funky" or "soulful." Norm and I raved over the band.

Right after Basie signed off, the station presented one black orchestra after another from clubs in Kansas City such as the State Line Tavern and the Cherry Blossom. The bands ranged in size from eight to twelve pieces, and they all sounded very similar to the Basie band. Kansas City really had a very distinctive and individual sound of its own that was readily distinguishable. From this night on, Norm and I rushed to the frequency of the high-fidelity station at the time the parade of the Kansas City orchestras began each night. Some nights, Basie or one of the other groups would broadcast twice in a span of two hours.

One night in the early spring of 1936, Mex and all the family were sitting around the front room of the house. It was one of the few nights that there were only a few visiting young neighbors present. There was still some chill in the night air outside, so the coal stove in the center of the room had a moderately warm kindling fire going, and several of those in the room were sitting in a ring around the stove. The front door at 1610 was never locked, and visitors came in and out freely throughout most of the day and early evening. No one took much notice when footsteps sounded on the rickety front porch. Suddenly, the front door burst open into the small hallway, and then the door to the front room was flung open, and into the room exploded Dude.

Mama and all the gang in the room went wild with glee as they pounced upon Dude with hugs, kisses, and shrieks. The cab driver who'd brought Dude from the railroad depot brought in bag after bag, plus Dude's footlocker. Dude was a fastidious dresser and now he looked very prosperous and healthy. He was dressed in the height of fashion. He was beautiful.

After all the excitement and surprise of Dude's arrival subsided and the last of the visitors left, all of us in the family gathered around him as he tried to relate all of his activities, experiences, and successes of the two-and-a-half years since he left home. One of his first acts was to present Mex with five twenty-dollar bills. Our eyes bulged. One hundred dollars was more cash money than Mama had had at one time in many years. A hundred dollars in an impoverished home in 1936 was a veritable fortune.

Dude was much impressed by the new room fashioned from the old shed porch and by Norm's sharp new furniture. Naturally, my half of the studio couch and Norm's room became Dude's, and I moved back into the room I had formerly shared with Dodda. Upon his return, Dude wasted no time getting a gig. Local bandleader Warren Webb was planning to organize a new band, so Dude quickly joined Warren Webb and His Spiders. Within days, Webb had driven to Topeka, Kansas, and brought back four young musicians: two saxophonists, a drummer, and a pianist to complement himself on bass, Dude on lead alto sax, and two local Omaha trumpet men. Daily rehearsals began in the front room of the Mansion.

The warm spring weather made them leave the doors and windows

Mexie Love at seventy-five in 1955.

open during the rehearsals, and the sounds of the orchestra caused quite a sensation in the neighborhood, especially when school was out for the kids at three o'clock each afternoon. The band played mostly popular and standard stock orchestrations, along with a few head arrangements and jam tunes they put together. Dude never played any of the solos except a couple of ballad melodies on numbers like "Stardust," but his beautiful tone danced on top of the three-man reed section. The sound of Dude in that reed section began to stir a mild interest in my mind for the saxophone. Dodda's tenor lay under the bed for months at a stretch before he would take it out and "doodle" on it occasionally. Upon his return to town, Dude had tried without success to rekindle Dodda's interest in the sax.

After about a week of rehearsals, Webb and His Spiders hit the road in the Midwest. They would be gone for several days before returning, and during Dude's absence I began to take Dodda's tenor surreptitiously from under the bed and try my hand at blowing it. Dodda came home a few times while I was in the midst of toying with the horn, and he readily

showed me the notes on the instrument from its top to bottom, and he instructed me how to lip the mouthpiece to get a truer sound from it.

I was very careful never to let Dude know I was fooling with the sax
when he returned from trips with the Spiders. Somehow, inwardly, I felt
that he would find it amusing and that I would be embarrassed. Toward
the end of the summer of that year, Webb was forced to replace his lead
trumpet player who was moving up to the Nat Towles Orchestra, Omaha's
top band of the moment. When the new first trumpet man joined the Spiders, Webb found it necessary to schedule several days of rehearsals at the
Mansion to break in the new man. Hawkins, the little drummer from
Topeka, took very sick the day of the first rehearsal after setting up his
drums in the front room with my help. I had always stood around intently
watching the rehearsals, and Hawkins had taught me how to set up nearly
as well as he could. Webb bemoaned the absence of a drummer and remarked several times that they weren't getting anything accomplished
without someone to keep the tempos. After a few minutes of this I spoke
up: "Mr. Webb, I can keep time for you-all."

Warren Webb turned to me and said, "O.K., kid, get on behind those
drums and just keep us some simple time with the brushes."

Since Webb agreed to it so quickly and good-naturedly, neither Dude
nor any of the others offered any objections. I mounted the drum stool
and picked up the brushes, and Webb kicked off their band arrangement of
"Swingtime in the Rockies." I immediately swung right into it as I had
heard Hawkins do so many times. When the number was over, all of the
fellows mumbled words of approval and encouragement. Webb grinned
and said, "I'll say one thing, he keeps the steadiest time any fifteen-year-old
could keep, I betcha."

Webb called a few more swing tunes and ballads, and then he asked,
"Can you keep time to a waltz, Little Dude?"
I said. "Sure."
He told the men to get out one of their waltz numbers and then
counted it off: one-two-three. I swung right into perfect waltz time and
even added a few crisp embellishments that seemed to please Webb as he
plucked his bass violin. When the rehearsal was over, Webb and all the fellows thanked me profusely. By now Hawkins was feeling better, after having lain down on the studio couch in Norm's room, and he slapped me on
the back.

"Little nigger," he said, "one of these days you goin' to be a great
drummer."

All of the musicians from Topeka except one of the saxophonists decided to leave the group and return to Topeka when they realized there

wasn't much future for Warren Webb's Spiders. They had also grown homesick. Webb had a number of gigs booked, which necessitated some quick replacements for the pianist, the drummer, and the one saxophonist who was leaving. Webb and the band members had heard about a fantastic young pianist in Parsons, Kansas. The word was out that the young cat wanted to get away from that small town, so Webb and Dude set out immediately in Webb's bus. In Parsons, they learned that the pianist was Charles Thompson, the seventeen-year-old son of a local minister. They also learned soon that Charlie's parents objected to his leaving home, but Dude was able to talk with Charles alone a few minutes and make arrangements for him to "elope" with him and Warren Webb that night after the parents were asleep. The next morning, Dude and Webb arrived at the Mansion with the very youthful Charles Thompson, who years later became nationally known as Sir Charles Thompson, a gifted orchestrator, pianist, and composer.

Webb was able to replace the saxophonist from Topeka easily enough, but on the day of their next gig Webb had difficulties finding a drummer. The gig was only a short distance out of Omaha, in Honey Creek, Iowa. Evening and the time to leave were approaching and no drummer. At about six, Webb called Dude at the Mansion and said, "Tommy, get the kid ready to leave. He's playing drums with us tonight." Dude and Webb chatted briefly, and I heard Dude say, "Yeah, I think we can get by with the kid for one night."

Dude instructed me to dress in my best clothes, after very casually announcing to me that I would be playing drums with them tonight. He explained that Warren Webb kept an old set of drums on hand that I would use. Nearly an hour passed, and then we heard Webb's old bus pull up out front at the Mansion. Dude and I hastily left the house, with Mex and the rest of the gang watching us to the door with disbelief and admiration.

Webb's bus was an ancient stretched-out Chevrolet body, but he kept it mechanically sound. When Dude and I tumbled into the bus, all the cats were laughing and talking animatedly. They began making jokes about fifteen-year-old me and seventeen-year-old Charles Thompson. This was to be Charlie's first professional engagement away from his hometown. Some of the musicians had half-pints of liquor, and already everybody was in a jovial mood. Dude, however, never drank liquor. It was Saturday night, and Webb was taking special pains to drive carefully on the hilly and curved highway north of Council Bluffs, which is directly across the river from Omaha. Most of the drivers in the area had learned that it was best to be cautious on that stretch of narrow highway on Saturday nights, with all the drinking drivers moving about between the small hamlets. To me, it

Tommy "Dude" Love.

seemed much further than seventeen miles between Council Bluffs and
Honey Creek, but soon we pulled up in front of the Aeroplane Inn, which
was a combination filling station, café, and dance hall situated right on
one of the curves on Highway 75. Honey Creek, Iowa, was little more
than a wide spot in the road, the Aeroplane Inn, a few houses, and a
Chevrolet garage located across from the Inn. Yet there were fine crowds
every Saturday for the dances at the Inn. The dance patrons were almost
entirely people from surrounding farms, with a few people who came from
Council Bluffs.

I can't claim truthfully that the gig at Honey Creek produced any novel
experiences or any exciting moments. I simply kept a steady beat for the
musicians and the provincial dancers as best I could. Honey Creek was
simply the first professional engagement of my life. The gig paid "line six"
or three dollars to the regular members of the band, but Webb paid me,

the novice, "line four," which was two dollars. Musicians used the line system then. In our esoteric musicians' language, "line" meant double the actual amount. Musicians used this code so that outsiders would think they made more than the feeble fees of that day.

The following Monday, Webb found a permanent drummer, and by the next weekend the band was sounding professional and well organized again. But that would be Dude's last weekend with the Spiders. His friend and mentor, Pluke Simmons, came by the Mansion one day in the middle of the week to tell Dude that there would be an opening in the twelve-piece band at Jim Bell's Club Harlem at North Twenty-fourth and Lake Streets. Dude would be in the four-man reed section, next to his idol, Pluke. They would alternate on first alto, and Pluke would play all the jazz solos. Dude was elated, and he informed Warren Webb that this weekend would be his last with the Spiders.

Jim Bell's Club Harlem was located a few yards from Omaha's legendary North Twenty-fourth and Lake Streets, the main corner of Omaha's black main stem, the hub of the Near North Side, as Omaha's black ghetto was known. The Club Harlem had a full line of chorus girls, a twelve-piece orchestra, and imported top-grade comedians, singers, emcees, and other acts for their floor shows. The club catered to all races and was frequented by a sizable percentage of rich whites from Omaha's Dundee section. Jim Bell was a large southern man who had experienced several ups and downs as Omaha's premier black entrepreneur and restauranteur. He was uneducated but shrewd and tenacious, as well as unafraid to gamble by investing in businesses in Omaha's ghetto. Many people in Omaha expressed the opinion that Mrs. Bell, his wife, was more instrumental in Jim Bell's successes than Jim himself. She was a tireless worker and the shrewd manager of all his business ventures. They had one daughter, Dorothy Bell, whom Jim worshiped and who was the envy of most of the less fortunate girls of the black community.

Everything at the Club Harlem was first-class, just like the famous eastern clubs. Dude felt he had made the big time. In spite of the semi-name performers Mr. Bell brought in from Kansas City, Chicago, and other points, he would also give budding local talent a chance at the Club Harlem. The word got around while Dude was working at the Harlem that a young man in town sounded just like the great Joe Turner, the blues singer from Kansas City, and Jim Bell sent for the young singer and took him on as one of the stars of the Club Harlem show. The hometown youngster's name was Wynonie Harris; years later he became famous as Wynonie "Mr. Blues" Harris.

I remember that every night, Dude would come home raving about

Pluke Simmons and the great Club Harlem. On a number of occasions a party of several wealthy white couples drove Dude home and came in with him. Usually the young men would have a bottle of liquor, and they would stay until the wee hours of the morning, fascinated by Dude, who was a great personality and conversationalist. His immaculate appearance seemed so incongruous with the dilapidated condition of 1610 with its outdoor privy and ramshackle furniture, but he never made any apologies to his guests for the Mansion. Presently, some of the girls in the parties began to appear at the Mansion without their escorts after Club Harlem closed some nights. Their only escort now would be Dude Love. My brothers Norman and Billy were very handsome young men, near Dude's age, and it seemed this fact was suddenly discovered by quite a number of the rich girls after the Club Harlem closed at night. I was just at the age to observe all this with more than casual interest.

Having a "big time" club like the Club Harlem only twelve blocks from the Mansion was like being near New York's famous Cotton Club or Chicago's Grand Terrace or one of the other renowned nightclubs we had heard about. The lure of the Club Harlem was like a giant magnet near a pile of nails. Every night would find a crowd of us teenagers glued to the back windows in the alley behind the club. There we could see and hear all of the action inside. I always stationed myself where I could observe Dude in the sax section of the swinging Club Harlem Band. Occasionally Jim Bell would slip out the back door and shoo us away, but we were usually permitted to stay and ogle until we got tired and dispersed to our respective homes.

Wynonie Harris had been one of the boys who frequented the Mansion when I was younger, because he was my brother Norman's close friend. So watching him sing and dance in the floor show gave me a big thrill. Even today I feel that Wynonie was a much more gifted dancer than singer. At the Club Harlem he was integrated into some of the dance routines with the chorus girls during his singing performance, and he comported himself very well.

Shortly after New Year's in 1937, business began to drop off at the Club Harlem, and Jim Bell had to cut three men from the twelve-piece band as well as shave other expenses from the floor show. Two of those laid off were Dude and a trumpet player from Chicago named Joe Rembrandt. Mex and Dude were soft touches for people in distress, so Joe was permitted to move into the Mansion for the rest of the winter, ensconced as brother Billy's roommate. Billy was now twenty-five years old, two years younger than Dude, and he demurred at having the obese Joe Rembrandt as a bedmate; but it will never be said that any Love allowed a person in distress to sleep in the street as long as there was an empty inch of space at the Love Mansion.

Within a week after the gig at the Club Harlem folded for Joe and Dude, they found a four-piece gig at the Harvard Bar on Twenty-fourth and Farnam Streets that paid $1.50 per night and tips. They worked every night except Sundays and Mondays. The four pieces consisted of drums, piano, Dude on sax, and Joe on trumpet. During that era there was always a reservoir of piano players, drummers, and bass players for these cheap tavern gigs. Usually these musicians couldn't read music or qualify for one of the bigger and more prestigious bands, but they knew nearly every old and new tune by heart, or they could fake almost any tune in whatever key the horn players or singers required. It was essential that they know many tunes, because these small tavern groups depended on tips from requests as much as on their wages. The little bandstands on these tavern gigs always included a "kitty," which was a box for the band's tips. The kitty was usually a wooden or cardboard receptacle carved or constructed into the image of a cat with a built-in blinker light in the cat's eyes to make it appear that the cat was winking. If no such elaborate kitty was supplied, there was at least a cigar box or a large glass on the piano or somewhere at the front of the bandstand, because the bar owner or club owner was anxious to see the band make all the tips it could, since that saved the owner from paying bigger wages if the band made up the difference in tips. Also, it kept the customers happier and caused them to buy more drinks when the band played all the request numbers asked of them.

The Harvard Bar was a narrow and not very long room with a small bandstand at its rear. There was no rear window from which to see or hear the band, and I was too young to be permitted in a bar; so the only way I could hear Dude and Joe there was to stand outside the front window of the bar. Whenever patrons entered or exited, I could catch a few bars of the music before the front door closed. I did this quite often on the nights that weren't extremely cold. From the front window I could see Dude and the band pretty clearly, except that the management of the Harvard Bar seldom washed the windows, which were always dingy from dirt or steamed up from the cold during those winter months. The pianist with the quartet was a little woman who played most of the bar or tavern jobs around Omaha with different groups, and she knew nearly every standard tune. She could even read sheet music well, and she had a stack of piano-vocal sheets on the floor by the piano. She carried two satchels of sheet music to the gig every night and placed them in a stack where she could refer to them conveniently if the band received a request for some tune that she didn't remember too well.

Preston Love, Omaha North High graduation picture, 1938.

The people who patronized the Harvard were a collection of working men and their wives, farmers, and cattlemen who were in town overnight and staying at the several second-rate hotels in the area. While in Omaha they didn't bother to dress up, even though they would be out on the town looking for a bit of diversion. They often wore overalls or cowboy attire and boots. Peering through the window, I noticed that most of the male patrons went straight for the woman pianist to make their requests, handing her the money directly although the flashing kitty was right in the middle of the bandstand in front of Dude and Joe. The farmers would hang around and make small talk with the pianist, and as soon as they departed she would pass the money over to Joe, who would drop it in the kitty's mouth. On weekends, the group would often receive more tips than their entire salary. There was no leader of the combo, therefore everything was split exactly even four ways, including the nightly six-dollar fee from the bar owner, which he handed to one or another of the group every night as they passed the long bar on their way to the front door at closing time. The tips on weeknights were sometimes as good as those on weekends if one or two good spenders came in and requested a few of their favorite numbers. At least once every week, some stockman or farmer would come in after having made a big sale at Omaha's stockyards. When the farmer began flashing a big roll and buying the band drinks, they knew the kitty would be fat that night.

Joe Rembrandt did most of the singing. He was from Chicago, and his idol was Walter Fuller, the well-known trumpet man and scat singer, then with Earl Hines. Joe was proud of knowing Fuller personally and tried to imitate and emulate him in every way. Joe's ambition and dream was one day to get a call to return home to Chicago to join Earl Hines and sit in the same trumpet section beside his idol. He spoke with some enthusiasm of joining Fletcher Henderson or one of the other great Chicago groups, but the big one would be joining Hines. Neither Joe's playing nor his singing was good enough to make it with one of the big names, but Dude encouraged him and acted as though the summons to join Hines was imminent. He even concocted little imaginary scenes and situations depicting how Joe would look and act on the bandstand with the great Hines brass section or with one of the other big Chicago groups at the Grand Terrace or the Club DeLisa. Joe got a great kick out of these little fantasies, which encouraged Dude to pour them on. The tune that Joe received the most requests for at the Harvard Bar was "The Sheik of Araby." While Joe scatted the words, the other three intoned in the background, "with no pants on . . . ," "naked as a Jaybird . . . ," and so on. On slow nights, the tips were very small, but the musicians' goal was at least to make the eighty cents fare for their round-trip transportation, so on the slow nights Joe would milk the few patrons by doing "The Sheik" over and over during the night.

Ernie Ritchie, a tall and very handsome ex-baseball pitcher, was their jitney driver. Ernie was feeling the same effects of the Depression as most other Omaha blacks, and he was surviving as best he could. He picked up the four band members at their respective homes before the gig each night and delivered them to the Harvard Bar in plenty of time for their kickoff. Every night after the gig, Ernie would be sitting right out front waiting for them in his 1931 Model A Ford, with the motor idling and the heater running, so the band members would be entering a warm interior. For all the service, each member paid ten cents each way, or twenty cents per night each. A dime, even a penny, went a long way in Omaha in 1937. Around eleven one cold Monday night in March of that year, Dude, Joe, and several members of the family were sitting around the front-room stove enjoying

In Omaha at the age of twenty-one, 1942.

the usual laughing and talking when there was a knock at the front door. I noticed Mama looking at Dude guardedly with a wistfully sad expression before he leapt up to answer the door. In a few seconds, Dude returned with a small, Indian-looking black man whom I recognized as one of the Patterson Brothers.

This brother was slightly crippled and drove a fairly recent model Packard around the community. I had seen him many times. All of the Pattersons, especially the younger brothers, Francis and Alladin, were very good-looking and likable people. I also had seen their oldest brother, Bruce, around town and knew that he was a most fantastic banjo player. Years later, I was to have the opportunity to back Bruce Patterson on several shows with my bands in 1950 and 1951. I also had the pleasure of backing the famous white banjo player, Gene Sheldon, at New York's Roxy in 1946 when I was with Basie. I'm completely convinced that if Bruce Patterson had been white instead of black, he would have been recognized as the greatest banjo player in history.

When the crippled Patterson brother entered the front room, Mex made him welcome. Dude and Joe Rembrandt retreated hastily to their respective bedrooms. It seemed like only seconds before Dude and Joe reappeared with their suitcases and instrument cases in hand. We were all surprised except Mex, because she was the only one Dude had told of their plans to go to Minneapolis for a steady location with Bruce Patterson's combo. Dude and Joe were somewhat skeptical as to whether the Minneapolis trip would actually materialize; hence they hadn't packed their bags or talked much about the prospective gig to anyone around the Mansion but Mex. They had tentatively quit the gig at the Harvard by telling the pianist and drummer to be prepared to replace them Tuesday night, but they left the door open to return there if the Minneapolis gig fell through.

Dude and Joe hugged and kissed Mama and instructed her to call the drummer the next day to inform him to replace them at the Harvard. Then they unceremoniously waved good-bye to the rest of us and were gone. Both Dude and Joe were sentimental people, and they didn't want the farewell to turn into an emotional scene. Dude was gone again.

CHAPTER TWO

Enter Earle Warren

✳

With Dude gone, I began to practice Dodda's tenor more seriously, and it wasn't long before I had passed Dodda in every department—reading, tone, technique, and execution. Dodda enjoyed my progress as much as I, and he continued diligently to supply me with reeds, mouthpieces, and other saxophone accessories. After Dude had been gone a few months in the summer of 1937, Count Basie caught a two-sided hit recording of "Boogie Woogie" and "Exactly Like You." Both sides featured Jimmy Rushing vocals. The Basie rhythm sound was new to all the country. Hit recordings endured more than a few weeks or months in that day, so for months on end "Boogie Woogie" and "Exactly Like You" could be heard all through the night on the jukeboxes along North Twenty-fourth Street from Caldwell to Lake Streets, the main stem of Omaha's black community. This record probably did more to establish Basie as a new big name in the orchestra field than any other single record. "One O'Clock Jump" was a big record for Basie, but "Boogie Woogie" had already started the ball rolling by the time "One O'Clock Jump" came along.

I was sixteen years old at this time, and naturally I was excited about the hit records of the moment, as was nearly every other young person. Norm and I had the added excitement of recognizing Basie's name and style from having followed his progress on the radio broadcasts from Kansas City. On "Boogie Woogie" I especially liked Lester Young's tasty new style and the new driving four-four rhythm of Jo Jones and Walter Page. Basie's piano style was also new and catchy to all of us young jitterbug dancers. On the "Exactly Like You" side, the opening chorus featured Basie's reed section on the tune's melody. Caughey (called "Couchie") Roberts played some very rhythmic and characteristically Kansas City–styled lead alto work that caught my ear, and even today I look back to that early Count Basie recording with great appreciation for Couchie's work in that reed section which also included Jack Washington, Lester Young, and Herschel Evans.

In spite of my tenor sax studies and my progress on the instrument, by 1938 I hadn't embraced any special favorites on the saxophone. I simply followed the trend and accepted Chu Berry, Johnny Hodges, Joe Thomas, Willie Smith, and a few others as being the best, since they were generally rated and recognized as the top of their field. No special solo style had commanded my attention or my affection. Dodda was a Chu Berry fan, but I was unable to generate much enthusiasm for Chu Berry, although I was much impressed with his technical speed. Early in 1938, Norm bought a record player with a miniature transmitter that played through any radio at a certain frequency. One could take the small turntable into any room in the house and clearly pick up the recording being played on any radio in that part of the house. In fact, several houses within a block radius could also tune in to our record player. Norm set out to accumulate recordings by Duke Ellington, Earl Hines, and other favorites of ours, but money was scarce, and our collection didn't grow very rapidly.

One night Norm came home a trifle earlier than usual and instructed me to go into his room and tune the Zenith to the record player's frequency while he stayed in the front room with the turntable. Norm had a package with him, which I suspected contained a new recording by Ellington or the Mills Brothers, which were his favorites. I stationed myself at the Zenith back in Norm's room, and soon the strains of a lovely trombone solo came through the set, and then the vocal began on the beautiful tune. I was quite impressed with the tune, the trombone solo, the fine-sounding orchestra, and the pleasant vocal.

I hollered out to Norm, "Hey, man, *who* is that?"

Norm hollered back, "Wait 'til you hear this."

Then he started the other side of the record. My excitement mounted with every second until the record ended. I rushed into the front room and excitedly asked Norm, "Who in the hell was that?"

Norm reached down, took the record off the table, and, full of smiles, handed it to me. I read the title: "Let Me Dream," vocal Earle Warren, "Time Out," both sides by Count Basie and His Orchestra. The solos on the "Time Out" side and the orchestration itself immediately captured my imagination. We were equally impressed by the warmth and charm of "Let Me Dream." This was a new and refined Count Basie from the Basie we had heard on radio from Kansas City and the Basie of the two 1937 hit records, yet a degree of the purest Kansas City sound remained. For Norm and me, this Count Basie band demanded more investigation. Soon there was a proliferation of Basie hits: "One O'Clock Jump," "Jumpin' at the

Woodside," "Every Tub," and so on. Either Norm or I pounced upon each one as soon as it was released, and we brought it to the Mansion for thorough examination.

One thing I noticed about all the Basie recordings was the rich sound of his reed section. One sound or tone stood out in the sax section even when the section played unison notes. This strident and incisive alto sax sound was detectable even on the speediest saxophone passages, but it was even prettier and more pervasive on harmony parts and on slower tunes. Norm, Dodda, and I all began to take special notice of the alto sax lead in Basie's saxophone section. This was my first full awareness of lead sax work in the section, and my first serious interest in the alto sax as opposed to the tenor. Of course, I had unconsciously noticed other lead sax men's work, such as that of Willie Smith with Jimmie Lunceford, Otto Hardwicke with Duke Ellington, and Hymie Schertzer with Benny Goodman. But here with Basie was something so new—a lead man who played sweet but never syrupy or schmaltzy. He played daintily but full and with power and very rhythmically. I never stopped to consider whether this was the same alto man who led Basie's section on "Exactly Like You." Upon closer examination during that succession of Basie hits, I did notice that the short alto sax solos in "Jumpin' at the Woodside" and "Doggin' Around" sounded totally similar to the lead alto tone on all the recordings. In the summer of 1938, I purchased a copy of one of the music publications, and the mystery of this alto man's identity was solved. There was a picture of Basie's band, listing the personnel in their seating order, and in the accompanying article the writer identified the lead alto man as Earle Warren.

I had just graduated from Omaha's North High School in June and had taken a job as a porter-bellhop in one of the local men's clubs, so I set out feverishly to save enough money for an alto sax. From here on there was no more tenor sax for me. It was alto sax all the way; but I did continue to practice on Dodda's tenor, and I also continued to have a standing order with the record store for any Basie recording before it was released. Thank God there were new Basie recordings released regularly and at short intervals. Then, early in August, placards appeared in all the business establishments on North Twenty-fourth Street announcing that Count Basie and His Orchestra would appear at the Dreamland Ballroom later that month. All of Omaha's black community buzzed with excitement about the coming dance and the new big-name band whose hit recordings had saturated the country. The excitement was high, but not epidemic. My excitement was equally divided between anticipation and curiosity.

The night of the dance arrived, and I stationed myself right in front of the reed section even before all the band members arrived. Finally, Earle

Warren arrived and took his seat and assembled his alto sax and clarinet. I told him that we had his recording of "Let Me Dream," and he was pleased. A big crowd surrounded Jo Jones because he had many friends in Omaha from having spent several years in the city before leaving to join Basie in 1935. Jo was still married to an Omaha girl, Vivien Green. Soon the band was ready to start, and Basie kicked off one of their more exciting numbers. On that August night in 1938 I heard for the first time the group of musicians who had revolutionized the whole style of big-band jazz or swing. The band's personnel included Count Basie on piano, Walter Page on bass, Freddie Green on guitar, Jo Jones on drums, Buck Clayton, Harry Edison, and Ed Lewis on trumpets, Benny Morton, Eddie Durham, and Dicky Wells on trombones, Lester Young, and Herschel Evans on tenor sax, Earle Warren on alto sax, Jack Washington on alto and baritone sax, with Jimmy Rushing and Helen Humes as the band vocalists. My big surprise came when Jimmy Rushing came out front to sing his first number. From first having heard him on the high-fidelity station from Kansas City, I had the impression that he was a small man. Here he was, a very fat man of over three hundred pounds.

I was hardly prepared for the incredible night of musical thrills that ensued, nor was I prepared for any sound or any concept as ideal as Earle Warren's on the alto sax. Earle played only a few short ad-lib solos, but they were startling, as was his ubiquitous lead work over the sax section. Basie spotlighted most of the members of the band, but the key features were the tenor sax contrasts between Lester Young and Herschel Evans, the trumpet contrasts between Buck Clayton and "Sweets" Edison, and the trombone features of Dicky Wells and Benny Morton. The Basie rhythm section of that era was also delectable beyond description. One of the big moments of the evening for Norm and me was when Benny Morton glided into the opening trombone solo on "Let Me Dream," followed by Earle's vocal.

After that August night in 1938, I became a fanatical fan of the Count Basie Orchestra and a devout worshipper of Earle Warren's lead alto playing. By now I had saved up slightly over one hundred dollars from my job at the men's club. My salary there was only thirty-five dollars a month for ten hours, seven days every week, but tips were good from the bellhopping. Considering that my mother supported nine children with a total income of about fifteen dollars a week for several years, one hundred dollars was a veritable fortune during those Depression years. I was now prepared to seek a used alto sax. Soon I learned that a Mr. Orlando Beck had an alto sax for sale at $18.50. The price was right, because I was too thrifty to go overboard and buy an expensive new horn. Mr. Beck had been a professional musician in his younger life, but now he had very little use for the instrument. The Becks lived only two and a half blocks from the Mansion, so on a cool crisp evening in November I strolled down to their house on Decatur Street and knocked on the door. Mrs. Beck came to the door and gave me a cordial greeting because she recognized me as one of the Love boys. I informed her that I was interested in the alto sax that Mr. Beck had for sale and she didn't seem at all surprised. She stepped into the adjoining dining room and quickly brought the horn to me for my examination. I opened the case and was a bit disappointed that that Buescher horn was silver and not gold lacquer, because the gold-colored horns had now become stylish and prevalent. However, I put the horn together and blew a few notes on it. It was in perfect condition, so without any further discussion I took the $18.50 from my pocket and handed it to Mrs. Beck. She thanked me and accompanied me to the door. As I started across the porch, Mrs. Beck called, "I hope you have lots of good luck with the horn, young man, and hello to Mrs. Love."

I could hardly wait to walk the two and a half blocks back home. When I reached the front room of the Mansion, I hurriedly opened the case and stared at the silver Buescher. At last, my own horn, an alto! Soon, I had the horn together and was making runs trying to sound exactly like Earle Warren. I set up the record player and put on several Basie records and imitated Warren as nearly as I could. Only a few members of the family were around, and they paid very little attention to me because by now everyone was used to our blowing horns around the house. Dodda wasn't home when I first arrived, but soon he came and seemed fascinated by the alto. He claimed that I sounded like Earle Warren already. Dodda seemed to fall in love with the alto himself; he continued to toot on it long after I tired of playing it that night. Norm didn't come home until later that night. Dodda and I waited up for him. We were listening to the big-band broadcasts when we heard Norm approaching on the porch, so I rushed into his bedroom and started Basie's "Jumpin' at the Woodside." Just as Norm reached the front room, the record had reached Earle Warren's solo, and I played the short solo along with the record. There was a folding door between the front room and Norm's bedroom. With the doors open, the two rooms were one. Norm peered around the corner into his room to where I was standing with the alto, and put on a great display of surprise and approval. At times like these, Norm's jovial personality was similar to Dude's. I showed him the alto and played a few things for him. Then he requested me to play the "Woodside" solo again. I was getting pretty good at the eight-bar bridge, or middle part, and Norm yelled in a voice similar to Dude's, "Look out, Earle Warren, your rival's comin' to get your butt!"

Lucky Millinder's reed section at the Plantation Club in Watts, December 1944, on a bill with Billie Holiday and T-Bone Walker. Left to right: Bull Moose Jackson, Ernest Leavy, Preston Love (twenty-three years old), Kent Pope, Elmer Williams, Lucky Millinder in back.

I went to bed that night with pleasant visions of someday replacing Earle Warren in Basie's reed section. How or why this would come about was vague in my dreams, however, because I felt that Earle Warren was born to play the Basie style and that Basie's band was created to give Earle and the other original members the fulfillment of their life's purpose and their destiny. This group of musicians was born to play together. This, I feel, was the most important part of their existence and their destiny. I feel the same about the original Duke Ellington band members and those of the original Jimmie Lunceford orchestra.

Nineteen thirty-nine arrived with my dedication to Earle Warren and Count Basie reaching obsessive proportions. I ate, slept, and talked Earle Warren and Count Basie. A number of my friends even called me Earle or Count. My Basie scrapbook was one of the most complete chronologies of

the band anywhere, and I became something of a Basie historian. I feverishly collected recordings of the band and simply existed between broadcasts from the Famous Door on Fifty-second Street in New York or from
other locations where they had coast-to-coast air time. Then in the early
part of the year, a bomb exploded. The word spread through Omaha that
our own Buddy Tate was leaving to replace Herschel Evans, who had just
died, in Basie's band.

Buddy Tate was a popular figure on Omaha's North Twenty-fourth
Street, having came to town three years earlier from Texas with the fine
Nat Towles Orchestra. Buddy's tenor sax style and his lovable personality
had captivated nearly every one of Omaha's 16,000 black people, and at
least the musicians and jazz fans among Omaha's white population. The
name Buddy Tate was a household word in Omaha and in much of the
Midwest. As one who considered himself an authority on the Basie style, I
approved wholeheartedly of Buddy's selection to replace Herschel, although we had heard several tenor sax virtuosos had tried out for Herschel's chair. Both tenor sax chairs in Basie's band were key positions because Basie was known to have a weakness for dual tenor sax solos and
powerful or "shouting" brass sections.

After Tate's installation in the band became official, all of the Basie fans
around town waited anxiously for the first record to be released with Tate
as the "other" tenor to balance Lester Young's unique virtuosity. Soon a
succession of records with Buddy Tate solos with Basie were available, but
midway in 1939 Buddy played a solo on record that must be his master-
piece: his solo on "Rockabye Basie." "Rockabye Basie" swept the country
and became a big hit record, establishing Tate as a famous tenor saxophonist. Every tenor player learned the melodic and fitting solo that Tate created on the recording, and even his detractors conceded that Buddy Tate
was a nearly ideal replacement for Herschel Evans. Yet Buddy continued to
be overshadowed by Lester Young because a soloist of Lester's stature
comes along only once in lifetime. Not long after "Rockabye Basie" became a hit, Basie was scheduled at the Dreamland. Buddy Tate brought his
ex-Omahan wife, Viola, back for the homecoming, and Omaha turned out
in force to welcome Buddy back and to see for ourselves how Buddy fit
into the fantastic Count Basie Orchestra.

Basie's band was practically the same as in 1938, except for more refine-
ments: the addition of a fourth trumpet, and Benny Morton and Ed
Durham had been replaced in the trombone section by Dan Minor and Ed
Cuffee. The addition of Shad Collins as the fourth trumpet man was the
beginning of a Basie trademark, the high-note trumpet player in a four-
man trumpet section to complement the regular lead trumpet player and

the soloists in the section. The band didn't appear in Omaha again until the spring of 1940, but I had kept pace with its activities by purchasing their every record and by listening to their broadcasts. I also sought every available music publication with articles and pictures of Basie's band. When the band appeared at the Dreamland in 1940, it had been enlarged to five saxes, with Jack Washington playing baritone sax exclusively while a fine alto-sax soloist, Tab Smith, had been added on second alto-sax. Tab Smith played second harmony under Earle Warren in the section, but for the first time ever Basie's band featured numerous long solos by an alto-sax player. The band had lost some of the primitive Basie and characteristic Kansas City flavor, but this was more than compensated for by its technical advances, which enhanced the primitive features that they retained. As usual, I spent every second of the dance glued to the front of the reed section, only inches from Earle Warren. I now understand how many people in middle age become mired in the past. To relive one hour of those moments standing before the early Basie bands would be in itself a form of complete fulfillment.

CHAPTER THREE

The Beginning of a Career

*

Each appearance of Earle Warren and the band in Omaha spurred me on to harder practice and closer scrutiny of Basie recordings. By now I could read stock orchestrations and the easier jazz scores pretty proficiently, and the word got around among the older musicians that "that Love boy has the right bite on the alto sax." I guess my sound was as close to Earle Warren's as is possible for one individual to imitate another.

One day, without having had any previous contact with me, a casual acquaintance of mine, Claude "Buster" Coates, came up to the Mansion and approached me about going to St. Paul with an orchestra that was being formed for a good-paying location job there. Buster Coates was a guitar player, and I recognized him from having seen him at several jam sessions in bars around town. I had never participated in a jam session, but some of my friends and I had sneaked in to hear musicians jam until the bar owner noticed our youth and ejected us. Buster had never heard me play, but he was impressed with the little reputation I was making in the musical circles in Omaha. He was four years older than me and much further advanced in his instrument than me from having played gigs and from participating in countless jam sessions at the popular jam spots in the ghetto.

I was most impressed and flattered that one of the "hip" musicians would ask me to leave town with a band. I didn't know that I wasn't his first choice, however, and that he had asked several other more experienced alto players to leave with him, but they had declined through skepticism. Buster had been contacted by phone from St. Paul, Minnesota, by one of the men organizing the band for the location and he had been delegated to enlist an alto-sax player who could read and fake. If Buster or the band manager had known that I was completely inexperienced at faking and playing gigs, I probably would have been eliminated from consideration. Nevertheless, I agreed to leave with the group, and the next evening,

August 15, 1940, Buster drove up to the Mansion in a 1939 Nash sedan with two men, one white and one black. They had called an hour or so earlier to inform me that they would be by to pick me up, so I was sitting on our rickety four-foot-high porch with my horn and a suitcase borrowed from Norm. As soon as the car pulled up, I leapt to the sidewalk and hurried to the car parked on the dirt road in front of the Mansion at 1610 North Twenty-eighth Street.

Mama, Norm, and Billy were standing inside the hallway peering resignedly out the screen door at the front entrance. After putting my bags in the back beside Buster, I paused to wave to Mex and my brothers, who waved back. Then I was in the car. The white man driving smiled and waved to the three inside the screen door, and we were off for St. Paul. When I had told Mama earlier that I was going to St. Paul, she didn't feel so bad, because Dude was in Minneapolis, and also she had two aunts and some other relatives in Minneapolis whom she told me several times to contact as soon as I got to the Twin Cities. I had met both of my great-aunts some years before when they came to Omaha to see Mama. They were practically the same age as Mex, and they had all been raised together between Fort Worth, Texas, and Minden, Louisiana.

Once we were under way, Buster introduced me to the driver, Ed Lippert, and to the other man, who was black. His name was Carl Pugh, and I quickly noticed his right arm was amputated nearly to the shoulder. Both men appeared to be in their mid-fifties. Driving along the highway, we had plenty of time for conversation, and before long I knew that Ed Lippert was the one organizing and financing the whole venture. He had owned the black variety show on several carnivals for a number of years. These shows were always referred to as "jig shows." Carl Pugh had been Lippert's associate, his friend, and the bass player on the jig shows during most of his career as a carny operator. Pugh had lost his right arm in an accident a few years back, and now he played bass tuba with his left arm. Pugh's tuba playing was of another era, but he played very well otherwise. He had a wife, two sons, and two daughters ranging in age from mid-teens to mid-twenties who lived with him in a modest dwelling in St. Paul.

When the conversation subsided, it was around midnight, and I dropped off to sleep. I didn't awaken until the car's motion completely ceased. It was daylight, and we were parked in front of a small three-story building with a sign across its front: Keystone Hotel. Soon Lippert came out the front door of the hotel and instructed Buster and me to get our bags and come on in. He had already checked us in. Carl Pugh was standing in the lobby chatting with the hotel's apparent owner, who was Afro-American but very white skinned.

Carl turned to us and said, "Mr. Burris here will take care of you cats. I live only a couple of blocks from here; and when you-all get up this afternoon he'll show you how to get to my house. My wife will cook dinner for you-all tonight." With this, he and Lippert left.

I was only nineteen years old, and all this seemed very adventuresome and exciting to me. Buster and I retired to our little barren room and slept most of the day. That evening Mr. Burris directed us to Carl Pugh's house, barely two blocks from the hotel. Buster and I quickly made friends with Carl's wife, and after dinner we sat around laughing and talking with his family and several young friends of theirs who dropped by. Most of the time was spent inside the house once we arrived, because August in St. Paul was more like early October in Omaha. I remember being disappointed that it wasn't summer at all as it would be in Omaha at this time. At about eleven-thirty that night Buster and I bade the Pughs goodnight and strolled back to the Keystone. Buster took out his guitar once we were in our room and softly strummed the chord changes to a few tunes while we chatted. He and I were really practically strangers, so we chatted until very late getting acquainted. We had many mutual friends and acquaintances in Omaha, and he knew my brothers Norm and Billy pretty well, which in itself was a form of familiarity. I noticed that throughout any activities or conversation, Buster constantly nodded, his mouth half open and his tongue slightly protruding. As the night wore on he would remain asleep for periods of several minutes, so I suggested we knock off the conversation for the night.

The next morning in a state of semiconsciousness I heard the soulful and beautiful strains of a tune I had never heard before. I jerked awake, sitting beside my bed playing my alto was a small dark man. He introduced himself to me as Julius Jacquet, and after introducing myself I asked him the name of the number he was playing. He looked at me in amazement.

"Man, ain't you never heard 'The Sunny Side of the Street'?"

I answered, "No, but you sure play it pretty."

Jacquet then resumed playing for me. The type of sound he used and the kinds of melodies and chords he wove in were new and thrilling to me. I had the "fat" lead alto tone and was considered a very good reader for that era, but I hadn't explored at all the mechanics of playing ad-lib solos or improvising. Jazz soloing was a wonderful mystery to me at this stage. Oh, how I wished to play like Jacquet! I even admired the little dainty tone that he used for jazz.

After he played a few tunes for me, Julius Jacquet explained to us that he was one of five musicians Ed Lippert had stopped to see on the jig show at Owatonna during our trip to St. Paul. The railroad car that carried the show and their equipment had burned a few days earlier and the musicians

Preston Love playing behind "Mr. Blues," Wynonie Harris, at Loew's State on Broadway in New York City, May 1944. Picture autographed by Wynonie Harris to Preston Love's mother, Mexie. (Photo by Norbert Hess)

had lost all their belongings, including their instruments. When we stopped in Owatonna, Ed Lippert had offered to buy the men instruments and clothing if they joined us in St. Paul. They agreed, and he had left them enough money to come to St. Paul on the early morning bus.

As soon as Julius left, I arose and practiced diligently, trying to get the sound and feeling with which he played. It was futile. I still sounded like Earle Warren or one of the legitimate first alto men.

Later that afternoon we all got together in the hotel and I met the four other members from the carnival band. They were Oliver Humphrey, piano; Isadore Pollard, drums; Booker Samuels, trumpet; and Wilbur Hoops, trombone. Hoops was by far the oldest of all our group, including Carl Pugh. The very next day Ed Lippert drove us to a house he had rented, and within a couple of days all the carnival members had instruments. Carl Pugh naturally lived at home with his family.

The home Lippert rented for us was a large but neat older-style home at 984 Iglehart in St. Paul. The owners of the house lived next door with their family in a house that was the twin to ours. The wife in the home, Mrs. Clemmons, was a plump woman in her mid-thirties. She was kind to the members of our band, but she emphasized that she didn't want a lot of drinking or carousing on her property. She especially didn't want a parade of girls or women coming in and out of the house. We almost never saw Mr. Clemmons, but Mrs. Clemmons and her young children were in evidence next door throughout every morning and afternoon. Our house was sparsely furnished at first, but Mrs. Clemmons continued to add chairs, tables, bedding, cooking utensils, and other household accoutrements for the first few days after we moved in. She even prepared some delicious food items and desserts the first few days. Since I was the youngest and most playful member of the group, she chided and scolded me good-naturedly nearly every time she came in contact with me.

Soon after we got settled in the house, we began to rehearse daily for the St. Paul nightclub engagement, which was to begin in about two weeks. All of our repertoire was standard jam tunes. Musicians who played with carnival bands knew all the standard tunes and all the standard riffs, and therefore most of our arrangements were head arrangements without actual written scores. In other words, we made up the arrangements in our heads and remembered them. However, after a few rehearsals, Lippert and Pugh arrived one day with a suitcase full of stock orchestrations. The orchestration included the newest hits or popular numbers, such as "Imagination," "I'll Never Smile Again," and such numbers as "The Woodchopper's Ball." Lippert had also brought several waltzes, polkas, and numerous old standard favorites such as "Tiger Rag," "Stardust," and so on. The written arrangements were brand new, because Lippert and Pugh had spent the early part of that very morning selecting them and purchasing them at one of the downtown music stores across the river in Minneapolis.

The rehearsals began at one each day, but Lippert called us together at about noon that day so we could pass out the parts to the "stocks" (as they were called) and number each arrangement. There were thirty-one stocks, so now we had thirty-one new arrangements to rehearse and to add to our head arrangements. I noticed an uneasiness in the carnival group and that they ridiculed each stock part as it was distributed. Booker Samuels complained that we didn't have any music stands to put the music on, and Julius Jacquet agreed. But Carl Pugh calmly instructed us to use our horn cases or extra cases as music stands temporarily. Pugh was a sly old fox, and he knew the reason for their uneasiness. With a glint in his eyes he assured us that Lippert would have one of the best sets of music stands before the week was out.

Finally, the parts were distributed and each was numbered, and Pugh selected one of the medium tempo stock orchestrations for rehearsal. This was the moment of reckoning, and soon we knew why the carnival musicians were eschewing the written music. Reading music simply wasn't their forte. We struggled through the arrangement a few bars at a time as Carl Pugh covertly shook with laughter behind his big tuba in the background.

Aside from my exercise-book studies at the Mansion, I had practiced relentlessly on stock orchestration since 1937. Dude had left a number of old stocks around the house; also, Dodda had brought me countless stocks from the music stores in Omaha to practice on. Therefore when Pugh kicked off with the stocks at this rehearsal, I devoured it as though I had been playing it all my life. Already I was a pretty good sight reader, which startled these older and more experienced musicians who were stumbling feebly through the arrangement. If they had only known how I would gladly have traded my reading ability and my tone for their ability to play solos and their ability to fake and create with that tasty black feeling.

Buster Coates was an excellent reader of chord symbols, but he, too, had difficulty with single string lines that were written. For the next few rehearsals, Ed Lippert commanded that we devote every moment to rehearsing the stocks because we had so many numbers to prepare for the coming engagement. In fact, for several days he continued to bring in a new stock or two of old favorite tunes or of things he knew we would have requests for. Several of the stocks he bought were of standards that the carnival musicians knew by heart, and they tried to convince Lippert that they could fake the tunes or make up better head arrangements than the stock orchestrations of them. They told Lippert he was wasting his money to buy stocks of certain standards, but Lippert was adamant that we should have the written notes whenever possible. I was happy that he took this position, because "heading" or faking was still difficult for me in my inexperienced state. By the time we had rehearsed the stocks a week, the group began to come together and to sound professional because all these players had quick minds and good ears for music. Also, I practically led the horns through the orchestrations until we learned them well. When you condense or cut down a big-band orchestration to only four horns as we had, the trumpet carries the lead part or melody most of the time, and Booker, our trumpet player, caught on quickly.

Our rehearsals at the big house attracted much attention, especially from the teenaged kids in the neighborhood. Soon a horde of young teenaged girls discovered there was a young contemporary of theirs in the band, and they began to hang around the area throughout our rehearsals. After one of our rehearsals, I made friends with the group, which encouraged them even more to haunt our rehearsals. Soon I was in hot water with Mrs. Clemmons. By now she treated me as a son, but she scolded me and threatened to evict the whole band if something wasn't done about the congregating on and near her property. This was soon resolved, however, because it was now the beginning of September and time for school to begin.

The band members were getting anxious to work, as the band began to weld itself into a unit. Each day Ed Lippert promised us that he would finalize our union membership in the St. Paul musicians' union local, which was necessary before our opening at the club, but we were in for a rude awakening, because only days before our scheduled opening at the location, the St. Paul union local rejected our application for membership. The reason they gave to Lippert was that we had violated a strict union law against coming into a local's jurisdiction "with job in pocket" when we came to the city with an engagement already booked before establishing membership in the union local. We all yelled foul, and there was great consternation in camp, but Ed Lippert was undaunted. He instructed us to resume rehearsal while he continued to stock our house with groceries and continued to advance us small sums of pocket money for each man's personal requirements.

When we first arrived in St. Paul nearly two weeks earlier, I had called my brother Dude, across the river in Minneapolis. He was incredulous when I told him that his little brother Preston had come to town with an orchestra. He screamed into the phone with his high-pitched voice, "With an *orchestra*? Doing *what*?"

I explained that I was playing alto sax and clarinet. (I had purchased a clarinet a year earlier but I was still in the earliest stages of development on the instrument.) I could hear Dude call out, "Hey, Joe, Connie, come on down here to the phone. Guess what! Little Pres is up here playing alto with a band over in St. Paul."

I talked to Joe Rembrandt, and he explained to me that Dude had married a girl named Connie only three days before. After a very excited conversation between us, Joe turned the phone over to Connie. She told me

With Count Basie and His Orchestra, Los Angeles, 1945. Preston Love, front row, third from right.

how wonderful it was to be married to Dude and how anxious she was to meet me and the rest of his family. Dude took the phone back shortly and fired a barrage of questions at me about my sax playing. He was completely surprised and astounded, because no one from home had mentioned one word in letters to him about my playing sax, nor had anyone said anything when he called occasionally to talk to Mama and all the family. I promised to get over to Minneapolis to visit them in a day or two. I then called Mama's Aunt Ludie and her Aunt Emma. They, too, were excited by my presence in the Twin Cities, and I promised to visit them when I came over to see Dude.

A couple of days later I called Aunt Emma who was the matriarch of the few remaining blood relatives Mex had left in the world. She and Aunt Ludie were sisters to Mex's mother, who had died when Mex was five years old. Aunt Emma informed me that "Sister" had been rushed to the hospital the day before. She was very disturbed, because Ludie was her only remaining sibling of the eight children in the Frazier family that began many years before in Minden, Louisiana. Since Aunt Emma felt so despondent, I postponed my visit with her and called Dude. He instructed me how to reach his house by streetcar from St. Paul, and within the hour I was at 42 Highland Avenue with Dude, Joe, and Connie.

The three of them shared an apartment located upstairs from over their landlord and landlady. Dude and Joe were working on a small combo gig in downtown Minneapolis. Their salary was twenty-one dollars per week and tips, and they regarded this as a mild degree of affluence. Connie was a beautiful young blonde, twenty-one, and she was fascinated at meeting one of Dude's family, since he and Joe had talked so much about Mex and all the members of the clan.

Dude's landlord was Eli Rice. He and his wife occupied the downstairs of the large old house, and Dude enthusiastically took me down to meet them. He bubbled over with pride in his kid brother. Eli Rice was formerly the leader of the Eli Rice orchestra, the best-known band ever to come from the Minneapolis area. Three years before, when I was about sixteen years old, I had attended a dance at the Dreamland Ballroom, which was the last time Eli's band ever played Omaha. Eli was very fat then and much older than the picture he used on the posters for advertising his dances. Being a budding young horn player, I had stayed right in front of the bandstand that night at the Dreamland to "dig" the band closely. Eli sat at the side of the bandstand in a chair that seemed to sigh beneath his girth. He was very congenial to us few youngsters who chatted with him during the dance, and he seemed exhausted from his age and his obesity. At intermission he asked me if I would go up front to the concession stand and bring him a soft drink if he bought me one also. I consented and quickly made the round trip to the stand, bringing him a Coke and one for myself.

Now in 1940 and at his own house I related every minute detail of this 1937 experience, and Eli seemed most pleased and flattered. He had now grown quite old and was much thinner than he had been at that time. He had the appearance of a man who had lost much weight from an illness or from a prescribed, rigid diet. Rice took an immediate liking to me and praised me to Dude and Joe. He was now a venerable but interesting old man.

Ed Lippert and Carl Pugh would occasionally disappear for several days, but the rest of us would diligently rehearse five or six days of every week. The others in the group were happy to see them gone because they felt that the tuba was too old-fashioned and an encumbrance. After we had been in St. Paul for about two months, Ed Lippert arrived at the house on Iglehart one day and announced that we would pull up stakes at the end of the week and move to St. Cloud, Minnesota, where he had secured a location for us. The indefinite contract would be at the 400 Club in St. Cloud, which is sixty-five miles northwest of the Twin Cities. I knew Ed was a "wheeler and dealer," a smooth talker and a con man who could convince almost anyone of anything, but I'm still astonished that he came up with that gig in St. Cloud.

During our weeks in St. Paul, I made friends with several young aspiring musicians and even made several rehearsals with one of the kid orchestras at the Hallie Q. Brown Community House. These fellows were all about my age, and we had lots of fun playing stock orchestrations of Duke Ellington's band as well as Basie and Lunceford stock arrangements. The leader of the band, Bobby Anderson, and another member, Arlie Reece, had become good friends of mine, so leaving St. Paul was going to be difficult. Nevertheless, I told all of my young friends I would be leaving, and on the following Saturday morning Lippert came by our house with a rented trailer hooked to the Nash. We loaded all of our belongings and the equipment that we had accumulated and four of us set out for St. Cloud. In the first load Lippert decided to take Hoops, Buster, and me, and he instructed Jacquet, Isadore, Booker, and Oliver to be ready to leave when he got back from St. Cloud that afternoon. By evening on that mid-October night of 1940, the Ed Lippert Orchestra was ensconced in the Merchants Hotel near downtown St. Cloud, Minnesota.

Within a few days we had met the Majors family, the only black family in St. Cloud. There were only three other black men in St. Cloud, one of whom lived at the Merchants Hotel down the hall from us. He was a shine man–porter at one of the barbershops in town. Mr. and Mrs. Majors were middle-aged people, and they were raising a teen-age girl, Martha, who was Mr. Majors' niece. The Majors and Martha made us very welcome. They were so happy to see some young people of their race because all the other Afro-Americans in town were older men. All of us members of the band visited the Majors regularly except for Hoops, our aging trombone player.

Life in St. Cloud was very dull and uneventful, especially when the dreary cold nights came; but for me this was just another way station on the path of my mounting ambitions. At the hotel we had one big bedroom with a kitchen next door to it. Hoops, the senior citizen of the band, had a small private room upstairs on the third floor, and he rarely came out of it except to go to the bathroom or to get his meals, which he took back to his room to eat after his plate was prepared in the kitchen. The big bedroom had three double beds that accommodated six of us. It also contained several chairs and tables that we used for playing cards and dominoes and for writing our letters home. We had a vintage Majestic radio that played very well. The radio sat on one of the tables between two of the beds. The kitchen contained an old-fashioned gas range and an equally old-fashioned refrigerator, four chairs, and a small table.

Except for the three or four hours of rehearsal, we would sleep all day or sit around the hotel playing cards and dominoes. Some of the fellows would go uptown to visit the Majors at their apartment. Toward evening, everyone would usually be on hand while our one big meal of the day was being prepared. Isadore Pollard, the drummer, was the chef of the band, and I was his assistant or second cook. Isadore knew most of the good soul-food recipes that could be prepared economically, and I learned some of my most cherished recipes watching him prepare our meals in St. Paul and in St. Cloud. Since our budget was limited, we had to rely upon the one big pot each evening for most of our eating requirements. Isadore was adept at concocting tasty dishes of beans with various hog parts, and at creating fine stews, biscuits, corn bread, and so on.

In this small and desolate place we still found it somewhat inspiring because each of us entertained his own brand of daydreams of someday working his way to the top, to be a part of one of the big-name bands and of playing the big cities at famous places such as the Apollo Theater in New York and the Regal in Chicago. We talked starry-eyed about someday playing the Savoy Ballroom in New York and other famous ballrooms and nightclubs that we read about and from which we heard broadcasts on the radio networks. The folks who owned the hotel were a white couple in their early thirties who seemed to be of Swedish or Norwegian descent. They were very hospitable to us, and they supplied us with a space at the bottom of the basement steps for our daily rehearsals.

The Lipperts had rented a neat, two-story house overlooking the Mississippi River, which splits St. Cloud east and west, and they provided Carl Pugh with a room on their second floor. Pugh was off with Ed Lippert most of the time, and neither attended many of the St. Cloud rehearsals. With no bass rhythm present most of the time, Buster Coates soon learned how to pick on the lower strings of his guitar and at times sound very similar to a bass. My daily routine was to sleep until the very last moment possible, arise and snatch a few morsels of food, and descend the stairs in time for our noon rehearsal. The rehearsal usually lasted until about three. The hotel owners' three smaller children spent nearly every moment of our rehearsals sitting on the steps, watching and listening with fascination. On some days after rehearsal, I would remain in the basement and practice until it was time for me to assist Isadore with preparing the evening meal. On occasion, Buster or Oliver Humphrey, the piano player, would remain a while to teach me the chords to popular jazz tunes, or Julius Jacquet would stay to show me standard runs and figures that good jazz soloists incorporated into their solos. It was interesting and challenging to discover some of the mysteries of harmonics and ad-lib soloing, but my whole existence was still wrapped up in playing lead alto sax à la Earle Warren.

The big event of every day and night, even bigger than the daily dinner pot, was yet to come. Every night after the ten o'clock news program ended, there would be a parade of big bands on the several major radio networks. Oh, how anxious we would be when the last seconds of the news broadcast approached as we sat there breathlessly waiting for the introduction of the first big-name band and then the strains of the theme song of Basie, Duke, Jimmie Lunceford, Earl Hines, or one of the other great bands coming from one of the famous clubs in Chicago, New York, or one of the other major cities. We knew we would now have about two-and-a-half hours of pure musical heaven although we were buried all those many miles from nowhere in this frozen hinterland.

In the present era of fast transportation and close communication, St. Cloud nor anywhere else in the country would hardly seem remote at all, nor would it be remote as it was in 1940. The few hundred miles from Omaha to St. Cloud would be less than an hour by jet, and with the commonness of travel today, one would hardly feel buried or stranded as we did, even in that backwoods. Next to listening to the broadcasts, our greatest pleasure each day and night was debating among ourselves which of the big bands was the greatest after the last big-band broadcast went off the air about 1:00 A.M. Even in our small group we had the Ellington faction, the Basie faction, and the Lunceford faction. Naturally, I was the leader of the Basie faction, which consisted of Buster Coates and me. Sometimes the debates among the factions developed into very heated exchanges. At these times the owner of the hotel or his wife would come upstairs from their first-floor quarters and plead with us to lower our voices for the sake of the other guests, who were mostly railroad crewmen and traveling salesmen who had to get up early in the morning.

After we had been in St. Cloud for several days, Ed Lippert instructed us to go down to the Home Furniture Store at each member's convenience and submit an application for membership in the St. Cloud's musicians' union local to Dan Freedman, the secretary treasurer of the local. The application was a mere formality, because Lippert had already paid Mr. Freedman for nine memberships (Lippert joined also), and within a couple of days all of the members of the Ed Lippert Orchestra were also members of American Federation of Musicians Local #536, St. Cloud, Minnesota.

We soon learned that our opening at the 400 Club had been pushed back to mid-November and that Ed Lippert had decided to make a quick booking and have us play a Saturday night dance at the armory in St. Cloud. Being the carny-show character that he was, Lippert bought some quick radio spots on the local radio station and had several hundred handbills printed up to advertise the Saturday night dance. The dance night was exactly three weeks from our arrival in St. Cloud. We were all as enthusiastic about the gig as Lippert, because it would mean a few bucks in our pockets plus a chance to play before an audience and a chance possibly to

Jimmy Rushing, Ann Moore, Count Basie, Betty Love, and Preston Love, Greystone Ballroom, Cincinnati, 1946.

make a few friends in the town. The handbills and radio advertisements were out several days before the dance date, and the prospects of a large crowd looked very good on Friday, the day before the gig. Since we would be playing the gig strictly on a percentage basis of 50 percent to Lippert and 50 percent to the musicians, our pay would be determined by the size of the crowd. The night before the engagement was a clear and crisp November evening, and several of us in the band went up on St. Germain Street to sound out the reaction of the young people towards the coming dance. There seemed to be a considerable enthusiasm for the dance and the "colored" band, so we went back to the hotel feeling pleased about the whole affair.

That night we listened to several bands from the East, and on the last broadcast before the networks went off the air for the night we heard Cootie Williams and his band from the Savoy Ballroom, the Home of the Happy Feet. Cootie had some fine men in that 1940 band, including Butch Ballard on drums and Eddie "Cleanhead" Vinson on first alto and vocals; we were stunned at how well Cootie's band compared to the best bands of the moment. In fact, that was one of the swingingest bands I ever heard before or since. We hung on to the last notes of his sign-off, because it meant the end of the music for the night and the beginning of another long night of nothing to do but play cards or dominoes until we were drowsy enough to drop off to sleep for the night.

Buster Coates and I had a personal feud going playing cooncan, so we were still playing cards long after the others were snoring. At about three, I got up to go down the hall to the bathroom, and as I passed one of the hall windows I noticed that snow was falling outside. It was the heavy and moist snow that falls whenever they have snow in early November in that part of the country, and it seemed to be piling up pretty deep on the ground. I proceeded to the bathroom after taking note of the pretty snow and then returned to our room where I remarked casually to Buster that it was beginning to snow outside.

Buster pulled one of our curtains aside and remarked, "Yeah, it's snowing up a breeze out there."

After a few more hard-fought games of cooncan, Buster and I decided to knock it off for the night, and we turned in. Being an inveterate late sleeper already at nineteen, I didn't even stir until nearly noon the next day; and when I awakened the first thing I noticed was a steady roar of the wind outside. The lighting in the room wasn't exceptionally bright like sunlight, but its color was very white from the reflection of the new, clean, white snow outside the three windows in our room. I got up and went to the bathroom and then into the kitchen to see what we had in the refrigerator for an early snack, and through every window all I could see was snow and more snow. The wind was very high; we had a full-scale blizzard going on. Blizzards were nothing new to me, being from Omaha, but we seldom had severe snowstorms before late November or early December. There were still a few automobiles and trucks struggling through the streets below our windows, but we could see that it was becoming impossible for them to negotiate the deep snow. There was something about snow and very cold weather that seemed to strike terror in the minds of those from warmer climates, and although we were safely sheltered in the warmth of the hotel, Isadore Pollard and Julius Jacquet continuously lamented the state of the weather outside. Booker Samuels, the trumpet player, was from Kansas City, which experiences nearly the same weather conditions as Omaha, and he took very little notice of the blizzard; but finally after one of Isadore's remarks about the snow, Booker mumbled, "Man, I ain't worried about nothing but that gig tonight. If it keeps on snowing and blowing like this, that gig will be canceled."

Booker probably simply voiced what most of us had been thinking, but now it was brought out in the open, and for the rest of the day each of us took turns going to one of the windows and assessing our chances of the gig's being saved. Finally, just before dark, the last few cars that tried to make it down the street in front and at the side of the hotel had to give it up. One by one their drivers would try to push and pull their cars out of the deep snowdrifts and then give up and leave the vehicles stuck on the street in the snow. As far as we were concerned, the gig was hopelessly wiped out, but a short time after dark at about five-thirty, Ed Lippert phoned us downstairs at the hotel and assured us that wintry weather didn't deter these northern people in the least. He explained that he had seen them go out in this kind of weather dressed only in lightweight clothing. He also instructed us to get dressed in our secondhand tuxedoes, which he had bought for the 400 Club engagement, and for us to be at the armory, ready to hit at nine. He ordered us to stay together as a convoy and walk to the armory, which was about six blocks from our hotel. We were somewhat reassured by Lippert's optimism, but as the evening progressed the blizzard grew worse.

At about seven, we all began to dress. In spite of the increasing crescendo of the wind we were all in a happy mood about the approaching night of playing our instruments under real gig conditions. Even old Hoops was in a buoyant mood. With the secondhand tuxes, Lippert had bought us each a bright orange shirt with ruffled sleeves and black patent-leather shoes. The shirts were to be worn open at the neck, and the ruffled sleeve ends protruded far out of the sleeves of our tuxedo coats. Looking back, I think of how weird we must have looked in this strange ensemble, but as compared to some of the ludicrous costumes worn by today's popular performers we were dressed in sartorial splendor. At least we weren't striving for some weird effect for the purpose of attracting notice as is true of most people in show business now.

Since we felt ten or fifteen minutes would be plenty of time to walk the six blocks to the armory, we decided to embark upon the journey at about eight. A few minutes before eight, we all assembled in the hotel lobby, resplendent in our tuxes and with our horns. Besides his horn, each man kept his own music folder with the repertoire, so each of us except Oliver, the piano player, had both hands occupied. Oliver, therefore, agreed to help Isadore carry one of his drum packs. Promptly at eight we assembled before the door of the hotel, and one of us pushed it open with much difficulty against the strong wind. In fact, before we could get the door fully open it took two or three of us to push on it and hold it open. Isadore with his drums, and Buster with both guitar and amplifier, had the heaviest loads, so we held the door for them to exit first. The walk in front of the hotel had been cleaned of snow several times that day, so there was just a light accumulation of snow there, but everywhere else was a sea of knee-deep snow, and in some places the snow had drifted to depths of four or five feet. The seven of us stood there shivering in the bitter cold wind, trying to decide which direction to embark on our six-block journey to the armory and the gig. We decided it best that each of us take turns in helping with the drums and Buster's amplifiers. Luckily, the guitar amplifiers were a relatively new innovation then and were usually quite light. The amplifiers used in modern rock groups are often taller than a good-sized man and weigh many times more than amplifiers of the forties.

We decided to take a route around the courthouse square, down Main Street and then turn into the street that led to the armory. Then we started the great struggle against the wind and the deep snow. Two or three of us carried all of the music folders, and the first serious trouble we had was with music blowing out of the folders. Visibility was very poor in the blowing snow, but we were able to retrieve the pieces of music as they blew about. At no time were we able to go very far without stopping to rest and change pieces of the drum packs. At times the trip seemed impossible to continue, but somehow we kept going, traveling mostly in the middle of the streets where there still were slight indentations from where cars had traveled hours before. Finally, after about forty minutes we arrived at the armory and tumbled into the warmth of the interior. By now all of us were numb from the cold and the snow, but by some near miracle we had made it. It was plain to see that the arduous trip had been in vain. Although it was nearing nine and gig time, there were only eight people in the big armory, and all of them had business there. They were Dan Freedman, the union secretary, who had come to collect the union tax (we were surprised that he could make it there), Ed Lippert and his wife, Carl Pugh (who came with the Lipperts), a ticket taker and his wife, and two people who were there to operate the refreshment stand. Nevertheless, Lippert instructed us to set up and be ready to hit on time. We arranged the bandstand enthusiastically, using some music stands that were on hand at the armory, and at just a few minutes past nine we hit our first number.

We played an hour or so just as though the house were full. Finally, Ed signaled us to take an intermission. All of the members of the band immediately headed for the refreshment counter, and the man and woman who ran the concession gave us all of the coffee, soda pop, and sandwiches we wanted without charge. After eating our snack we stood around a few minutes, and finally Ed decided to call it off, since we hadn't sold one single ticket nor had one single person shown up at the door in the raging blizzard. We were determined to go back to our warm rooms at the hotel, but everyone urged us to remain at the armory overnight until the blizzard subsided. After a vote among ourselves, we decided to leave all of the equipment at the armory until such time as we could come back and get it, and then set out on the journey back to the hotel. After a trip that was much easier without the equipment, we arrived at the hotel in time to catch the last half of a thrilling broadcast of one of the big bands from New York City. The broadcast and the warmth of our quarters seemed to make it worth all we had been through in this unbelievable night.

Our opening at the 400 Club was definitely set for the following Thursday night. We would receive twenty-one dollars per week. Since we hadn't had more than a few cents in our pockets since August, we looked forward anxiously to the completion of our first week. The pay seemed like affluence to us, and the 400 Club was a rather fine club for that area. It was out from town a few miles and catered mostly to middle-aged people who regarded us with a bit of curiosity. These white liberals from the area didn't see many black people in St. Cloud, so we were something of a novelty, but they paid very little attention to us in the band other than to receive our music with courteous approval. After the first week was completed, as he drove us home from the club, Ed Lippert told us that he would be around to the hotel the next day to settle up. The next day we waited with anticipation for Lippert and Pugh to bring our money. Pugh stayed with the Lipperts at the house they rented when we moved up from St. Paul, and, every time we saw either Carl or Ed, they were together.

When Ed and Carl arrived shortly after noon that day, they summoned all of us to meet in the big bedroom. We sat on chairs or on the beds, and Ed seated himself at one of the tables in the room. From the inside pocket of his heavy overcoat he drew a large envelope, which we could see was thick from its contents. From the envelope Lippert withdrew a thick roll of typing paper that he unfolded and began passing the sheets of paper around the room one by one to the band members. There, neatly typed and itemized, was a record of every dime Ed Lippert had spent for our food, lodging, the uniforms he bought, and a few other incidental expenses he had incurred in organizing the band. Mrs. Lippert had evidently been a secretary or a bookkeeper, because everything was laid out in a legal fashion and was typed very neatly. After each or us briefly inspected the sheets of paper, Lippert returned them to his coat pocket and began to outline to

Preston Love at the Royal Theater, Baltimore, Maryland, 1946 or 1947.

us what the program could be from here on. He would continue to pay the eighteen dollars per week total for the rooms at the Merchants Hotel, and he would continue to advance the money to buy the groceries. From now on, there would be a regular breakfast every day for those who wished it. We would receive four dollars apiece every payday for our own personal needs, and all of the other money would go toward erasing the several hundred dollars we owed him for subsistence for the three months since August. In that day of deflated currency, twenty-five dollars per week bought plenty of groceries for seven men who ate as inexpensively as we did. We had no idea what the actual total price of the contract at the 400 Club was, but Ed Lippert probably ended up with nearly two hundred dollars a week, according to my estimates. This was a veritable fortune in prewar 1940. For all of our self-denial and hardships, we would be left with a bare subsistence and four dollars in cash after each week's work.

From this moment on, I formulated my plan to get back home to Omaha. I was determined to get back for two reasons. First of all, I was very unhappy about the situation in St. Cloud, and I was beginning to yearn more with the passing of each day to see Betty Riggs. Betty and I had fallen madly in love before I left Omaha, and the exchange of letters between us had grown more and more impassioned. I used ninety cents of my first four dollars to call Betty long-distance, and we agreed that I should write off the Lippert venture as a failure. Whatever value I could get from the experience had already been gained, and as soon as I could save up the bus fare to Omaha and a few extra bucks I would head for home. We set Christmas as my target date for my return. I told no one in the band that I intended to leave, including my buddy, Buster. I thought it best to be secretive about my escape, because I knew Ed Lippert was the type who might try to prevent my leaving or at least try his best to discourage me from doing so. Then, too, I thought it best not to have the others in the band know that I was leaving them. I was intrigued by the surprise aspect of my escape. When we were paid off December 22, I had a little over ten dollars, which would be about five dollars more than the six-dollar bus fare from St. Cloud to Omaha. Later that afternoon, all of the fellows except Hoops decided to go down on Main Street and do whatever little Christmas shopping they could. Their shopping would consist mostly of watching all the hometown people do *their* Christmas shopping, as the downtown section of the little town was now packed every day with parents and children from in town and from the outlying farming area.

The Majors family lived downstairs over a drugstore right in the heart of town on Main Street, and we always visited them when we went downtown, so I told the fellows I would meet them at the Majors' in about an hour. As soon as everyone had departed from our room, I went down to the little room that Hoops occupied to make sure he wasn't up and about. He was lying down listening to a little old-fashioned radio he had bought, and I talked casually with him for a few moments and left. I then went back to the big room and gathered up my few belongings and my horn and quietly slipped down the stairs and out of the Merchants Hotel. I took the opposite route from the one the fellows would take toward Main Street and walked the few blocks to the Greyhound bus terminal. The next bus for Omaha left in about an hour and a half, so I bought my ticket and found the least conspicuous part of the bus station to spend the time waiting. It seemed like forever, but finally the man behind the ticket counter announced the bus, the many little towns on its route to Omaha, and at last "Council Bluffs and Omaha." It was practically dark when the bus pulled out of the terminal, and with a twinge of sadness I looked down to the right at the lights of the Christmas decorations on St. Germain Street. I knew the fellows would be at the Majors' place now and expecting me to show up any minute.

The trip to Omaha took slightly more than twelve hours, so I arrived home early in the morning on December 23, 1940. At that time of year it was still as dark as midnight. I was anxious to call Betty and to go by Buster's mother's house and report to her, but I knew I would have to wait for a more respectable hour of the morning to do both. I took one of the cabs in front of the Greyhound bus station in Omaha and directed it to take me to 1610 North Twenty-eighth Street, the Mansion. Our door was never locked, so I walked in and put my bags down and went in the back bedroom and hollered hello to Norm and Dodda. The house was cold as usual at night, since we seldom kept a fire going in the front room all night for economy reasons. The Loves were all inveterate late sleepers, so Norm and Dodda didn't get up. Mama stayed with one or the other of my three married sisters during most of the coldest season, so she wasn't at home. I knew my brother Billy would be home in the next hour from his night job at a bakery, so I got a few pieces of kindling and the coal scuttle from the closet in the front room and started a fire.

As early as respectfulness would permit, I called Betty to inform her that I had arrived, and we made arrangements to meet later that afternoon. I then walked the four blocks down to Twenty-fourth and Seward Streets to Pop's Buffet where Buster's mother, "Miss Georgia," ran a small food counter in the rear. I reported to Miss Georgia all of the details of the St. Cloud situation and told her that I had sneaked off without letting anyone know I was leaving. She was very concerned for Buster, because he had had sleeping sickness since he was a little boy, and Miss Georgia was very protective about her only son. The sleeping sickness had subsided considerably, but Buster still would often doze off in the midst of a conversation, a card game, and sometimes in the middle of playing a number in the band.

The day after Christmas, Miss Georgia received a letter from Buster telling her of their great surprise when I didn't show up and relating all of the news about St. Cloud since I left. First of all, as soon as it became evident that I was gone for good, Ed Lippert informed them that he was cutting their total weekly allowance to thirty-two dollars, which would expedite his recouping of the debt owed him. They all felt trapped so no one protested. While I was there, Buster and I were considered a sort of Omaha clique that slightly balanced the carnival clique; since I was known to be rather young and pugilistic if the situation called for it, Buster and I were able to avoid our complete domination by the carnival clique. Now that I had left, Buster was alone against them, and they had begun completely to outnumber him in any decision or any discussion. Buster put a short note to me in his mother's letter. In the note he ran down the musical policy of the group since I left.

While I was there we played all of the stock orchestrations of the popular tunes, in addition to which we had several of the standard corny tunes. In this part of the country we would get zany requests for them, especially since we were playing mostly for middle-aged and middle-class people at the 400 Club. The boys from the carnival could barely read music, and they secretly resented the fact that I, an excellent reader, practically had to lead the whole band through these orchestrations. They didn't like the standard numbers anyway and preferred to play the head arrangements on the jazz tunes that they had played with their band in the carnival. Buster and I weren't as familiar with their head arrangements, nor was I very adept at heading arrangements. Ed Lippert could appreciate head arrangements and the standard riffs and the good solos that Julius Jacquet played, but he recognized the necessity of sounding organized and of playing the type of music the patrons appreciated most, so he kept the heading down to a minimum. Somehow the carnival boys held me responsible for this policy, and now that I was gone they were able to convince Lippert that the stock orchestrations were unplayable without a lead alto sax. Buster lamented in his note that now they were nothing but just a jam combo, and he hated bands or combos that sounded disorganized, like a jam session. Buster was outnumbered, so there was nothing he could do but sit there and suffer it. He expressed his anxiousness to come home in the letter to Miss Georgia, but he had no way of getting his bus fare. Money was very scarce with Miss Georgia, as with everyone in the ghetto in Omaha then, but she and I got enough together to call Buster at the Merchants Hotel to tell him to hold on until we could send for him.

It was almost traditional in Omaha that every musician would have a gig on New Year's Eve, whether the musician was old or young, and even if he didn't work another gig all the rest of the year. Even the worst musicians always had a gig on New Year's Eve either in town or out a few miles in the Omaha area in one of the hundreds of little towns that had New Year's Eve affairs. I was no exception. I got a call from E-Flat Bryant to make a gig with him in a little town over in Iowa, about forty miles from Omaha. The gig paid $7.50, which seemed like all the money in the world to me. Up until then, the most I had ever made for one night's work on my horn was $3.50.

On New Year's Day of 1941, Miss Georgia scraped together a few dollars. I matched hers, and we wired Buster his fare. We had told him to check with Western Union every day, because I knew that if we wired the fare to the hotel, Ed Lippert would learn of it, and Buster might encounter some difficulty in leaving. I never asked Buster the details of his departure from St. Cloud, but he arrived home right on schedule the day after we had wired the bus fare. Buster had always been quite fat, but he was slimmed down some from when his mother had last seen him, and she remarked that she would have to fatten him back up with her good soul food. Shortly after his return, Buster was working on a steady gig at one of the beer joints downtown in Omaha with a small combo.

From January 1941 on, I continued to practice my sax and clarinet. My obsession with Earle Warren's lead alto work, and with Basie's orchestra, grew more with the passing of each day. I played a few gigs with local combos, but I realized with each gig that combo work wasn't my forte because I didn't know enough of the standard jazz numbers nor many of the popular riffs of the moment. I also found it hard to adjust to playing a tune well in keys different from the one I had first learned it in.

A few weeks after the first of the year, my brothers Norman and Billy received their "greetings" from the Selective Service board, and on March 15, 1941, they left with the first peacetime draft contingent from Omaha. They were supposedly drafted for just one year, and I would replace Norman on his job as porter at the local office of the MGM film distributors. Norman had been working there for several years, and several of my friends and I had gone down many times to help him clean the offices, so it was an easy matter for me to take over for him while he was gone in the army. I would now be the main financial support at the Mansion. I didn't have to be at work at MGM until one-thirty in the afternoon and could leave any time I finished my cleaning, so the job worked out wonderfully for me as far as my practicing my horn and courting Betty were concerned. Also, I now had a few bucks in my pocket all of the time, which was a new experience for me.

One day around the first of June of that year I was outside at MGM washing the windows when Lloyd Hunter's bus pulled up in front of the building and stopped. It was fully loaded with the band members and equipment obviously on the way out of town. Although Lloyd's bus was a miserable-looking old school bus, to me at this moment it looked as glamorous as one of the big highway cruisers that the name bands traveled in. Lloyd parked the bus and came up to me where I stood with my

Earle Warren in New York City, circa 1949.

window-washing equipment and told me he would like me to join his band when they returned in a few days. Lloyd had come close to making the big time on several occasions and was second only to Nat Towles in musical prestige in the Midwest; naturally I was thrilled and excited and quickly agreed to join him. Lloyd said he would contact me upon their return from the trip. Several days later, on June 8, 1941, Lloyd, who used the bus also as his family car, drove up to my house and made the arrangements for my joining his band and told me to be at a rehearsal that afternoon at the "colored" union local's headquarters, which was in a rickety old building on Omaha's main black thoroughfare, North Twenty-fourth Street.

I remember very vividly the first number Lloyd decided I would play to audition. It was a stock orchestration of Duke Ellington's "The Sergeant

Was Shy." I knew most of the band members casually, or had seen them many times when I attended the dances at which I had "dug" Hunter's band, but now came the big moment. I felt very alone and afraid. The arrangement of "The Sergeant Was Shy" had one brief but beautifully voiced spot with saxophone soli near its middle, and when we came to it and I sang out, boldly leading the section, I could feel the pulsation of the whole band's approval and also see the reaction of the spectators who came to the rehearsal. Lloyd, who was a rather obstreperous person in a lovable way, suddenly leapt from his place in the trumpet section and had the reed section play the good reed figure over for him several times, loudly proclaiming, "Here I've been looking all over for a first alto man, and one of the greatest has been here right under my nose all this time in Omaha."

Needless for me to say, this was a great moment for me. But within myself I knew how far I had to go to justify fully the praise he and the other band members heaped on me after the rehearsal. That night, we left at seven to play a small town in Iowa, about twenty miles from Omaha across the Missouri River, and my big-band career was officially launched.

Lloyd's bus was a 1933 Ford school bus and very inadequate for sixteen or seventeen adults and luggage, but we spent many carefree and happy moments traveling to the engagements although the conditions were most uncomfortable physically. In the winter we were very cold and we were always cramped, but the band almost always played as though inspired, even in the middle of cornfields and in cow barns where many of the dance halls were located in the Midwest. Each man's incentive was always the hope of being discovered by a name band and escaping the small-time conditions. Lloyd was a beloved individual, and people felt that the only things that prevented his moving into a higher bracket were his carelessness about the appearance of the band and his own appearance, because at that time great notice was always taken of a band's physical appearance and appearance of its transportation and other equipment. Lloyd was never an urbane person in his dealings with the agents and operators who hired the band, so although they usually liked him they never took him or his band very seriously. When I visited the mortuary to view Lloyd's body in 1961, there was no one there but his remains and me for quite some time. I felt a wave of indescribable sadness as I stared endlessly at the somber death mask of this man with whom I had shared so many meaningful experiences and carefree, youthful moments.

Very soon after I joined Lloyd in 1941, we were booked for four weeks at the College Inn in Boulder, Colorado, where the University of Colorado is located. Since Boulder is only thirty miles from Denver, we stayed in Denver at the Rossonian Hotel on Denver's famous Five Points, which was the main corner of the black business section. We commuted the thirty miles to Boulder nightly in our bus. Directly across from the Rossonian was located Benny Hooper's Bar, which had a downstairs nightclub where big jam sessions were held nightly: sometimes even in the afternoons. I was never attracted very strongly to jam sessions, either as a participant or as an observer, but Benny Hooper's was a meeting place for the local musicians and the place to be for young musicians, so I attended the jam sessions as regularly as most of the other musicians in town. At every session at Benny's I noticed a tall and slender white kid who either sat in on drums or on the vibraphones. I also began to see the same kid around the Rossonian dining room when I ate there, and before long I began to see him in the company of our drummer, Bobby Parker. Bobby Parker and I enjoyed a fine rapport, so inevitably I was soon introduced to Bobby's friend, Johnny Otis. Bobby Parker informed me of Johnny Otis's obsession with Jo Jones and Basie's band, and made it known to Johnny that I was also a Basie fanatic with Earle Warren as my particular obsession. Naturally, it didn't take long for Johnny Otis and me to gravitate toward each other. He and I also soon discovered that we were nearly identical philosophically and intellectually. No two men ever agreed more completely and spontaneously than Johnny Otis and Preston Love. By the time the four-week engagement at Boulder ended, Johnny and I had become devoted friends.

Johnny and his young wife, Phyllis, were rooming with a family only a few doors north of the Rossonian. He and Phyllis had eloped from their hometown, Berkeley, California, only weeks before when Johnny joined a small orchestra that was leaving Berkeley for a gig in Reno, Nevada. After the Reno engagement, Johnny and Phyllis had come on to Denver with the orchestra, which soon disbanded, leaving them practically stranded there. After my friendship with Johnny blossomed, I was soon spending most of my free time with him and Phyllis, even eating most of my meals with them at their rooming house. Phyllis left Johnny and me to our ravings, which were divided between discussions about the Basie band and our social and political philosophies. There is no fascination like the meeting of two minds that concur, especially in the early stages of the discovery. Immediately, Johnny and I fell under each other's influence. Johnny had a greater gift of expression than me, which was even more fascinating to me, but he deferred to me because of his preoccupation with the mystique of Afro-Americans. Since Phyllis was Afro-American, and since Johnny's entire musical interest was black music, Johnny identified himself completely with black people.

In mid-July, when the Boulder engagement ended, Lloyd Hunter's band headed back to the Omaha area, where we resumed our itinerary of one-nighters through Nebraska, Iowa, Kansas, and the other neighboring midwestern states. A few days before we left Denver, Johnny Otis had joined the George Morrison combo on a steady location in Denver, but before we parted Johnny pledged me to get him the drummer spot with Lloyd if for any reason Bobby Parker should leave the band. By the end of the four-week gig at the College Inn, Lloyd's band had begun to sound closer to a big-name band than most territory orchestras had ever sounded. Upon our arrival in Denver four weeks earlier, Lloyd had engaged a young tenor sax player who sounded very similar to the great Lester Young of Basie's band. The young sax man was named Paul Quinichette. Paul was spending the summer vacation at home in Denver from Tennessee State University, where he was attending school. Since many of the arrangements in Lloyd's book were built around Paul's solo chair, Lloyd's band took on the Basie flavor, which naturally made me and the other young players in the band very happy, inspiring us to imitate the Basie sound even more than we would have anyway. We knew our little moment of utopia would end when Paul returned to college in September, but it was still fun while it lasted. For at least those few months I could pretend to be Earle Warren, and the others could play at being Lester Young, Walter Page, and other Basie sidemen.

On August 11, 1941, after one of our week-long trips, Lloyd's band returned to Omaha to spend a few days in town. It was early morning when the bus dropped me off at the Mansion. Since Norm and Billy were away in the army, and Mex was now living with my sister, Phylis, no one was at the Mansion but Dodda. He and I were the only two members of the Love clan now living at 1610. Parked in front of the house was a 1937 Chevrolet that I recognized as the car of Dodda's lifelong friend, Blik Avant. I awoke Dodda and inquired about the car, and Dodda informed me that Blik was going to be out of town for a few days, so he left the car with Dodda. Blik Avant was also a good friend of mine; therefore I knew he would have no objection to my using his car. I also knew Dodda would probably sleep until the afternoon. So I said, "Hey, Dodda, I'd like to use Blik's car for a few hours."

Dodda motioned sleepily to the keys on the stand by his bed and turned over to resume his sleep. I heated some water on the kerosene stove in the kitchen and washed and groomed myself from the overnight ride in Lloyd's cramped bus, and then it seemed late enough in the morning to phone Betty. She knew I would be coming in that morning, and she had prearranged it that she would sleep by the phone at her home, which would enable her to answer it before her mother would be awakened or could reach it. I dialed Betty's number, Harney 4567, and before it could ring the second time my girl's voice softly answered on the other end,

"Hello."

Without any further embellishments I announced, "Baby, get dressed and slip out of the back door. I'll pick you up in ten minutes. We're going to get married today."

Betty simply replied, "All right. I'll be watching for you to come."

It was only five blocks from the Mansion to Betty's house, so within five minutes I had pulled up in the driveway leading to her back door. I parked a few yards away, and in a few minutes Betty quietly eased out of her back door and quickly spotted me since mine was the only car in sight. In a few seconds she was beside me in the car and we were on our way to Papillion, Nebraska, a small town six miles from Omaha's city limit. Omaha couples who wished to be married secretly went to Papillion, because it was in another county from Omaha and the notice of the marriage would not appear in the Omaha papers. The marriages in Papillion were very quick and uncomplicated, including the license acquisition and the wedding ceremony itself. Nearly every young lover in Omaha was aware of this. Papillion marriages for Omaha couples were very popular.

Betty and I drove leisurely to Papillion. The only discussion between us was of how enormous our love was for each other. Marriage just seemed automatic and predestined for us at this moment. Before noon on the morning of August 11, 1941, Betty Riggs and I became one. There was hardly any reason for secrecy because we drove directly back to Omaha and announced our marriage to Betty's mother, packed Betty's clothing, and moved forthwith to the Mansion. Although concerned for her only daughter's welfare, Betty's mother agreed that Betty and I should be together since we had exhibited such extreme affection for each other for the past couple of years. Bravely, but sadly, my new mother-in-law watched as her young daughter drove away with me toward 1610. With Norm absent in the army, I inherited his room, complete with the studio couch, the console radio, and his other sharp furnishings. Now the room became mine and Betty's.

We had been married hardly a week when Lloyd Hunter announced that he had booked a return engagement at the College Inn in Boulder. The booking would be for eighteen days right after school began in September. This was especially good news for me, because I would see my friend Johnny Otis again, and Betty and I could use the stay in Denver as a belated honeymoon. In my next letter to Johnny, I informed him that the band would arrive in Denver in the first week of September and that my new wife would be traveling there by train. I also instructed him to find a small apartment for Betty and me since it would be less expensive than the hotel rate, and we could also economize by having our own cooking facilities. The gig in Boulder paid only twenty-two dollars per week, but with these arrangements we could make ends meet very well.

Upon the band's arrival in Denver I went immediately to see Johnny and Phyllis, since they lived only a few doors from the hotel where the rest of the band members were busily checking in. Johnny and Phyllis were anxious to meet my wife, and they had made arrangements for an apartment for Betty and me only three blocks from their place and the Five Points. For seven dollars per week we had a furnished kitchenette upstairs over a flat occupied by an older woman who had been recently widowed. She was the owner of the house, and she was happy to have some young people around for the three weeks we would be in town. Betty's train arrived within an hour after the band's arrival, and I met her at the Rossonian Hotel and took her directly up to meet Johnny and Phyllis. This was the beginning of a friendship between Phyllis and Betty that has lasted throughout their lifetimes, the same as my friendship with Johnny.

A few days before the Boulder engagement, Lloyd was forced to replace our pianist, Fletcher Smith, who was leaving the band for a more lucrative engagement with a small combo. Lloyd had heard about a pianist in Kansas named George Salisbury. When Lloyd called Kansas City and offered the piano chair to Salisbury, the pianist readily accepted and instructed Lloyd to wire him a ticket to meet the band in Omaha. George Salisbury arrived the day before we were to leave Omaha for Denver and came directly from the depot to our rehearsal at the musicians' union hall. All of us band members were incredulous at Salisbury's solo technique and his command of chord changes, but I was hardly prepared for the display of jazz virtuosity that he demonstrated during the engagement in Boulder. He left us shortly afterward, however.

Conditions were ideal at the little rustic cabin-styled College Inn to make a band sound the best, and the University of Colorado fans were both enthusiastic and congenial toward the band members and our music, which inspired the band to its best performance every night. A jazz buff from Denver named Jimmy Thompson and his wife Arleen attended nearly every night of our stay at the College Inn, and Jimmy recorded our entire program nightly on his wire recorder, which was a new and exotic innovation. This was the first time I heard myself on a recording with an orchestra, and I was able to listen to myself critically and objectively.

At the end of the eighteen-day engagement at the College Inn in Boulder, Lloyd's band played a dance for blacks in Denver that was Paul Quinichette's last night with us before he returned to Tennessee State University. His hometown friends turned out in large numbers, which was a fitting tribute to him and the fine solo work he did in Lloyd's band. Before leaving Denver, Betty and I encouraged Phyllis and Johnny to move to Omaha, but Johnny's gig with George Morrison's combo was a good one, and he chose to keep it. However, they promised to move to Omaha if the drummer spot in Lloyd's band ever became open. Lloyd had already verbally committed to both Johnny and me that the job was Johnny's if Bobby Parker ever left the band.

Upon our return to Omaha from Denver, Nat Towles, leader of the Midwest's top band, began to seek my services. Naturally, I was excited, because Nat's band would be considered a step up for me in every way. Towles was the diametric opposite of Lloyd as a bandleader and individual. Nat shared none of Lloyd's carelessness as a businessman and ruled his band rather despotically. Where Lloyd Hunter was loved by his musicians, Nat never enjoyed the affection of his personnel, nor did he especially seek it. Where agents and operators were charitable but disrespectful in their relationship with Lloyd, they felt compelled to treat Nat Towles with the utmost respect and a certain admiration. Nat was a stickler for neat appearance in his band, both for the personnel and for his band equipment. Towles always kept a big sleeper bus, which made for a glamorous appearance. Towles's operation was never haphazard, as Lloyd's was sometimes, and I was most impressed with the fact that only two years earlier Buddy Tate had gone directly from the Nat Towles band to replace Herschel Evans with Basie. Nevertheless, through loyalty to Lloyd and an esprit de corps that existed in Lloyd's band, I repeatedly declined Towles's offers to join his band.

He continued to talk to me, however, and to send emissaries who pointed out to me that I would be improving myself and furthering my career by joining Towles, so in April 1942 I gave notice to Lloyd Hunter and joined the Nat Towles band. I wasn't with Towles very long before I realized this was a step upward, although I missed Lloyd, his fellows, and the spirit of his band. Nat's library was more along the Jimmy Lunceford style, where Lloyd's had been Basie-ish and much easier to play than Nat's. Playing Towles's repertoire represented a challenge for me and a chance to gain valuable experience and knowledge. If a musician, especially a first saxophonist, could play Nat's books, he could play any repertoire in the bigband business.

After I had been with Towles about three months, I was instrumental in getting him to hire Buster Coates on guitar. This was the summer of 1942. Buster's sleeping sickness wasn't as controlled as it had been in 1940, and he dozed off rather frequently. The first time Buster dozed off the bandstand in the middle of a number, the fellows in the band found it very humorous and kidded him mercilessly. But not Nat Towles. When Buster fell asleep for those few seconds on Towles's bandstand, he had sealed his doom as far as working with Nat was concerned. He was dropped at the end of his first trip.

In early September of that year we headed for the South, which was my first time ever south of the Mason-Dixon line. On a September day in 1942, near Texarkana, Texas, I saw cotton growing for the first time in my life. For young blacks in the North, picking cotton was a legend, since most of us only heard of it from the older black people who had migrated from the South. In fact, cotton was referred to jokingly, and not having picked it or seen it growing represented something of a status symbol among blacks in northern cities.

We had played several nights in the South when I called home one night to talk with my wife, Betty. Her first words were, "Guess who's in town! Phyllis and Johnny. Lloyd Hunter sent for Johnny to join his band, and he and Phyllis came in three days ago. Lloyd has a whole bunch of new young guys from Wichita and Tulsa, and Johnny said they are just waiting for you to come back and join them—and Lloyd has a new bus."

Johnny and I had kept in touch ever since I last saw him, but I didn't know his joining Lloyd was in the works. I immediately entered my notice with Towles and told him I would like to leave for Omaha as soon as he could find a suitable replacement for me. Towles began nightly to audition alto players for my chair in each town, but each night it seemed more futile. When we arrived in town, Nat would make it known through the musicians' union local or by word of mouth to the local musicians that he was looking for a first alto saxophonist. Each night at the gig several alto players would usually show up and take their turns at trying to play a number or two in my first saxophone book. This had gone on nearly ten days when we arrived in Baton Rouge, Louisiana, to play the Black Masonic Temple where public dances were held. The band had played about half an hour when a large young man arrived on the bandstand with his alto in hand, ready for action. I made a place for him beside me and made the next scheduled arrangement ready for him. Towles kicked off the number, and after a few bars I knew that Towles had found my replacement. Between numbers I learned that his name was Porter Kilbert and that he was attending Southern University, a black school in Baton Rouge. He informed me that he would take a sabbatical from school if Towles hired him.

Since Porter was doing so well with the repertoire, I left the bandstand and called the railroad station to inquire when I could get the first train for Omaha. The man informed me, in a heavy southern accent, that I could get a train to Kansas City connecting to a train to Omaha if I got to the station in one hour. I hastily gathered my luggage from Nat's sleeper bus and caught a cab for the railroad depot after bidding Towles and the other musicians good-bye. Within an hour I was on the way to Omaha.

Later, I was to become good friends with Porter Kilbert as we crossed paths in various cities with various bands. Before his death in Chicago in 1960, Porter became one of the great alto sax players of the world and played with many bands including Duke Ellington, Roy Eldridge, Billy Eckstine, Illinois Jacquet, and for years with the Red Saunders house band at Chicago's Club DeLisa.

When I arrived in Omaha it was late September. Betty and I had become parents of a son in July, and it was good to get back to my family after an absence of nearly three weeks. After the reunion with my wife and young son, I called Johnny Otis to inform him that I was back. Within hours I had been rehired by Lloyd Hunter. A rehearsal was called for the following day, which would be the last day off for the band before beginning a two-week trip through the Midwest. All of the new fellows with Lloyd were young men near the same age as Johnny and I, and they too were Count Basie fanatics. The new band promised to be lots of fun.

Personnel changes in bands had become very frequent now because of the war, but most of Lloyd's men enjoyed exempt status from the military. However, Dave Finney, who had played guitar with Lloyd for many years, was forced to take a job at the bomber plant near Omaha. I recommended Buster Coates to replace Finney, and Lloyd readily hired him. The fellows rode Buster about his falling asleep on the bandstand and in the card games, but he took it good-naturedly and retaliated with his own chiding. With Buster, Johnny Otis, and all the new young musicians in the band, life was one big round of laughing, joking, and kidding around. This was the most jovial band I have ever played with, but we were still very conscientious about self-improvement and about striving to prepare ourselves to replace one of our idols in a big-name band.

Johnny and I carried our fishing gear and our shotguns in the bus that Lloyd had purchased. It was a later model sleeper bus sold to him by a midwestern orchestra leader who was being drafted into military service. Most of Lloyd's bookings were played on an outright percentage basis of 70 percent of the gross gate receipts going to our band and 30 percent going to the promoter. There were also bookings where we received a nominal guarantee with an added percentage privilege. Only a minor percentage of Lloyd's contracts were for outright flat guaranteed fees. Lloyd's band was operated on the so-called co-op basis. Each night, the travel expenses and other operating costs for the engagement were deducted and the remainder from the gross was divided equally among the sixteen members of the band. As leader, Lloyd Hunter received one-half share more than each sideman. Lloyd was ten or twelve years older than most of his personnel, but he had a great sense of humor and joined in all the fun. On all percentage jobs, just before we hit the first number, Lloyd would bellow out in the direction of the admission gate, "Let them on in there, Mr. Charlie. We're on P.C. tonight!" All the young cats would double up with laughter.

The ratio between percentage engagements and guarantees had been reversed with Nat Towles's bookings, but even the percentage engagements were usually very lucrative because Nat was the biggest drawing card of the territory bands. With Towles, we received a five-dollar nightly guaranteed salary, which was more than we usually received on most of Lloyd's engagements. Before I left Towles he had offered me eight dollars per night to induce me to stay. Towles averaged nearly six nights per week, which was also a slightly higher weekly average than Lloyd Hunter's. Before I made up my mind irrevocably to leave Towles, I did some quick figures in my mind. With Nat I would average nearly fifty dollars a week, which was unheard of for territory-band musicians up to that time. Nevertheless, I stuck to my decision to leave.

On my first night back with Lloyd, we played a percentage engagement at a skating rink in Nebraska City, Nebraska. The dance was known as a jitney dance, where each couple paid ten cents for each dance number on which they entered the dance floor. Our percentage would be 70 percent of the gross gate receipts, so the band cut each number short and took little time between numbers to insure the biggest possible receipts. The dance started at nine, and by ten-thirty we realized it was a bomb. We struggled through the four hours until one, but after deducting the night's expenses the band's split came to sixty-five cents per man. We were undaunted, however, and moved on happily to the next night's gig, because it would mean another opportunity to emulate our idols in the famous bands.

On our nights off in Omaha during this period with Lloyd, most of us band members would go down to the Barrel House or to McGill's Blue Room, both of which had house bands and featured nightly jam sessions. McGill's was in the heart of the black community, and the Barrel House was a white-owned club located a few blocks from downtown Omaha. Usually when jazz musicians with big names came through town, they would seek a jam session if they had a night or two off, and these big-name instrumentalists would always end up at McGill's or the Barrel. Both clubs experienced some monumental jam sessions with a mixture of out-of-town greats and Omaha's better jazz players.

The Barrel House was unique because it was the first spot in the white area of Omaha that catered prevalently to clientele of both races. Also, the Barrel House had a large following of cattlemen and cowboy types who were in Omaha in association with Omaha's big meat-packing industry. These Western types preferred country-and-western music, but they affably accepted jazz with a certain appreciation. The whole concept of racial and musical mixtures was considered revolutionary for Omaha of the 1940s, and the Franklins (owners of the Barrel House) were far ahead of their time. They were anachronistic because they enjoyed every moment of the unusual mixture of races and types at their club, Even more phenomenal for 1942 was the fact that there was never a serious racial incident at the Barrel House, in spite of the mixture of races.

A black pianist, Vi Anderson, was the leader of the house combo at the Barrel House for several years, and she became a personally beloved favorite of the Franklins and of the Barrel House clientele. However, in the early summer of 1943, after Johnny had been with Lloyd for eight months, Vi Anderson began to have disagreements with the owners of the Barrel House, and they approached Johnny and me about our bringing a five-piece combo into the club as house band. Johnny and I pondered the move for a while, and in June 1943 we gave our notices to Lloyd Hunter and left his band to open at the Barrel House.

With two avid young jazz performers like Johnny and me at the Barrel House, the jam sessions flourished. The Barrel became even more so the gathering place for all the hip young musicians and for the hip music fans, both black and white. Johnny became the darling of the white jazz lovers in Omaha and of the white musicians who aspired to play jazz. They were mystified by Johnny's complete immersion in the black community and in our way of life. As the only white member of otherwise entirely black orchestras, naturally Johnny stood out visually, but he was also a dynamic drummer and vibraphonist, which increased his conspicuousness.

We had been at the Barrel House slightly over a month when one day we saw in the *Omaha World-Herald* newspaper that Count Basie, his band, and show would open at the Orpheum Theater for one week on August 3. The impact was comparable to the explosion of an atomic bomb to us two Basie fanatics. Johnny was as fanatical about Jo Jones, Basie's drummer, as I was about Earle Warren's alto sax work in the band. From the moment we read Basie was coming to the theater, we began to count the seconds until the band's arrival. Neither of us had ever had the opportunity to catch Basie on a theater stage. We had only seen the band at dances, where the conditions weren't nearly as perfect as the vantage point of a theater stage with its good acoustics. Eventually, after what seemed like ages, their opening day at the Orpheum arrived. Johnny and I stationed ourselves in the balcony to witness the incredible spectacle of our gods on the stage. When the band struck up its theme, "One O'Clock

Jump," behind the curtain, both Johnny and I were literally close to having heart failure. Then the curtain was open, with the band into a fast, up-tempo version of "I Found a New Baby." There on stage before our eyes were Walter Page, Buck Clayton, Sweets Edison, Dicky Wells, Jack Washington, Jo Jones, Freddie Green, Earle Warren, and all the individuals whose names we had grown to worship. Even today, I often wonder how I survived the excitement of observing that great aggregation on a theater stage for the first time.

In 1943, the downtown theaters in Omaha still insisted that blacks sit in the balconies, but Johnny and I were so overwhelmed with the band and show that we almost convinced ourselves that the balcony was an even better vantage point from which to observe a stage show than the first floor. We caught every show, every day of their stay in Omaha, except for the two late shows on the nights we had to go to our gig at the Barrel House. After the theater engagement in Omaha, Basie's band left for a week's stand at the Tower Theater in Kansas City, and for a few one-night engagements in the Midwest. Several days passed before Johnny and I recovered from the thrill of their stay at the Orpheum.

The reputation of our combo spread quickly around Omaha, and soon after Basie closed at the Orpheum the owner of Sloppy Joe's Tavern approached us about coming to work at his club. Sloppy Joe's was several blocks from the Barrel House, more in the heart of downtown Omaha, and the owner offered us a considerably higher salary than we were receiving at the Barrel House, so we decided to switch to the new spot. Shortly after we opened at Sloppy Joe's, placards were posted for a coming appearance of Count Basie and the band at the Dreamland Ballroom on North Twenty-fourth Street on September 6. When the night of the Dreamland engagement arrived, we had been at Sloppy Joe's only a couple of weeks or so, but we made it plain to the owner that we *would* be taking the night off to hear Basie, and he reluctantly let us have the time off.

On the way to the Dreamland that night after parking our 1931 Chevrolet convertible, Johnny and I and our wives passed Earle Warren as he, too, was on his way to the ballroom. My heart almost stopped at being so close to "god." Earle had grown to recognize me because I was always in front of him before every dance they had played in Omaha since 1938, and I stayed there throughout the dance and talked to him about reeds, mouthpieces, and the other things that starry-eyed kids talked about with their idols. But Earle didn't recognize Johnny and me in the darkness. Also, I learned later that he was driven to distraction by the stomach pains he was having. After we arrived at the ballroom and stationed ourselves at our usual place in front of where the saxes would sit, Earle came onto the bandstand and seated himself and began to take out his sax. When he saw me down front, he said, "Hey, boy, I've been looking for you. I sent a fellow named Emmett James to find you."

I couldn't imagine what he wanted me for, but he quickly told me he wanted me to work in his place. He went on to tell me that he had heard around town and when he was in Los Angeles that there was a boy in Omaha that played just like him. I thought he was joking and kept laughing, but he assured me that he was serious, because his stomach ulcer was forcing him to take some time off and travel back to Johns Hopkins Hospital in Baltimore for treatment and further diagnosis. I almost panicked with fear, but Earle reassured me, telling me to go get my horn and audition right then and there.

The thought of auditioning before all the hometown people and for my idol's chair with the great Count Basie band was chilling, but Johnny, my wife, and our circle of immediate friends standing around us expressed their confidence in me. Johnny quickly turned from the discussion and headed for the front door of the Dreamland. In a few minutes he was back with my alto. He had driven our jointly owned 1931 Chevrolet convertible the few blocks to my apartment and back in probably the record time for that trip. Many of the hometown people knew of my extreme worship of Earle Warren and the Count Basie band, and there was a murmur from the sea of faces when I pulled myself up on the stage and began to remove my horn from its case. Earle made a place for me and for the chair that had been placed beside him for me, and he got the music out for the next tune Basie had called. The number was "As Time Goes By," which featured a vocal by Thelma Carpenter.

Most of what happened next was like a dream or trance, but I remember that there was a fabulously beautiful alto-sax introduction and some beautiful reed-section figures before the vocal began. There was also some beautiful reed-section background during the vocal. Basie motioned to all the band to play softly so he could hear me more plainly, and I remember it sounding as though I was all alone, with no sound but mine on the stage.

I was an exceptional reader, which made the repertoire easy. I had studied Earle's phrasing and his inflections, which made it seem as though I had been playing with the band for some time. I could hear members of the band expressing amazement in the background, and I could see the looks of amazement on the faces of the audience down front. Nat Towles's repertoire or book was much more difficult than Basie's, and now I was so happy that I had received the opportunity and experience of playing Nat's book for those several months.

After I had auditioned with the band for an hour or so, Basie called the band valet, Henry Snodgrasss, and instructed him to tell me to be at the Union Station the next morning at eight-thirty. I could hardly believe my ears. I was up bright and early the next morning and packed and ready to leave. My wife, Betty, called a cab and we headed for the Union Station. At the station, the various members of the band were milling around. The ex-Omahan, Buddy Tate, was surrounded by a group of friends who had come to see him off, but he proceeded to take me under his wing. Soon Earle Warren arrived, and naturally I left Tate to be with him. Earle reassured Betty that all would go well. Presently, I bade her good-bye, as it became time to board the train.

CHAPTER 4

The Count Basie Band

❋

Aboard the Missouri Pacific Eagle, I was excited at being surrounded by the fabled Basie personnel as we headed for our first stop, which was St. Louis, Missouri. Earle Warren was very gracious to me, but the person who paid me the most attention was Jimmy Rushing, the rotund blues singer of the band. Rush was almost paternal in his attention to me. He and I struck up a friendship that was to grow and last until his death in May 1972.

Upon our arrival in St. Louis, we checked into one of the black hotels, the Booker Washington. That night we played a dance at the Kiel Auditorium. Earle Warren sat on the stage beside me most of the night, helping me to find my parts and generally instructing me. Basie's band played many head arrangements for which there was no music, and Earle had to help me with all of these. By the time the gig ended, my confidence had grown, and I was anxious to get my teeth more deeply into the repertoire.

The next night would be spent at liberty in St. Louis before we headed for the next engagement: a week at the Regal Theater in Chicago. Since I was a stranger in St. Louis, Sweets Edison asked me if I would like to spend the night off making the rounds of the city with him and his wife, Birdie. I was happy to accept and at ten o'clock that night, we set out from the hotel in the Edisons' sharp convertible that Birdie had driven from New York to spend some days with Sweets.

Harry "Sweets" Edison considered St. Louis home because he had spent several years there playing with the Jeter-Pillars Orchestra before moving to New York. Sweets had worked several months with Jeter-Pillars at the Club Plantation, where the orchestra had been for several years, so that was the first place we visited. Upon our arrival at the Plantation, the white club owners and members of the Jeter-Pillars band were very cordial

Portions of this chapter derive from my interview with Stanley Dance, originally published in *The World of Count Basie* (New York: DaCapo, 1985).

to Sweets. He introduced me to Hayes Pillars as Basie's new first alto man, which evinced a wave of excitement in the co-bandleader. Pillars explained that they had rehearsed a new show that day, the Joe Ziggy Johnson Revue, for that night's opening, and their first alto sax man had been taken suddenly ill, only moments ago, with the opening scheduled for a half-hour hence. Jeter was the other half of the bandleader team, and although he was a competent third alto player, the lead alto chair was not his forte. Sweets assured Pillars and the club managers that I could play the show's first alto sax book at sight, and I was rushed onto the bandstand a few minutes ahead of showtime to organize the show repertoire. So many times in my career I have wished that I had been born with that gift for improvising and conceiving clever melodic passages while soloing on tunes with difficult chord changes. I have always marveled at those jazz soloists with this innate facility. But on this night, my gift for sight reading and phrasing and interpreting as I read the music enabled me to play the lengthy show repertoire with precision. After I played the opening show amid all the excitement and anxiety of the opening night of a new show, Pillars thanked me profusely. He and the club management offered me money and food, and I accepted the Plantation's choicest steak dinner.

Sweets and his wife watched the show from a front-row table, and while I was eating my steak during the intermission Sweets came back to where the members of the band were and introduced me to all the members. Two of the musicians in that Jeter-Pillars band were Clark Terry (who was to become one of the all-time trumpet greats) and Rene Hall (who played guitar and trombone in the band and wrote most of the band's arrangements). From this night in 1943 on Rene and Clark have continued to be good friends of mine, and I had the pleasure of playing numerous recording dates and other engagements for Rene in Los Angeles between 1966 and 1971.

After the night off in St. Louis, Basie's itinerary called for a trip to Chicago early the next morning. The band had another day off before we would open at the Regal Theater in the Windy City, and the last night off before the opening would be spent in Chicago. We arrived in Chicago in the afternoon, and since I knew that Nat Towles's band was playing a six-week engagement at the Rumboogie there, I set out immediately to find the members of the band after we checked in at the DuSable Hotel, one of Chicago's top black hotels. It was easy to track down the hotel where the Towles band was staying because nearly all orchestra members either stayed at the DuSable or at the Oakwood Manor. I had many friends in Nat's band from my days with that organization, and several of my friends from Lloyd Hunter's band were now with Towles.

The first member of Towles's band with whom I talked at the Oakwood was James Von Streeter, who had been my special buddy when we worked together in Lloyd's reed section. He and the other Towles members were incredulous when I told them I was in town playing first sax with Basie. I promised to meet them at their gig at the Rumboogie that night after taking a few hours' sleep. At about ten that night I caught a cab from the DuSable to the Rumboogie, and since Towles and the band were on an intermission, I found my way to their dressing room. When I heard familiar voices behind the dressing-room door, I burst into the room and received a hero's welcome from all the cats.

Towles had an excellent band, and they played the backup music for the show performers exceptionally well. I had great pangs of nostalgia for my old chair in the band and my many young friends in the group. After the last show, several of us went to an all-night café and ate amid much joviality and reminiscing. We then took a cab for our respective hotels. Upon bidding me good night, the members all assured me that they would be there tomorrow morning for the first show at the Regal Theater.

I had never played a theater before, nor had I had enough time to become familiar with Basie's repertoire, so anticipating their presence the next morning didn't help my anxiety any. When the lights went up on stage, I was already wracked with nervousness with all the newness of stage work. Then the curtain opened, and there in the front row sat all of the Nat Towles band, including my ex-boss, Nat himself. Somehow I made it through that first show. Being a very impatient individual, I strove hard to learn the many facets of playing theaters. Within a few days I felt like a veteran of stage work.

We were scheduled for four straight weeks of the old "Negro" theater circuit, which was the Regal in Chicago, the Howard in Washington, the Royal in Baltimore, the Paradise in Detroit, and the Apollo in New York. The only one of these we would miss on this trip was the Paradise in Detroit. By the time we had played the third theater, I was accustomed to the rigors and the differentness of stage work, and I now began to love playing theaters. One day I was sitting on stage while an act was performing and we had nothing to play for a few minutes. I casually looked around me on the stage when suddenly I realized that I was surrounded by Jo Jones, Buck Clayton, Harry Edison, Dicky Wells, Buddy Tate, Jack Washington, Freddie Green, and all the men I had held so in awe. I experienced cold chills and thrill bumps for the first time in my adult life. I actually felt like pinching myself to see if I was dreaming. Until today I have never experienced a greater thrill than the thought of Basie's great brass section and the world's greatest rhythm section being there behind me. The only other comparable thrill was playing with Jo Jones on one of his better nights during that period.

While we were at the Regal one day after an afternoon show, Sweets Edison called me as I came off stage. With him was a handsome young man who looked vaguely familiar to me. When Sweets introduced him as Trevor Bacon, I remembered having seen him on stage a few months earlier at the Orpheum Theater in Omaha with Lucky Millinder's band and show. Trevor had sung two big hit songs with Lucky Millinder, "I Want a Big Fat Mama" and "When the Lights Go on Again All Over the World." He was now on his way back to New York from California at the end of a tour with Millinder's band, the Ink Spots, and other Moe Gale Agency stars. Quickly after our introduction, Trevor Bacon began to heap praise upon me. He said he had stayed to see two shows and moved to several areas of the theater to listen to my lead-alto playing. He then informed me that Tab Smith was planning to vacate his lead-sax chair with Millinder and urged me to consider joining Millinder's band when Earle Warren returned to his chair with Basie, which I was holding temporarily. I eagerly accepted Trevor's offer and assured him that I would join Millinder as soon as Earle returned, if I heard from Lucky.

Earle Warren recovered from his illness in about six weeks and returned to his job. We had played several weeks of theaters and a week of one-nighters, and with these under my belt I felt much better prepared for any big-band offer that might come my way. My last week with Basie was at the Apollo Theater in New York. Earle Warren elected to come in for some shows each day and I would play the other two or three.

Don Byas had replaced Lester Young, the original Basie featured tenor-sax soloist, in 1941, so Don was in the band throughout my weeks there. However, when I arrived at the Apollo to do my first show, I walked on stage to take my chair and there sat the great Lester Young in the first tenor chair. Don Byas's absence that week was unexplained, but shortly afterward Lester rejoined the band permanently. I regarded Byas as one of the greatest tenor-sax virtuosos in history, but Lester Young was an original part of the Basie style and possibly the most unique tenor-sax innovator of all time. This was the only experience I had working with Lester Young.

I arrived back in Omaha in late October after Earle's return. Since I had nothing else scheduled, Lloyd Hunter asked me to make the few gigs he had lined up through New Year's Eve. Wartime had decimated Lloyd's once-fine band. What few good men he was able to recruit soon moved on to Nat Towles after they came to Omaha and saw the superiority of Nat's present situation to Lloyd's. Lloyd was now reduced to playing his few meager bookings with a small combo and traveling in two ancient cars.

Nevertheless, I felt good about playing Lloyd's few gigs because I realized this was a very low ebb in his career. We had the actual dregs of the country's musicians and the dregs of the Midwest bookings, but Lloyd was still his usual good-natured and undaunted self. Only Lloyd and I of the present personnel had been around during the good days of his bands, so we shared an unspoken camaraderie during this low time.

Most of our gigs paid five dollars per night, so we all looked forward anxiously to our New Year's Eve gig, which Lloyd had announced as more than fifteen dollars per man, which was a lot of money in the Midwest of 1943. One of the two cars we used was an ancient seven-passenger limousine that Lloyd rented from a former traveling bandleader in Omaha. Since we had only seven men, Lloyd decided to take just one car, while pulling a trailer with the equipment. On every trip the old limousine developed some mechanical problem, but each time Lloyd would "get out and get under" and keep the old vehicle alive. Finally, on the morning of New Year's Eve we loaded up the trailer with the equipment and hitched it to the limousine and set out for the big gig, which was in a small town nearly four hundred miles from Omaha in western Nebraska. From the very beginning the old limousine would falter after running smoothly for a few miles, but Lloyd would work on the ignition system or the carburetor and keep it going. Finally, shortly after it became dark, the old car quit, near Alma, Nebraska, and nothing Lloyd did got us going again.

Lloyd's band had once been a favorite in Alma and its vicinity, so he was able to get a mechanic to come out from town to look at the car, but the car refused to budge. By now it was getting near the time for us to start the gig, and we still had over a hundred miles to travel. As Lloyd and the mechanic worked on the car, the band members became quite chilled. The mechanic directed us to go to a nearby farmhouse and to tell the family that he had sent us there to keep warm. We arrived at the farmhouse, which was only yards away, and the farmer and his wife congenially accepted us. It was now shortly after eight-thirty and apparent that the big New Year's Eve job was lost. We settled down to enjoy the warmth of the farmhouse while Lloyd and the mechanic worked on the car several yards down the road. The farmer's wife gave us coffee and cookies and turned their radio on for our entertainment while the old farmer plied us with questions about various subjects. At ten we listened to the nightly news, and then suddenly at the end of the newscast the strains of "One O'Clock Jump" burst forth from the radio as an announcer exclaimed, "From Maria Kramer's Lincoln Hotel in the heart of New York, we bring you the music of Count Basie and His Orchestra, with vocals by Jimmy Rushing, Earle Warren, and Thelma Carpenter."

I felt pangs of mixed emotions as I sat there in the bleak surroundings of this remote farmhouse listening to the same notes that I had read and played only weeks before in the same great New York City from where my idols were now broadcasting. Here we sat in the provincial area of Alma, Nebraska, after missing our coveted New Year's Eve engagement, while my associates of a few weeks ago were performing in the plush and glamorous surroundings of the Lincoln Hotel's main dining room in New York, the Big Apple. It seems the other members of Lloyd's band sensed my mixed emotions, because for the most part they remained in respectful silence throughout the broadcast. This was an unusual reaction for small-town musicians when they listened to Basie or to any one of the other big-time bands on radio, on records, or in person.

Around midnight, Lloyd arrived at the farmhouse with the limousine, which he and the mechanic had repaired sufficiently to get us back to Omaha if we were fortunate. So at midnight, while most other people were reveling and bringing in 1944, we were heading down the dark highway bound for Omaha, without money in a barely heated antique limousine. I had worked my last job ever with my friend Lloyd Hunter's band. The events of this night made me realize for the first time in my young life that life is a game of extremes—feast or famine.

Four days later, on January 4, 1944, I received a telegram from Trevor Bacon in New York, instructing me to call Lucky at the Hotel Theresa there. Upon receiving the wire, I quickly made the call, and Lucky Millinder told me of Trevor's high recommendation, then made me a salary offer, which I accepted. Two days later I received a wire for train fare and expenses to join his band at the Fay's Theater in North Philadelphia. Lucky had an excellent band with some fine jazz soloists, such as Joe Guy on trumpet, and Sam "The Man" Taylor on tenor sax. The band stressed precision more than the Basie band, whose strength was in its loose and relaxed style.

Tab Smith had played third alto sax with Basie to Earle Warren's lead from 1940 until 1942. Basie had never featured an alto-sax soloist before. Tab had played both lead in the section and was the featured soloist with Millinder's band for several years before he joined Basie in 1940. Back with Lucky's band in 1944, Tab was the first or lead alto sax man as well as the most featured soloist in the orchestra. Tab also wrote most of the orchestrations for Millinder. When I arrived at Fay's Theater on about the eighth of January, Lucky immediately installed me in the third-alto chair beside Tab Smith. In all my youthful brashness, I quickly informed Lucky that I played only *first* sax and that I would not play third sax under any man alive including Earle Warren, whom I certainly conceded as my superior as a lead sax man. Lucky constantly assured me that Tab Smith would soon be leaving to form his own combo, but one night in Charlotte, North Carolina, Tab took me aside in a café and confided to me that the first chair in Lucky's band was his "home," the same as the first chair in Basie's band was Earle Warren's home.

Within a few days I had contacted Nat Towles, who was on tour on the black theater circuit with Ethel Waters. Nat urged me to put in my notice with Millinder. Nat's band was soon to go on a seven-week tour of the South and the East with Marva Louis, the wife of the heavyweight champion, Joe Louis. After playing out a two-week notice with Lucky, I left him in Jacksonville, Florida, and met Nat Towles in Philadelphia. Towles's band comprised a number of friends of mine from Lloyd Hunter's band, as well as several promising young players and the few original members from Nat's earlier bands. The band was lodged at the old Dupree Hotel on the main corner of Philadelphia's black community, Broad and South Streets. The tour with Ethel Waters had ended a couple of weeks past, and the tour with Marva Louis was three weeks off, so Nat booked a couple of one-nighters to keep his members in pocket money. With the passing of each day, we became anxious to begin playing regularly. Soon, the Marva Louis tour was only four days off. The first of the rehearsals with Marva was scheduled for the next afternoon, which was Monday, and on the Sunday night several of us band members gathered in my room for drinks and reveling. The merrymaking subsided at about four, and the revelers retired to their respective rooms with great enthusiasm about the afternoon's scheduled rehearsal. Within minutes I was in bed snoring.

In about two hours, I awoke nauseated and hurriedly made for the nearest toilet. I seldom vomited, so I became alarmed when the nausea persisted for some hours. On one of my trips to the bathroom a band member became aware of my distress and went to Towles's room and informed him. Towles quickly donned his bathrobe and came to the bathroom. He knew with one glance that I was seriously ill, and within minutes he had gone to his room and dressed and returned to take me to a doctor. Nat and I walked around the corner to a physician's office where I was given a blood-count test. Upon seeing the results of the test, the doctor hastily called the Mercy Hospital, which was Philadelphia's all-black-staffed hospital, and made arrangements for me to have emergency surgery. He then called a cab company and instructed them to send a cab to his office "on the double." The physician informed Towles and me that my appendix was probably only minutes from rupturing.

Less than an hour later, I was on the operating table at the Mercy Hospital being prepared for an appendectomy. Before being anesthetized I instructed one of the nurses to call my wife, Betty, in Omaha, and inform her of my operation as soon as the results appeared successful. Two-and-a-half days later Betty arrived in Philadelphia by train on the same morning Towles and the band were scheduled to leave on the tour with Marva Louis. Betty checked into the Dupree Hotel in my vacated room. Before the band departed, Towles gave Betty the tour itinerary, instructed her to keep him posted on my progress, and gave her money for our subsistence. Naturally, I was very disappointed at missing the opening of the big tour, but within eight days I was out of the hospital and beginning to feel stronger each day. Towles called us daily, and six days later Betty was on her way back to Omaha and I was en route to Savannah, Georgia, to rejoin the band. The train arrived in Savannah at 6:00 P.M., and Nat met me at the depot. At nine I was sitting on stage at the Savannah Auditorium in my first-sax chair. I had missed sixteen days of the Marva Louis tour.

A few weeks after the tour Lucky Millinder and I began to correspond, and he soon sent me a wire that Tab Smith was leaving and the first chair was mine in the Lucky Millinder reed section. It wasn't Basie, but I felt it was at least a step closer to my goal of being with Basie permanently. Lucky Millinder's band had been a stepping-stone or way station for numerous top musicians who had gone on to the top name bands. I rejoined Millinder in New York in May 1944. My train arrived in town in the early evening, and I checked into the Braddock Hotel at 126th Street and Eighth Avenue in Harlem. The band was in the middle of a four-week stand at the former Savoy Ballroom, and I was scheduled to start with the band the next night. With the night off, I took a short nap and at about eleven I dressed and headed for the Savoy. When I arrived at the Savoy at 140th Street and Lenox Avenue, the marquee showed that Lucky's band was sharing the stand with the Erskine Hawkins band. The Savoy billing often included two groups booked by the Moe Gale Agency, because Gale was associated with the Savoy and used it to rest its bands and troupes from one-nighter tours as well as for the Savoy's network radio exposure.

As I went up the wide steps that led to the ballroom, I recognized the sound of Millinder's band. I edged unobtrusively to the front of the band-stand where my appearance created a mild sensation among the band members, most of whom had been with the band when I left four months earlier. But I was electrified at seeing the male vocalist who was sitting on the far right end of the bandstand. It was Wynonie Harris, my dear friend from my boyhood in Omaha. Wynonie and I had a big brother–little brother reunion, and when the band took its intermission my reunion with the other band members was completed. They informed me that Trevor Bacon and Tab Smith had made it known to Lucky months before in California that they would be leaving to organize their own unit, and it was then that Wynonie had been contacted to join the band in the spring. Wynonie was enjoying great prominence in Los Angeles as a blues singer and nightclub performer.

Within days after I arrived, Lucky began to rehearse the band for a scheduled recording date at Decca Records. I had never recorded before, and my excitement and anticipation were at a high pitch. On May 24, we recorded five sides. Two of the sides featuring Wynonie Harris were instant hits. They were "Hurry Hurry" and "Who Threw the Whiskey in the Well?" Two sides featuring vocalist Judy Carol were also very successful. They were "Darlin'" and "I Just Can't See for Lookin'." Because of the record hits, Wynonie became an overnight big name and left us in the middle of his first southern tour to go on his own.

The next week we opened a week-long stand at Loew's State Theater, which was my first Broadway engagement, providing me with another of my biggest thrills. Lucky's band was a well-rehearsed and bright professional organization. With several new hits and "Sweet Slumber" still popular, our tours were nearly as successful as any of the top names. In November we headed for a four-month tour of California, which meant a reunion for me with my friend, Johnny Otis, and my oldest brother, Sonny, who was also living in Los Angeles. While on the coast, we toured in the Northwest and northern California extensively before doing a week-long stint at the Orpheum Theater in Los Angeles. Our next stand was a seven-week stay at the Club Plantation in Watts. The bill featured T-Bone Walker and Billie Holiday. Billie was making the picture *New Orleans* during the daytime, but she managed to sing with great inspiration and expressiveness every night. Our reed section was Kent Pope on alto sax, Elmer Williams on tenor sax, Bull Moose Jackson on tenor sax, Ernest Leavy on baritone sax, and myself on alto. From the standpoint of precision, balance, and phrasing, this was by far the finest reed section with which I have ever performed. Lucky had a number of arrangements made featuring just the reed section with rhythm accompaniment. But I had the Basie bug worse than ever. I was therefore discontented in any other setting, and Lucky and I soon became disaffected. Upon the band's return to New York in April of the new year (1945), the Lucky Millinder band and I came to a parting of the ways, and I returned to Omaha.

After I returned, I soon went to work at the Barrel House with a small group that included Lloyd Hunter on trumpet. Lloyd was having some personal problems, and it wasn't a happy time for him, but it was wonderful being around him nightly and sharing half-pints with him on our intermissions. Lloyd was a beautiful cat. After a couple of months at the Barrel

House, I began to hear from Count Basie from New York. I had heard through various sources that Earle Warren intended to leave the band and form his own group. Now Basie confirmed it. Basie encouraged me to come to New York at least a week early to give myself the chance to listen to the band carefully backstage at the Roxy Theatre, where they would be winding up a five-week stand. I really didn't need too much encouragement; on May 29 I entrained for New York City at my own expense. Basie had assured me that he would reimburse me for my expenses.

I took a cab to the Braddock Hotel at 126th Street and Eighth Avenue, where I had stayed before when in New York with Lucky Millinder. I deposited my things in my room and hastily took the subway downtown to the Roxy Theatre where Basie was playing. The band was onstage and I eased into a place between the curtains only a few feet from the reed section. The wings of a theater are by far the best spot from which to hear an orchestra. Hearing that great Basie band backing up acts on a stage show is a thrill that every musician should have the opportunity to experience.

Buddy Tate was nearest me, and when he caught sight of me, he nudged the other sax players: Earle, Jimmy Powell, Lucky Thompson, and Rudy Rutherford (on baritone sax). Jimmy Powell had played third alto in the 1943 band, so we knew each other well. I had worked with Lucky Thompson on two occasions with Lucky Millinder's band in 1944. Rudy Rutherford was the only one in the reeds with whom I had never worked. There were several new faces in key positions in this wartime Basie band, but it was still fantastic and still very much "Basie." It retained nearly all of the early Basie style, flavor, and aura. Shadow Wilson had replaced Jo Jones on drums when Jo went into the army, but Basie, Freddie Green, and Rodney Richardson were there as in 1943. Rodney was the perfect replacement for Walter Page, because he admired Page and was like I was about Earle's style. Rodney was dedicated to retaining the true Count Basie style and purpose.

Karl George was on trumpet, having replaced Joe Newman some weeks earlier, and J. J. Johnson and Ted Donnelly were on trombones. These were the only three members who were new to me, except that I had seen Donnelly with Andy Kirk's band in Omaha around 1936. The tune "Mutton Leg," which we recorded in 1946, was a tribute to Ted Donnelly, since the title of that number was his nickname in the band. It was actually another version of the early Basie recording, "Every Tub." The final day of the Roxy Theatre engagement came, and, at last, on June 6, the first-alto chair with Count Basie was mine. Earle Warren came down to our charter bus in front of the Theresa Hotel on 125th Street and took me aside to encourage me about my future in the band and to counsel me about my negotiations with Basie's management, which had a rather bad name in the orchestra business of that day. I detected a little melancholy in his manner, but he couldn't know how happy he had made my life. The bus was more than an hour late leaving for a one-nighter in Johnstown, Pennsylvania, so I spent the time talking with Earle and with Jimmy Rushing, who "adopted" me immediately and became my guardian, as he had done when I joined the band my first time in 1943.

That 1945 band was a formidable group of musicians, but without Jo Jones, Jack Washington, Walter Page, Buck Clayton, and Earle Warren, there had to be differences. I constantly measured my performance against Earle's and came up very short in my own estimation. I actually resented it when fans and columnists compared me favorably with that great lead-alto man. One reviewer caught us at a Cleveland theater and wrote: "At least Basie's reed section has gotten together, thanks to the presence of a fine young lead sax man who replaced the erratic Earle Warren." I called him the next day and told him that he knew nothing about lead sax, that Earle was the greatest lead man in history, and that to compare me with him, especially in Basie's band, was stupid. After many years and much more experience, I am even more amazed at lead men like Earle and Willie Smith. They are as incredible in their way of leading a section as were geniuses such as Art Tatum, Lester Young, Charlie Parker, and Clifford Brown in their solos.

On October 15, 1945, I had the great personal thrill of making my first records with the band at CBS in Hollywood: "Queer Street," "Jivin' Joe Jackson," "High Tide," and "Blue Skies." That night, our road manager handed out a new itinerary for our trip back east. My heart almost stopped when at the top of the list I saw "Orpheum Theatre, Omaha, October 22–28"! Ever since I was ten years old I had been going to the Orpheum to see all the famous bands and their stage shows: Duke Ellington, Cab Calloway, Erskine Hawkins, Jan Garber, Lucky Millinder, Charlie Spivak, and for the first time, Count Basie. To go from the poverty of the Love Mansion and Omaha's ghetto to the Orpheum stage seemed too farfetched to a black kid of my generation. Nearly every kid I knew, musician or not, had dreams of performing on that glittering stage some day. The Orpheum simply represented the "big time" of Omaha.

I began counting the seconds when the Union Pacific Challenger pulled out of Los Angeles and headed east for Omaha. The Union Station seemed to be crowded with members of the Love family and friends. They were there to greet me and Buddy Tate, who they thought of as an ex-Omahan. If Jo Jones hadn't been in the army, there would have been a contingent of his friends there, too. After directing some of the band members to the best rooming houses in the ghetto, I was whisked off to one of the night-clubs on the main street of the black community. North Twenty-fourth Street was buzzing like a bee that night, with Count Basie's band in town and with a night off before the Orpheum opening. I almost got tired of taking bows at the clubs on the "Avenue," the term we used for the area of Twenty-fourth and Lake streets, the main intersection in our part of town. My wife and I still maintained our Omaha apartment. She and our three-year-old son had been with me in California for three months, but they had left a few days ahead of the band's departure. I awoke earlier than usual on the opening morning of the Orpheum engagement because I had invited Bill Doggett to breakfast. Being an early riser, he arrived promptly on time at ten. He was traveling with the band as staff arranger, and occasionally Basie would let him sit in on piano. We had our bacon and eggs and set off in good time for the theater. I stopped on the way to pick up some accessories at Hospe's Music Store, sauntered south on Fifteenth Street, and turned into the alley leading to the Orpheum stage door.

The movie was on and I could see that the band valet had been there earlier that morning before the film began to set up the bandstand. The five chairs for the reed section were on the side nearest me. A lot of friends and well-wishers were standing around, but I finally found one of the better dressing rooms upstairs that Buddy Tate had staked out for me and him. In a few minutes they called the "half hour" before the show, so I changed clothes and warmed up my horn. It seemed like no time at all before someone yelled "All on!" Down the steps and into my seat I went. I remember Basie's piano intro to "One O'Clock Jump" and his signaling "Line Ten," which meant for the reed section to begin its opening riff on the number. All the lights were bright onstage and the curtain began to open as the movable stage rolled forward. Here I was before a hometown audience at the Omaha Orpheum Theater. Blacks were still "requested" to sit in the balcony in downtown theaters then, but there in the front row were a gang of my lifelong buddies, among them "Brother" Joe Allen, Maxine "The Red Fox" Parker, Basie Givens, Bernice Donaldson, and Bernard Butler. They cheered and pointed to me, and I could also hear a murmur of excitement from the balcony, where other ghetto friends were seated.

After a short version of "One O'Clock Jump," the band launched into an up-tempo number called "B-Flat." For the next hour, Basie and his stage show kept the audience wild with delight. He never gave any special recognition to band members when the band was playing their hometowns. That was the band policy, so I had only a short solo on each of the five daily shows — the eight-bar bridge Earle Warren had played on "Jumpin' at the

Woodside" or the one on "Rockabye Basie." But Pop, the backstage door-man, soon learned I was a hometown boy by the number of visitors who came to see me. He had instructions from the management to curtail the number of people backstage, but he realized this was my moment of glory, so throughout our stay there was always a big crowd of my friends and rel-atives backstage, in the wings, or in our dressing room.

My mother had purchased a fine home in 1944 with money sent by my brothers, Norm and Dodda, from their army pay, and during the week my sisters gave several huge parties there for the entire Basie band and show cast. At each of these affairs, Jimmy Rushing and Sweets Edison were the life of the party. What with playing piano and telling jokes, they kept everybody lively. I think of them as two of the cleverest individuals ever in show business. The night we closed at the Orpheum, we had to hurry to the Union Station to catch a late train to Minneapolis, where we were to open at another Orpheum. I was very excited at the thought of seeing my brother Dude there again, when he would get to hear his kid brother play first sax with Count Basie for the first time. When the band returned to Omaha the following year, it was an added pleasure for me because my two other brothers were home from the war in Europe.

Nineteen forty-six was really the most significant year of my stay with the band, because Jo Jones and Walter Page returned to reunite the famous Basie rhythm section. Jack Washington was back from the army on bari-tone saxophone, and in some ways this little giant was the greatest saxo-phonist ever to play in the band. If Buck Clayton and Earle Warren had only been there, it would have been one of Basie's best bands. In the sum-mer of 1946, too, we "discovered" a young tenor-sax man named Paul Gonsalves, who replaced Illinois Jacquet, who had taken Lucky Thomp-son's place in October 1945. I never felt Paul's style fit Basie's band ideally, but he was a true virtuoso and we became very good friends. Of course, he went on to distinguish himself in the great Duke Ellington band.

Perhaps the most overlooked member of the original Basie band was Ed Lewis, the lead trumpet player. Ed played nearly all the lead parts on the classic recordings when Basie had only three trumpets, Buck Clayton and Sweets Edison being the other two. In concert, Buck or Sweets would oc-casionally relieve Ed by playing the lead on a riff or a prolonged number, but even after Basie added a fourth trumpet, Ed still played a predominant part of the lead. Much of the Basie sound was Ed Lewis. He grew up with the original Basie style from Kansas City and captured the essence of the Basie feeling and the Kansas City charm. Ed had a sweet, delicate sound, but he played definitively. Basie's was the greatest swing band with the most relaxed feeling in jazz history, and Ed always swung like no other lead trumpet probably ever did. We always referred to his lead as "funky," long before the word came into common use in connection with rhythm and blues. I rate Snooky Young as the greatest of all jazz lead trumpets. For power, finesse, and the ability to interpret a part, he is without equal. But in Basie's band, Ed's lead had a very special quality that fit the Basie style. I heard Ed and Snooky together nightly for nearly three years, and although Ed was nearing the low end of the curve of his greatness as a lead man, he still gave a beautiful account of himself on the more characteristic Basie arrangements. He would still spit out the lead on numbers such as "It's Sand, Man" just as he had years before. Then, toward the climax of the arrangement, the younger Snooky would take over with high notes on "shouting out" choruses. Ed Lewis gave his all to the Basie band during its rise to the top. He may even have burned out his lip by playing *all* the lead parts in the powerhouse band of 1937, 1938, and early 1939. Unfortunately, his dedication was never properly rewarded.

Nineteen forty-six was really the last glory year for the Basie band of the thirties and forties. Bookings were still good, crowds were still large, and the band still played the most prestigious nightclubs, theaters, and ballrooms regularly. However, storm clouds were brewing. Bebop was becoming the popular craze in jazz, and Basie hadn't had a hit record or anything dramatic happen in quite some time. When the war ended, the country's economy changed drastically. Early in 1947, as if at some prearranged signal, things declined sharply for the Basie band. After a tour of the West Coast, we played a one-nighter at a ballroom in Philadelphia on our way back to New York. It was late January 1947, and the crowd and enthusiasm were much less than when we played there before. Before intermission, I noticed a group of young fellows standing attentively in front of the reed section. Occasionally, they would whisper to each other. From their manner, I judged them to be young musicians from the same orchestra or local clique. At intermission, they beckoned me to join them in front of the bandstand. A spokesman for the group said, "Man, we want to talk to because you're a young cat. How can you stand playing those old-fashioned arrangements, man? Diz was here with his big band, and that's what's happening! Basie better get hip and get some new stuff. We know if you tell him what's happening, he will listen to a hip young cat!" Then one of them pointed to Buddy Tate. "They don't play like that anymore," he said. "That other tenor man, [Paul Gonsalves] can kinda' get by, but that old cat has got to go!" The whole group laughed in agreement.

I was twenty-five years old, the youngest member of Basie's band, but I felt nothing in common with these beboppers. But I did realize that the mania for change and newness in both show business and the music business had finally caught up with even my beloved Count Basie band. Looking back to that night in 1947, I wonder how those young musical "revolutionaries" feel about youth, age, and changes in music now that they must all be in their early seventies. Buddy Tate has survived as a highly esteemed figure in jazz, but I wonder if any member of that clique ever made a name for posterity to remember. Buddy always played tastefully in the purest jazz idiom, compensating for a lack of virtuosity with expression, a big sound, a driving beat, and by always telling a meaningful and unpretentious story in his solos.

Bookings fell off sharply as 1947 progressed, as did the caliber of the places where we were forced to work and the size of the crowds. Some of the better bookings were retained, but there were more one-nighters, unpaid vacations, and "short weeks" in which we worked less than five days for reduced salaries. In early June, Basie called a meeting and announced that summer bookings were few, but that his manager had the opportunity to book the entire summer season at the Club Paradise in Atlantic City if the payroll were reduced to meet the club's top offer. It meant a sharp reduction for all of us, but we agreed to it rather than go through the summer unemployed. Although the cost of living in Atlantic City was staggering, by careful budgeting all of us were able to have our families with us to enjoy the resort atmosphere. The hours at the Paradise were brutally long, but we had a fine show, complete with Ziggy Johnson's revue and a line of attractive chorus girls. Like a well-conditioned athlete, any band shows the effect of a long location by becoming tighter, and on its better nights, the Count Basie band almost "burned down" that little Club Paradise.

Our competition in Atlantic City came from the other main black club, the Club Harlem, which presented the Coleridge Davis big band, Larry Steele's *Smart Affairs* revue with twelve beautiful chorus girls, Moms Mabley, Billy Daniels, Tops and Wilda, Derby Wilson, and others. The musicians and performers from both clubs soon had a wonderful rapport. Basie's band had a fine softball team organized by Paul Gonsalves, Jack Washington, Ted Donnelly, Sweets Edison, and me. We played several mornings each week after we got off at five in the morning. We played teams from the Harry James, Charlie Spivak, and Louis Prima bands when they were working in Atlantic City. We also played teams made up of bartenders and waiters from the black clubs, as well as teams formed by the black policemen and firemen of the city. I played third base and Paul Gonsalves played shortstop. If you could have combined my ability to catch sizzling grounders with Paul's rifle-like throwing arm, we would have had the finest shortstop–third base combination in jazz. But Paul was prone to miss a few catches, and I always had the worst throwing arm in the world.

We won only occasionally, but the games were great fun. The stands would be full of celebrities because nearly every star of black show business visited Atlantic City during the season. Some of them would play with us for laughs, and after each game there would be a big party.

Freddie Green, Ted Donnelly, my son, and I went crabbing once a week. We had bought ropes and crabbing baskets, and we would walk several miles to an inlet where we stood on a little bridge and caught hundreds of ocean crabs. Freddie was from Charleston, South Carolina, so he was right at home on the seacoast with crabbing basket in hand. He was also a master swimmer. Emmett Berry, singer Bob Bailey, and I once made the mistake of trying to swim with him in the ocean. The three of us had a frightening time when we found ourselves far out beyond our safe limits! Snooky Young, his wife, their three children, C. Q. Price (the third alto man), and his wife Mildred, together with my wife, son, and me, shared a three-bedroom apartment, which reduced our costs to a minimum. The three families worked out the cooking arrangements very harmoniously, considering that there were ten of us in a rather small space.

The season at Atlantic City traditionally ends on Labor Day, but Basie's management got a booking at the Strand Theatre on Broadway in New York, so we closed at the Paradise on August 22. It had been a surprisingly enjoyable eight weeks. Hot Lips Page opened at the Paradise with a hastily put-together band the day after we closed. We stayed one day to catch his opening with the same show we had played. Hot Lips had a much smaller group and most of his men were good jazz players, but not adept at reading show music. It was a disaster, though Sweets Edison got up on the stand with his trumpet to help them. Sweets even conducted some of the more difficult show numbers. When he played for dancing after the show ended, Hot Lips rewarded us with some of the richest, purest Kansas City blues I ever heard.

We opened at the Strand on August 25 with the picture *Deep Valley*, featuring Ida Lupino and Dane Clark. We had an excellent stage show with the Edwards Sisters (tap dancers), Lewis and White (comedians), and Pearl Bailey as the headliner. This was Pearl's first Broadway appearance, and she was sensational. But a weak movie on Broadway meant a short run, so the Strand gig lasted only two-and-a-half weeks. After a two-week "vacation" without pay, we set out on a string of one-nighters. The Orpheum in Omaha passed on us this year, but we played a one-nighter at The Dreamland Ballroom, where I first saw Basie in 1938, and where I auditioned to replace Earle Warren in 1943. This 1947 gig was enjoyable because all my family and hometown friends could stand right in front and chat with me between numbers. Jo Jones and Buddy Tate were still sensations in Omaha, so coming there was a pleasure for them, too. The visit was marred for me, however, by the fact that I had the only argument with Count Basie that I ever had. He called all the members of the band into the office during intermission to discuss salaries for the rest of the tour, and somehow the road manager maneuvered the conversation to make it appear that I was being mercenary. I told him and Basie that if they couldn't pay my full salary, they could leave me in Omaha right then and there. I was contrite afterward, because Basie seemed surprised and disappointed by my outburst.

From Omaha, we went to Denver for a one-nighter and then to the Rainbow Rendezvous Ballroom in Salt Lake City for a week. The ballroom afforded Basie valuable airtime on a coast-to-coast network. I never quite got over the miracle of broadcasting on the networks, which enabled my family and friends to listen to us at the very moment of our performance thousands of miles away. By this time I had made hundreds of broadcasts with Basie, but it remained a novelty for me till the end. We went to Los Angeles from Salt Lake City in our private railroad Pullman car. Our arrival at Union Station had previously always been triumphant, with crowds of friends, relatives, and fans to greet us. But this November morning in 1947, only a small group showed up, although Les Hite, Basie's faithful friend and admirer, was on hand. Les was formerly leader of the top big band on the coast in the thirties and early forties. I realized then that the Basie magic was waning, but there was worse to come. We opened for a week at the Million Dollar Theatre, which had once been an ornate and prestigious venue, but it was on lower Broadway and it had declined. The Orpheum, where we had previously played, was on upper Broadway and was considered a higher-class place. Furthermore, attendance at the Million Dollar was far below what we had enjoyed at the Orpheum.

Next, we went off for some weeks of one-nighters in northern California, Oregon, Washington, and Vancouver. We played a week at the Golden Gate Theatre in San Francisco. In nearly all these places we had played to enormous crowds in 1945 and 1946. I had also played some of them in 1944 when I was with Lucky Millinder and we played from Seattle down to San Diego. Now we were playing to far smaller audiences than Lucky had drawn. I was alarmed and I felt personally affronted by any serious threat to the sacred Basie "thing." We returned to Los Angeles for a four-week stand at the Meadowbrook Club in Culver City, which had been the Casa Manana when we triumphed there in 1945. Previously, during Les Hite's great days, it had been Sebastian's Cotton Club. After the first week, the owners told Milt Ebbins, Basie's personal manager, that they couldn't honor the remaining three weeks of the contract because of the miserably poor attendance. Ebbins reached a compromise whereby the band would work only three nights over the weekends. Everybody in the band had to accept a large reduction in salary, and, with Christmas approaching, spirits were very low. The lack of enthusiasm on the part of the fans was also damaging to morale, but this didn't touch me deeply, because I was still with Basie and felt sure something would turn up to improve the band's fortunes.

On the first night of the last three-day arrangement, I arrived at the club with Jimmy Rushing in the jitney we shared each night. Milt Ebbins was in my dressing room, and he motioned for me to closet with him.

"Prez," Milt began, "Earle is coming back to the band."

"I had heard rumors about that," I said. "I even heard the tape Basie made telling Earle that he missed him."

Milt became all flustered and protested nervously, "No, Prez, Basie loves your playing and wants you to stay on and play with Earle. Isn't that what you've always wanted, to play in the same section as your man?"

I knew the gesture of offering me the third alto chair was halfhearted, because C. Q. Price had become an important member of Basie's arranging staff. I had personally gotten C.Q. into Lucky Millinder's band in 1944 and was instrumental with Buddy Tate in getting Basie to hire him, so I wouldn't have done anything to cause his dismissal, even if I had felt the third-chair gesture was sincere.

"Listen, Milt," I told Ebbins, "this band is Earle Warren's home. As long as Basie has a band it should include Earle as first alto if he needs a job. Furthermore, I wouldn't play third alto under anyone, including Earle, and I think you and Basie both know this."

We could hear Basie signaling the band from the piano, so I asked Milt to excuse me and started to put my alto and its stand together before heading for the stage. As I came around the back of the bandshell, I could see Earle Warren hurrying across the dance floor with his sax case in hand, heading for his chair in the middle of Count Basie's reed section. He had arrived in Los Angeles earlier that day without my knowledge. I rushed to greet him in front of the bandstand. We exchanged a few warm words, and within seconds I was listening to the greatest first alto sax man in the world, in the band that was now made complete again by his presence.

I always felt that my years with Count Basie were undistinguished and that I simply kept the chair warm until Earle Warren's inevitable return, so leaving the band represented no particular trauma for me, in spite of my love for it and my love of playing with it. Ironically, Johnny Otis and his seventeen-piece band were scheduled to open at the Meadowbrook the week after Basie's closing, so I agreed to stay over for two weeks and split the lead alto chair in Johnny's band with Buddy Collette, who has since become one of the most successful of Los Angeles studio men. During that two-week stand, I also had the pleasure of recording six big-band sides with Johnny's band on Otis Rene's Excelsior label. Bill Doggett was in town working, so he composed a ballad, featuring me on alto, called "Love's Nocturne," which we did on the session. I also was featured on a beautiful arrangement of "My Old Flame" done by Doggett. Doggett and I had worked together with Lucky Millinder for a year when he was the band's pianist, and he had also traveled with us in Basie's band as staff arranger for some months in 1945. Not many of his fans gained from the fame of his hit record "Honky Tonk" are aware that Bill Doggett was a great big-band arranger and pianist.

My dear friend Johnny begged me to remain in Los Angeles to be his colleague, but my love for Omaha was beckoning me back to my hometown. Then, too, I had been smitten with the bandleader bug. Not too long after I had gotten over the first thrill of joining Basie, I became obsessed with the desire to head my own traveling band, and I knew that Omaha and the Midwest was probably the only place I could accomplish organizing a band and establishing a foothold as a bandleader. Furthermore, I realized there was no future for me with Basie since the specter of Earle's inevitable return was always present. Basie often reassured me that a place would be made for me if Earle came back, but my youthful ego would never have permitted me to play third alto, even under my idol. In addition, since I wasn't a jazz soloist, I would have been buried completely in the third alto chair of any band. Then too, I felt that a move to any other band in the world would have been a step down, since Basie was the pinnacle of my ambitions up to then. Shortly after New Year's of 1948, I sent Betty back to Omaha with our son, Preston (Sandy), who was five years old now. Two weeks later, over Johnny's protests, I entrained for Omaha and home.

CHAPTER FIVE

Preston the Bandleader, Part 1

※

Secretly, I had always harbored the desire to lead a band, to call the shots and try my hand at deciding the way things would be done. In every band I had played with there seemed to be so many things that could have been done differently and improved upon. By nature I have always been for the underdog, a person strongly opposed to any injustice or inequity no matter how insignificant the injustice might seem. Perhaps it was naiveté on my part, but I envisioned a band that would be a utopia for every individual musician and for the nonmusician employees such as the valet and bus driver. In my conception of band leading, the business aspect of the organization shouldn't be treated carelessly, but a traveling orchestra should be a combination of pleasure, creativity, self-expression, and business.

Upon my arrival in Omaha in mid-January of 1948, I realized that I had a big image locally because of my few credits and successes, but I was ill-equipped to work as a freelance musician. With my obsession for playing lead alto in the Earle Warren tradition, I had neglected to broaden myself otherwise on my instrument. I had spent very little time learning my chord changes and practicing the necessary jazz figures and popular jazz cycles of the day. At twenty-six years of age I had almost deprived myself of a real career in jazz by not at least exploring my potential as a soloist. I didn't entertain any misgivings or doubts about Earle Warren's greatness as a lead man, but in order to be competitive I realized I must turn my back on that concept, at least partially. The Charlie Parker and bebop solo style and phrasing was now the complete order of the day, and I was steeped in the Basie style, which was rapidly waning in popularity.

Soon after I returned to Omaha, I found myself in demand for jobs with several of the medium-sized orchestras in the city's black community. Numerous young musicians and some of the older ones accorded me a form of idol worship because of my track record, but I detected that some of them were shocked at my limitations as a soloist when they launched into all the new hip Charlie Parker–Dizzy Gillespie improvisations of standards such as "Idaho," by Donna Lee, and the others that were sweeping the country. It was painful to me to play with one young player after another who wasn't one fifth the musician I was but who knew his way around a thousand times better in the mysteries of jazz improvisation and modern interpretation.

At this point in 1948, I opened my mind and heart to the study of chord progressions and began to learn all of the hip tunes that permeated the prevalent jazz of that era. My heart wasn't entirely in it, because I was then (and I am still) obsessed with my love for lead alto sax à la Earle Warren and other great lead men, but at least I detected some talent for soloing. Although it was too late for me to develop into another Sonny Stitt or one of the other gifted jazz soloists, I could occasionally get off a creditable solo. I made a rather halfhearted attempt at starting a band in 1948, but it was abortive. It wasn't until Easter of 1950 that I launched my first full-fledged orchestra operation. In the interim, between late 1948 and Easter of 1950, I played with Nat Towles briefly and with various combos of my own and of other leaders. By the time I motivated myself to organize a band seriously, my money was very "weak," so I was forced to start on a shoestring. However youth is youth, and somehow at a young age an individual usually manages to pull a thing off no matter how great the odds are against it.

In January 1950, when I realized that I would actually be starting a band, I wrote to my friend Johnny Otis. He sent me his entire big-band library, which I copied off with the help of Betty and several friends before returning it to him. Johnny's big band was now defunct and he was operating his Club Barrel House in the heart of Watts in Los Angeles. Many of the arrangements in Johnny's repertoire were things I had given him from Basie's book, because in 1945 Basie had given me permission to clean out arrangements that he didn't use from his book and to pass them on to Johnny. Some of these were excellent charts by such arrangers as Buck Clayton, Hugo Winterhalter, Buster Harding, and Bill Doggett. As soon as we copied off Johnny's library, I began to schedule rehearsals for all of the capable young players around Omaha. We practiced daily at the Urban League Community Center at Twenty-second and Lake Streets. By March, I had made contact with the Howard White Booking Agency of Omaha. This was the agency that "made" Nat Towles when Nat had his early successes in the Midwest from 1935 until he got a shot at the big time during World War II and signed with a big eastern agency. Howard White died shortly after I signed with the agency in 1950, and Howard's wife and her

Preston Love Orchestra, March 17, 1950, Ballerena Ballroom. (Photo by William W. White)

brother Augie took it over. The agency was pretty close to collapsing, but Augie was able to book some dates for me after I had a very impressive brochure made up and equally attractive posters printed.

Our first date was scheduled for the night before Easter in April 1950 at the Glovera Ballroom in Grand Island, Nebraska, which is 145 miles west of Omaha. As the first engagement approached, it became more and more apparent that I didn't have any means of transportation or other necessary band equipment such as music stands or a public-address system. As yet, we didn't have a good drummer available to us for a full time tie-up with the band. I can't remember all of the details of how I accomplished it, but we sent to Chicago for a drummer, Phil Thomas, who arrived in Omaha only the day before the first engagement. Somehow, I acquired music stands and a sound system only hours before departure time for Grand Island.

Several days earlier I had read an ad in the *Omaha World-Herald* about a bus for sale in Lincoln, Nebraska, for the price of three hundred dollars. Somehow I raised this small fortune and took a Trailways bus the fifty-five miles to Lincoln. The owner of the bus turned out to be the owner of a small bus line operating between Lincoln and several small towns near it.

The bus was a 1942 vintage school-type Chevrolet bus that was outfitted with comfortable seats and other improvements to its original construction. When I brought it back to Omaha two days before the approaching inaugural gig, my young band members and I beheld it with great pride and admiration. Several of my musicians had played with Nat Towles and other local bands that had much finer buses, but this was *ours!* We all felt that we were launching our collective bid for the big time. The bus still had the names of the bus company and several little Nebraska and Kansas towns printed on the sides, the front, and the back, so several of us immediately began painting over the lettering. The first thing I did the next morning was to find "Doodle Ree" Gibson, one of Omaha's gifted artists, to paint "PRESTON LOVE & HIS ORCHESTRA" on the front, back, and sides of the bus. Doodle Ree did a masterful job of painting, and somehow I scraped together his eight-dollar fee.

From our days with Towles and Hunter we learned not to leave for an engagement at the last possible minute. My fellows and I decided always to give ourselves plenty of time when leaving for a gig. There is nothing in the operation of a band worse than actually missing the gig, because this means no money for anyone when band members are paid on a nightly basis. In the orchestra business, you are in the transportation business first and the music business second. Not many people are aware of a band's musical ability beyond certain minimum professional standards, but even the best band in the world is no good if it doesn't get to the engagement. Arriving late is nearly as bad as missing the engagement because the fans and the promoters always think the lateness is caused by some negligence on the part of the leader or the group. Furthermore, if the band arrives late, many times the operator will dock the band for part of its fee. Many of the customers become skeptical and leave if the band arrives too late, and even if the engagement goes on, a late start creates an unpleasant atmosphere for everyone concerned. It is better to leave too early for the gig and allow for any reasonable contingency than to leave at the last minute and shave it too close to your arrival. The gig is sacred and inviolable, even if you are playing free of charge. Bandleaders become adept at improvising and getting to the engagement no matter how hopeless it might seem when adversities occur.

Many of the currently popular groups are notorious for getting to engagements late. With modern buses and airline travel, they are very careless about travel plans. These troupes fail to consider that even the finest transportation can break down or encounter unavoidable delays. Unlike the bands of our day, the prospect of being docked or missing a few thousand dollars is no deterrent to their taking a chance and missing the gig or being late. In the arithmetic of recent years, even worthless performers can earn incredible sums of money if they can accomplish popularity by some means or other. I have seen more money spent on narcotics by the pop stars of the sixties, seventies, and eighties than great performers earned in the days of Duke, Basie, and others. As far as I'm concerned, the lifestyle of young performers of this era nearly nullifies the thrill of becoming famous and rich.

The gig at Grand Island on Easter eve was a resounding success. Black groups had been in great demand in the thirties and forties, but now there were almost none operating in the Midwest. There were no blacks in any of the small Midwestern towns. Except for the bigger cities such as Omaha, Lincoln, Des Moines, and Sioux City, you could travel the Midwest for weeks without seeing a black person. Grand Island had two or three black families, but Afro-Americans were still quite a novelty even there, with their proximity to Lincoln and Omaha. The Glovera Ballroom was packed. My posters announced that I was formerly with Count Basie, but now I realize that this was of no value in those little Midwestern towns. They were intrigued by the prospect of a swinging, jazzy "colored" band.

Another thing I had learned with Nat Towles and Lloyd Hunter and other bands touring the Midwest was that no matter how good your repertoire was from the standpoint of swinging and playing jazz, you must play at least fifty percent of the music in the Lawrence Welk and Guy Lombardo style to please the dancers in that area. It was even more important to please the ballroom operators, because they considered their own taste as the final authority on a band's worth. There were other popular white recording hits and white stars whose songs were essential to any band's programming in this area. We considered Glenn Miller's version of "In the Mood" (written by a black musician, Joe Garland) and Tommy Dorsey's "Boogie Woogie" as corny and laughable, but we stocked our repertoire with several of these things, such as Lawrence Welk's "Josephine," to get us through the night on Midwest gigs. With talented young creative musicians, we often made some of those ricky-ticky corny tunes listenable and enjoyable to play. No bands ever played the middle-aged country-club two-beat dance rhythm more tastily and with a better groove than some of the Afro-American rhythm sections of that era, although we played this trite music only out of necessity. We often did so with humor.

The old stereotype that all blacks are born with rhythm is certainly a myth. Rhythm and expression aren't genetic with black Americans. They are simply parts of the African cultural tradition since the drums played such a big part in all of African tribal life. Because of the tradition of rhythm with blacks, a great emphasis has always been placed on the beat.

This consciousness of the rhythm or beat is cultural and environmental with most black people, and I'm sure if some Afro-American kid was born and raised in a provincial area of the country he or she would have no more consciousness of rhythm than the Caucasian kids of that area. To a large degree, each of us is a product of our environment and our conditioning. Thank God that the environment of the American ghetto has fostered the black creative genius of Ray Charles, Jo Jones, Aretha Franklin, Otis Redding, and Dicky Wells, among others.

For the first six months of 1950, my band struggled, always tottering on the brink of financial disaster. The Howard White Booking Agency was on the verge of going out of business, and bookings were very scarce and money equally so. We were very popular at a few spots in Minnesota, the Dakotas, Nebraska, Kansas, and Iowa, but any band needed a five-night-per-week average and about a one-thousand-dollar-a-week average gross to survive. We averaged three nights and five hundred dollars per week, and I just couldn't support ten men, a bus, and an agent much longer on this kind of money. My original musicians were Eli Wolinsky and myself on alto sax, Harry Lewis on tenor sax, Albert Winston on bass, Billy Cargile on piano, Donnie Kelly and General McCloud on trombones, and Nathaniel "Georgetown" Holmes and Jake Andrews on trumpets. Eli Wolinsky and Jake Andrews were the white members of the band, and many people in the small towns still considered the presence of whites in a black band quite a novelty. My men were very enthusiastic about our band and determined to stick it out even when we barely had enough gigs and enough money to survive physically. When we experienced hardships and privations they retained their confidence and suffered the hardships uncomplainingly.

In the Midwest we often played actual barns and dilapidated, makeshift ballrooms. We traveled for days on bumpy, unpaved roads in some areas, and in order to get engagements we usually had to make long overnight trips to the next gig. A six-hundred-mile jump was not unusual, and this only put a bigger strain on the transportation and on our resources. Eight of our ten members took turns driving, but I did most of the night driving after the gigs because I was conditioned to stay awake at night. I also feared that someone else might fall asleep at the wheel. After all, their lives were basically my responsibility. I needn't add that we didn't have one penny of insurance on the bus or liability for the passengers. We were new in the territory and our drawing power hadn't grown yet, so many of the operators were opportunistic or astute enough to accept my band only on a straight percentage arrangement. It seemed that every time we needed money the most urgently, we would have nothing but percentage gigs booked, and they would all turn out to be bombs. Either the weather would turn bad or the farmers would be in the midst of planting or harvesting. Another common cause for our small gate receipts was that Whoopee John, the Six Fat Dutchmen, or one of the popular Welk or Lombardo-style bands was playing somewhere in the area. Whether they were coming soon or had just been there, the size of our crowd would be drastically reduced.

After a taste of the major leagues with Millinder and Basie, including the Broadway theaters and nightclubs and all of the other rewards of the big time, my return to the sticks was sometimes distasteful. The fact that I had had my little brush with the big leagues and still endured the hardships of the sticks with consistent good nature seemed to impress my band members, and my perpetual pleasantness was infectious. In the face of nearly insurmountable odds, we still had a ball and looked forward anxiously to having our instruments in our hands on the bandstand even if it was in a cow barn. As an added bonus, several of us fished or hunted at every opportunity. Whenever possible, we had a big fish fry or pheasant and rabbit fry in one of the towns. The long trips between gigs never daunted us because of the around-the-clock card games (usually tonk) and the hilarious kidding around in the bus. Some of the cleverest comedy in history was gotten off in band buses of that era.

As August approached in 1950, my band was very close to folding. We had too few engagements and not enough money. In June, Augie, the manager of the Howard White agency, had ordered a new batch of my brochures and sent a mailing to all the old accounts from the days when Nat Towles's band was king of the Midwest and some areas of Texas. Late in July we received a response from a promoter in Big Spring, Texas, and Augie booked a date with him for $350 on August 10. Three hundred and fifty dollars was a fortune for us then. It was, by far, the biggest contract for one night I had secured to date. This was something we could build around. Even if it was the only date, we intended to make a Texas tour even if it meant driving all the way to Big Spring and back. My wife's first cousin, Steve Ritchie, was born and raised in Waxahachie, Texas, and was living in Omaha. Several times in the past, Steve had assured me that he could drive to Texas and Oklahoma and get bookings for us where we would all make plenty of money. We would play only the smaller towns where there was a constant demand for dance bands to play for a small guarantee or a percentage. Now, with the $350 gig at Big Spring in the bag, I contacted Steve. Within a few days he and his friend, "Cat" Wright, were loaded in Steve's new Buick and headed on the way to Texas. Only two or three days had passed when Steve began to call me to put dates in my book. He had secured dates in Salina, Kansas, and Guthrie, Oklahoma,

Preston Love, publicity photo, 1951.

to get us to Big Spring, and almost daily he called me to announce he had booked Sweetwater, Abilene, Corsicana, or some other Texas town. Most contracts were for 70 percent of the gross gate to us. In Steve's home, Waxahachie, we would receive all of the gate and stay with Steve's mother, Mayella, and other friends in the black neighborhood. The owner of the dance hall there, over the mortuary, was Steve's lifelong friend, and he gave the hall to us without fee.

My men and I were elated as the dates poured in. Going to Texas was like hitting the big time to most of my musicians. Also, we would be playing all-black dances. We could play our best arrangements all night. The first gig, at Salina on August 7, served its purpose. We played the black community center and took in enough money to split eight dollars apiece and buy gas to Guthrie. Warner Barber had promoted the black dances in Guthrie for years at several halls in town. He ran a nice café, and when we pulled into town we went straight there to eat and get directions to the hall. After the engagement, we would check into rooming houses for the night. Warner was a very friendly brother who knew the ropes in dance promoting. It was from him that I got the first hint of storm clouds brewing. He and I visited as I ate dinner at his café, and he began to stammer about such things as money being short in town around this time, and "if you fellows only had any kind of recording, I would have put it on boxes around town, and I know we would have a good crowd. As it is, maybe we won't do too bad." Warner was very kind and tactful, but I could tell he was also disappointed by our school bus. A glamorous bus might insure a better crowd. In the black communities of that era, new or unknown bands were usually judged by their "front"—a fine bus, sharp uniforms, and fancy music stands.

Warner Barber's misgivings were well founded. We grossed thirty-seven dollars in Guthrie, but we were more embarrassed by the small crowd than concerned about money. After all, we had a whole $350, a small fortune, coming two nights later in Big Spring. Since the band's bankroll was so short now, we decided to head for Big Spring after the gig in Guthrie. We would get to Big Spring a day early and check in there. After riding all night from Guthrie, we arrived in Big Spring the next evening, a couple of hours before dark. Walter Green ran a small business in the ghetto, and we found him easily. He, too, was a kind and paternal man in his late fifties. He directed us to a rooming house–style hotel where we could get the most reasonable accommodations. Before we left for the rooming house, Green took me aside and almost repeated the words that Warner Barber said about it being too bad we didn't have a recording and that money was short in the black community because it wasn't cotton-chopping time. Walter Green gave our 1942 school bus a doubtful glance, but he instructed me to ride around the ghetto as much as possible the next day to let the people know we were in town. He also said that if the girls saw all the good-looking young men in the band, the females would come to the dances and the local male dance fans would follow. Since we had ridden a night and a day in the intense August heat, we took advantage of the night off to get a good night's sleep. The next day we circulated about town, and everywhere we went people assured us that they would all be at the dance that night. I had already promised everyone twenty-five dollars each, which was an unheard-of large sum for a night's work in Midwest territory bands.

This would leave me $125 to pay the union tax (about seven dollars) and keep a bankroll for future contingencies, such as a bus breakdown or the purchase of a tire. Our next booking was in Abilene, Texas, in two days, and I estimated it would cost only about twenty dollars to get there. The dance hall in Big Spring was a Spanish hacienda-style building, and since it was a hot night all of the windows were thrown open for ventilation. Walter Green instructed me to open with several of our best blues numbers and for us to play loud so the people in the streets would hear us and come and buy tickets. He then set up his box office at the front door. We had played almost entirely for white audiences in the Midwest or for more swing-oriented black audiences in towns such as Omaha, Sioux City, Des Moines, and Wichita. Our entire blues repertoire consisted of "Cry Baby," a Johnny Otis hit of the moment, and about three boogie-woogie or shuffle-type tunes. Our best arrangements were in the Basie and Lionel Hampton big-band veins with brass and reed figures. Nevertheless, we followed Walter's instructions, and before long the streets were full of people. You could hear Georgetown Holmes spitting out the high lead trumpet parts for ten blocks in each direction. The entire area of the dance hall was full of people frolicking, lounging on the sidewalks and in cars. But an hour had passed and Walter hadn't sold a single ticket. He left someone at the door and came to the bandstand to talk to me.

"You boys sure have a good band. I think if we can get just one couple to buy tickets and come in, all the rest will follow, and we'll get a crowd. Have your singer do a couple numbers."

Then he headed back to his box office. We didn't have a singer per se. In the Midwest we could get by without a full-fledged singer, as Donnie Kelly and Georgetown Holmes would struggle through a few of the most essential vocal numbers each night. Donnie knew Mel Walker's popular rendition of Johnny Otis's "Cry Baby" and a couple up-tempo blues that we proceeded to do per Walter Green's instructions, but still no paid admissions. Then Green headed for the bandstand again. He instructed me to give the fellows an intermission and took me aside. He looked down sorrowfully and said,

"Look, Preston, we ain't gonna get nobody. I'm sorry but I don't have no $350 without selling any tickets. I know you probably need some money to get to your next job, so what if I give you a $100 and we call it off?"

I was sensible enough to realize this was all I could get, and we needed even the hundred or we would have been stranded. After all, this man was being as fair as possible. My men and I were somewhat taken aback by the turn of events, but we were young and hope springs eternal in youth. We set our hopes on the coming engagements, and by now Steve had booked a string of small Texas towns. With each call to me, he was optimistic about the future crowds.

When we arrived in the ghetto in Abilene we began to see Pee Wee Crayton dance posters. Upon closer inspection, I noticed the date on the posters was only one night before our engagement—last night. Pee Wee Crayton was riding the crest of several rhythm and blues hits and was touring the South with a strictly rhythm and blues troupe. The night before they had played the most prestigious dance hall the blacks used in Abilene. My posters beside his in several windows announced a different ballroom or hall. We sought out Abilene's main hotel, and there, parked in front, was Pee Wee's fancy big Flexible bus with his name emblazoned on its sides. It was apparently near the time for departure for their next booking, as several of his players were around the bus and standing around the hotel entrance. I parked our little feeble bus in back of Pee Wee's, and we made friends with him and his people who expressed surprise that they would book two dances on consecutive nights. Someone was going to be hurt, but it couldn't be them, because they had attracted a sellout crowd last night.

After seeking out a restaurant that featured tasty southern-style food at the most inexpensive prices, we ate and then inquired of the waitresses where we could find some rooms. They perceived that we were looking for just plain, clean rooms for a price we could afford, and they directed us to a rooming house run by an older woman who was known to rent rooms to musicians and to the black baseball teams when they came to town. The owner of the rooming house was "Mother" Williams, and she seemed happy to have us. She confided in me that a few years earlier she couldn't have accommodated the two white members, but now the police didn't bother her if there was a white boy or two in a band. The rooms were three dollars each, double; so the whole bill only came to fifteen dollars. I was thankful for this, because the band's entire bankroll was getting pretty small. An hour and a half before the gig's beginning, we arrived at the dance hall. It was a small lodge building, but I estimated it would hold 250 people, which would be wonderful if we could sell it out to capacity. At two dollars per head, our sixty percent of a sellout would be about three hundred dollars, a fortune. After Steve's fee and the union tax, the band would be in pretty good shape to face the rest of the tour. For two and a half hours, up to intermission, we watched the door anxiously, torn between trying to concentrate on playing with enthusiasm and thinking about getting enough money to eat and get to the next town. The man who promoted us in Abilene evidently needed money badly to meet his expenses also, because he, too, showed concern when only a trickle of people came through the entrance. At intermission we had twenty-five customers, and the promoter worriedly assured me we should catch a few more in the last hour. After intermission we sold two more tickets. For our share of the gate, we received thirty-three dollars. When the promoter handed me the money, I knew he was as unhappy about the bomb as I was.

At that moment it hit me smack in the face. "Here I am away down in Texas, hundreds of miles from home with nine fellows depending on me . . . almost no money, no hit recording, no repertoire for the music required in this area." The terror of all bands since the twenties was the thought of getting stranded away from their home base. I wasn't too terrified because before we left Omaha, Donnie Kelly had confided in me that he had a bankroll of about one hundred dollars. In all the bands that Kelly played with, including Nat Towles's, Donnie was known for being thrifty and shrewd with his money. No matter how bad things were, and no matter how broke all the other band members in any band he worked with, Donnie Kelly always had a nest egg stashed away. Buddy Tate was another musician well known for this propensity in all the bands in which he worked.

Every gig after Abilene was just a repetition of Abilene and Big Spring. After a few more days, I began to borrow money from Kelly until he was almost tapped out. After fifteen days we were booked in Brownwood, Texas. When we counted up the gate receipts after the dance, I realized that if we played one more night that didn't take in at least seventy-five dollars we would be stranded. Our top percentage so far had been eighty dollars. The next three nights were further south in the state which would mean greater expense to get back to Omaha, where we at least had homes and could manage to eat somehow. After dividing up the Brownwood take of fifty-eight dollars, I kept just enough to buy gas back to Omaha. I then called Steve, who was at his mother's home in Waxahachie, and instructed him to cancel all of the remaining bookings. I explained to him, and he understood.

None of us in the band was too disconsolate as we headed for Omaha. At least we'd be back in friendly surroundings, and I assured the fellows that I could make some quick bookings in and around Omaha. I would borrow some money from relatives to tide us over and stand good for their rent at their respective rooming houses in Omaha. Actually, there was a spirit of exhilaration as we headed north for Omaha. Luckily, the old Chevy school bus had performed perfectly throughout the trip, or we would have been in real trouble. We were bent, but not broken. We had missed no meals, and we had checked into some hotel or rooming house every night that it was necessary. By riding steadily all night, changing drivers every few hours, and only stopping for gas and quick bites to eat, our estimated time of arrival in Omaha would be late the next night. We became more anxious each mile to get back to Omaha, and after traveling several hundred miles the remaining two or three hundred seemed like a mere walk. The bus was purring along through familiar territory in Kansas. It was shortly before dark in the evening, and the band members were in the midst of their usual fun and games, when there was a sizzle and the bus motor ceased. We pulled to the side of the highway and attempted to start the motor without success. I stopped a passing motorist who drove me five miles to the nearest town. The owner of a filling station on the highway in the little Kansas town drove back to the bus with me and diagnosed our trouble as a broken timing chain. He hooked up a tow chain and pulled us into his filling station. His partner and he would work four hours or so and put in the timing chain. The repair would be approximately forty dollars. I checked with each member of the band, and we could scrape together sixteen dollars. We needed at least twelve dollars of this for gas to complete the trip to Omaha. Preston Love and His Orchestra was stranded. I instructed the mechanics to proceed with the repairs, and then I put in a hurried call to Betty. She would borrow the forty dollars from her mother and wire it to me, but we were not able to get the telegraphic money order until the bank opened in the little town next morning.

My first activity back in Omaha was to book some quick percentage jobs in the area. It was easy to set dates as long as we accepted sixty-forty or seventy-thirty with no guarantee, but none of the straight percentage ballrooms were popular spots. Bands learned that the crowds at these quick pickup gigs were usually small. But even if we only cleared a few bucks each, playing together meant staying together. We could at least avoid disbanding. Augie at Howard White booked what he could for us, but he was too busy with his regular job as a municipal bus driver, so I was doing most of our booking, such as it was. We tried hard to hold the band together, but it looked as though we would fold any day.

Around October 1, I heard about a new booking agency in Omaha that was doing wonders for a couple of territory bands. The agency was called Music Management Service. Its owner was an ex-band leader from the territory named Royce Stoenner. Since my October datebook was almost empty, in desperation, I contacted Stoenner and convinced him of my sobriety, my punctuality, and of the band's versatility. But he wanted to be sure. The following Saturday night, he and several friends drove the twenty-two miles to Missouri Valley, Iowa, to hear us play at a dilapidated hall out in the country. The band and I had driven all the way from North Dakota overnight to make the $150 gig at Missouri Valley, a distance of nearly six hundred miles. We had never played better, we made even "In the Mood" sound up-to-date and hip.

Early the next day, Stoenner called me to meet him at his office. After a few criticisms and suggestions, Stoenner signed me to a five-year contract. His main advice was that we were a bit too modern and jazzy for the Midwest dance business. As a booking agent, Royce Stoenner was an artist. Before nightfall that evening, he called to give me three fat gigs to put in my book. Our first one was only ten days hence, on a Tuesday night, in Allerton, Iowa, which is about two hundred miles from Omaha. The gig paid two hundred dollars: two hundred dollars on a Tuesday night, and barely two hundred miles to drive! We were used to driving three to four hundred for most gigs. Even our top Saturday gigs paid only $175. We hadn't played many midweek dates before this, and when we did they were usually percentage gigs or for $150 or less. By the end of October, Royce had us booked solid well into the spring of 1951. He even had a framework of our summer work booked for that coming year. Where we had averaged about three engagements a week before, with Royce we were averaging nearly six nights a week, and the distance of our jumps to bookings was cut nearly in half. I added a third trumpet, a third trombone, and a fantastic singer named Eddie Eugene, who would be a worthy subject for an entire book. We now began to play the finest ballrooms, country clubs, and schools in the Midwest, as well as an occasional officers' club or NCO club at the military bases that began to spring up in the area.

In mid-November, Johnny Otis called me from Washington, D.C. He announced that he was getting a newer and bigger bus. His bus driver would bring his Flexible to me in a few days and fly back to meet Johnny and his troupe. I couldn't believe my ears. Johnny and his troupe with Little Esther, Mel Walker, Redd Lyte, and others, had been to Omaha in the Flex a few months earlier, and I remembered the big, beautiful bus. Johnny had stayed with us, and I remembered how pitiful our little school bus looked when they pulled the Flexible up behind it. A few days later, Johnny's driver Lou arrived with the Flex. He handed me the title, had a bite to eat with us, and asked me to drive him to the airport in the Flex. He would instruct me on how to drive it en route to the airport. It was twice as big as the school bus, plush and beautiful, all mine, and gratis! Returning from the airport, I could hardly wait to let my fellows see our new bus, so I drove around to each one's house and picked them all up for a demonstration. They were ecstatic. I drove straight out to Royce Stoenner's office to show him the prize.

Preston, Betty, and Preston, Jr., in Santa Monica, California, 1952.

Royce lived in back of his office, and he was having dinner when we arrived. He came out to view the bus, and I noticed he was only mildly enthusiastic. In fact, he was rather restrained, although complimentary of the bus's beauty. I could see he didn't want to dampen our elation. The next day we were scheduled to leave at noon for an engagement not too far from Omaha. At around ten that morning I received a call from Royce. He obviously was choosing his words carefully.

"Preston, uh, are you taking the new bus today?"

I answered, "No, I don't think so, Royce. I want to have Johnny's name painted over and ours put on it and do a few other things before we start using it."

Royce paused again, then he continued, "I wouldn't try to use that bus if I were you. Several of us leaders in the territory tried using those big buses and they almost wiped us out. Maybe you could keep it as a spare for when the old bus breaks down or just use it when you are playing a big colored dance in Wichita, Denver, or Des Moines. I realize how the colored fans won't turn out if a band comes to town in a shabby bus, but I don't think you can afford to operate that big Flex."

Basie Givens and other local bandleaders around Omaha had cautioned me many times about keeping transportation inexpensive when I first organized the band, so Royce's message came through loud and clear now. We lived in the government project homes, and I parked the big beautiful Flexible under our window in the driveway, locked it up, and took off for our next gig in the old school bus. Where we had all been happy chugging down the highway in the school bus, which we called the Green Hornet, immediately a clamor arose among the men (now twelve of us) to use the new bus. The more I protested about the impracticality of using the new bus, the more they put subtle pressures on me to discard the Green Hornet and use the showy new bus. Eli Wolinsky and Donnie Kelly were my closest confidants in the band, but I detected no sympathy even in their faces when Phil Thomas and Harry Lewis led the clamor for using the new bus.

For the upcoming Thanksgiving holiday, we had the eve booked for an engagement for blacks in Sioux City, and on Thanksgiving night we were scheduled for a big promotion at the black Elks Club in Waterloo, Iowa. Two days before the Sioux City gig, as we were riding along the highway on the way back to Omaha from western Nebraska, Phil Thomas walked up to the front of the bus and stood beside me. I was driving.

"Count, I know you're gonna take the new bus to Sioux City and Waterloo. Man, those brothers and sisters will fall out when they see that fine thing."

I protested feebly, and Georgetown Holmes joined in from the rear of the bus, "Aw, come on, Count, this is our chance to show these folks around here that we're makin' it now."

I was hooked. I relented. "O.K., we'll take that Flex on that trip."

A chorus of cheers rang out in the bus. The contract in Sioux City was for two hundred and fifty dollars and the Waterloo gig paid two hundred and seventy-five dollars, which was good money for that part of the country and for those size towns, but I had to be careful to realize a profit. I now had eleven people to pay, and I had raised the salaries from ten dollars to twelve dollars each per night. The booking agency received twenty percent of the net after deducting ten cents per mile for transportation and deducting as well the nightly union tax, which was 10 percent of union scale for each man or about eight dollars a night. The agency's fee thus actually averaged about 16 percent of the gross contract. If I was careful with transportation costs, I could average about 20 percent profit across the board on all engagements, but there wasn't much latitude for setbacks and unexpected expenses.

Sioux City is only a hundred miles from Omaha, but I scheduled a one o'clock departure time on the afternoon of Thanksgiving Eve to give us enough time to get there early and parade around in the new bus. In anticipation of using the bus for this trip, I had Johnny's name expunged from the bus and ours painted on it. We had played many percentage jobs in Sioux City in the past six months while using the old bus, and the town was always good for nearly one hundred dollars, which many times saved our lives when bookings were especially bad. Now we would be returning in style.

We always departed from in front of one of the popular cafés on North Twenty-fourth Street. I drove to the leaving point a half hour or so early, and the fellows would gather at the café and eat or get snacks to take with us. This day, I parked the Flex in front of the café an hour earlier than departure time. It created quite a sensation as people walked or drove down Twenty-fourth Street. The band members milled proudly around the bus in front of the café. A psychoanalyst would have had a field day trying to label all of my hangups and inferiority complexes from the poverty and privations of my youth at the Love Mansion as he or she observed me in this moment of triumph. At precisely one o'clock, all of the fellows trooped in the bus and staked out their permanent seats. Until I taught some of them to drive this bus, I would have to do most of the driving. We took off down Twenty-fourth Street in the direction of the bridge leading across the Missouri River to Omaha's twin city, Council Bluffs, Iowa, and to Highway 75 for Sioux City. I had gassed up earlier that morning. A few miles out of Council Bluffs on the hilly and curving road one of the fellows in the rear of the long bus called out, "Hey, Count, something's smoking back here."

I immediately pulled to the side of the road and inspected the rear of the bus. The left dual wheels were smoking considerably. The next town was Honey Creek, Iowa, so I decided to continue the few miles to there. I pulled into the garage on the highway directly across from my old friend, the Aeroplane Inn, in Honey Creek. The garage attendant dropped what he was doing and inspected the source of the smoke for me. He then jacked the bus up and diagnosed the trouble as "draggin' brakes." The problem was soon corrected, and I paid the mechanic his four-dollar fee. On to Sioux City.

With the Sioux City and Waterloo gigs and the three weekend dates, we put slightly over a thousand miles on the new bus before returning to Omaha the following Monday. Nearly every day there was some minor repair necessary on the bus, and we had to add a little antifreeze and water constantly, because with its motor and radiator far in the rear, the Flex had quite a large plumbing system. The fluids just seemed to get away from us somehow, through attrition maybe. Outside of the inconveniences, the repairs hadn't been very expensive, but when I totaled up the receipts at the end of the trip, I noticed the bus had cut rather sharply into my small margin of profit. That was it. The Flex was parked for the winter. Back into the Green Hornet.

There was both good news and bad news ahead. Royce Stoenner, the "magician," booked an eight-hundred-dollar job for New Year's Eve, which seemed more like a million dollars to a band that had been so near to extinction only a few months earlier. I would pay the men twenty-five dollars each, and pay up some of the bills I had incurred keeping the band together during the very lean period. The bad news was that Donnie Kelly was being drafted into the army. He had delayed it as long as possible, but he had to report in mid-December. Donnie was very popular with all of us in the band. I had paid him the hundred dollars that I borrowed on the Texas fiasco, and everyone in the band could be thankful that he had been a shrewd person with a buck. There were occasions on the Texas trip that we would all have been unable to eat or pay rent if Kelly hadn't had his little stash of money.

Lent usually means reduced bookings in the Midwest, but even Lent didn't deter Royce Stoenner. We were rolling in fat, full weeks right on through January, February, and March of the new year of 1951. Easter and the end of Lent only increased the volume of our already good bookings. Shortly after Easter, we were en route to a big, fat, spring prom date at South Dakota State University in Brookings when the Green Hornet began to have troubles. She had given us many thousands of nearly trouble-free miles of service. Instead of pulling into the Chevrolet garage and having the old bus gone through completely, which would probably have cost a couple hundred dollars, I decided to put the Flex into service. Red Thompson, a cab-driver friend of mine in Omaha, had been pressing me to give him a job as our bus driver. He said he could be ready on a moment's notice, so I called him and asked him if he would bring the Flex up to Brookings, 230 miles north of Omaha. Red jumped at the opportunity and resigned his job at the Ritz Cab Company, Omaha's black-owned cab company. I asked one of the officials at the university if I could park the Green Hornet somewhere on the campus until we could pick it up in a couple of weeks on our way back to Omaha from deeper into the Dakotas. The official said I could leave the bus there indefinitely and gave me instructions to park it where it would be completely out of their way.

Red left Omaha with the Flex that evening, and shortly before we played our last set at the prom, in walked Red to announce the Flex was parked outside, "ready for action." We had a long jump to our next gig, which was in North Dakota, but now we had a bus driver. At the end of the prom, all the band members eagerly tumbled into the Flex, transferring their effects from the Green Hornet and loading our instruments in the spacious compartment in the rear of the bus. A stop to eat at a café on Highway 77, and then we were on our way north, to North Dakota. Red left the lights on inside the bus so we could play cards as we roared down the highway in the plush cruiser. The jovial scene inside the bus was priceless to me as I relaxed in my comfortable double seat, second from the front of the bus on the right-hand side. We had gone about fifty miles when the bus began to backfire occasionally, followed by a tapping sound in the motor at the rear. Red half turned to me from his driver's seat and said, "It was doing that on the way up from Omaha, but I don't think it's anything to worry about."

With this I reclined in my seat and soon dropped off to sleep. Red stopped to gas up early that morning and soon after giving him the cash to pay for the gas I dropped off to sleep again. When I finally awoke for good later in the morning, the backfiring and motor noise were more frequent. I instructed Red to go straight to a truck garage when we arrived in the town we were playing, even before checking the fellows in a hotel or motel. The town was quite near and we pulled in shortly after noon. Aside from me, all the men were asleep except a couple who played cards all morning. After the bus had been stopped for a while, everybody awoke to find us in the garage in the town of the gig. A mechanic was working noisily on the motor from the rear compartment, having set most of our instruments on the floor of the garage to enable him to get to the motor.

Pretty soon the mechanic asked for the band manager, and when I arrived at the back compartment he announced, "Mister, most of your push rods are bent or broken. I wouldn't try to drive this bus much further without getting them replaced." I asked him how big a job it would be, and he answered, "About a hundred dollars."

I authorized the mechanic to start the repair, and then we all picked out our luggage and adjourned to the nearest hotel. This was a scene that would be repeated almost to the letter over the next weeks and months. There was, however, a period of a few days without a major breakdown, and we began to feel pretty good about the bus. After all, it was the height of comfort and attractiveness. One night, a few days after the first breakdown, we stopped at the all-night truck-stop restaurant in Denison, Iowa, which was only a few miles from the gig we had just finished. Several of the fellows went in to eat, and some of us remained in the bus playing cards (tonk) while instructing others to bring us sandwiches and malts. While we were there, an old and rusty-looking school bus pulled up alongside us, with the name Eddie Skeets Orchestra printed on its sides. By now most of my men were back from the cafe. Some of us remarked that another band was on the lot, and by their remarks I could tell they were feeling very proud and smug about the comparison of the two buses. Pretty soon three or four musicians from the other band stepped up into our bus, and Eddie Skeets introduced himself to me.

"Hi, Preston. I've heard a lot about you guys, and this is my first chance to meet you. We played over at the Starline in Carroll tonight. We're going in to Omaha to play Peony Park tomorrow."

I proudly acknowledged Skeets's introduction and remarked, "I see you have a school bus. We used to use one almost just like yours. In fact, I still own it. It's parked on the parking lot up at the college in Brookings, South Dakota."

Skeets smiled and said, "You'd better go get your school bus and get rid of this. I used to have one identical to this one. It will bankrupt you. Several of us leaders used to operate Flexes, but we finally were glad to give them away." All of my men were in the bus by now, and there was a hush as he continued. "The Flexes are a good bus for bus companies because they have spare parts, spare motors, and mechanics on their payrolls with plenty of time to fix them before they break down. All of us leaders learned that you can't get parts for these Flexibles in the small towns or find mechanics who know how to do the repairs right."

As he left, Eddie Skeets laughingly called back, "If you stick with this bus, Preston, next time I see you, you'll be a hundred years older." As soon as Skeets was out of earshot, several of my men made such remarks as, "Aw man, that cat is just jealous," and "Man, I wouldn't go to a dog fight in that raggedy bus of theirs." But Eddie Skeets's words were prophetic. Soon there was hardly a day when the bus didn't break down. Sometimes it was twice a day. Even when the motor ran well, we were plagued with expensive repairs on the axles, the universal joints, the air compressor for the air brakes, wheel bearings, and the motor-ventilation system. With most repairs we pulled out of the garage in worse shape than before the "repair." Since we had to keep going to make the engagements on time, we couldn't turn back. When we would get just past the point of no return, the bus would break down with the same problem we had just spent big money to supposedly have corrected. En route to one gig we had three clutches put in. After each new clutch, we would get a hundred miles or so, and the new clutch would cease to function. Calling back to the garage that did the repair was a waste of time. They would give us some double talk and that was the end of it.

Nineteen fifty-one promised to be a big year in the history of my band, with all of the big bookings rolling in, but on April 30 I received some even bigger news. Johnny Otis called me from a southern city where they were playing on tour and announced that he had just wrapped up a deal with Ralph Bass and Syd Nathan of King Records for a recording contract for me and my band. I was so happy and surprised I could hardly believe he wasn't jesting. Ralph Bass had been Johnny's A&R man at Savoy Records when Johnny caught the big hit, "Double Crossin' Blues" with Little Esther and the Robins, and now he and Ralph had become good friends. Johnny also had a thing going with Syd Nathan, because Syd wanted Johnny to sign Little Esther to his company. Also, Syd and Johnny had negotiated for Johnny to be the A&R man and director of most recordings that King would make in Los Angeles.

Johnny asked if I had a good blues singer, and I answered "Yes, one of the greatest, Eddie Eugene." We made arrangements for my band to meet him in Cincinnati on the second Sunday in May. Cincinnati was the home of King Records and Johnny's troupe would be playing a one-nighter across the river from there in Kentucky, with two days off afterward. I was especially anxious to see Johnny and his troupe, because my brother Dude was now traveling with them as a general aide and companion for Johnny, and I hadn't seen Dude since 1948 when I left Los Angeles after leaving Basie. Also, Earle Warren was with them as road manager.

Royce juggled our bookings for the next few weeks, so that we would have Sunday, Monday, and Tuesday off the week we were to record. We would play Saturday night at the ballroom in St. Cloud, Minnesota, which was one of my strongest spots as far as drawing power, and then hightail it for Cincinnati to meet Johnny. All of our hopes for a hit recording rested on Eddie Eugene, because we realized that most hits were made at that time by rhythm and blues singers. Then, too, Johnny Otis was thoroughly steeped in this art form. Johnny had told me not to worry about material because he had hundreds of songs to choose from that he or others around him had written. I told him I had one tune I would especially like to do, and he said, "O.K., I'll take a look at it when you get here." We called this song "Unconscious Blues." It had been written by a girlfriend of one of the fellows in my band. Everything was in anticipation of the approaching trip to Cincinnati and the recording session. It would be the first recording for everyone in the band except Georgetown Holmes and me. But it would be the first I had ever recorded as the leader, under my name as the artist.

A few days before we left for the engagements that would lead to St. Cloud and the Cincinnati trip, Eddie Eugene went to Des Moines to see his friends there. On the day we were supposed to leave Omaha, Eddie had not arrived back from Des Moines, and we couldn't find him when we called his friends in Des Moines. Not wanting to foul my contract calling

Preston Love and Dennis Lyles in Denver, Colorado, 1953.

for a singer on all of our gigs, I called "Big George" Williams and asked him if he would like to make the trip with us. Big George was a fine tenor-sax player and a wonderful singer, so he could double at playing and singing. George was doing pretty badly in Omaha professionally and had told several of our band members when they saw him at jam sessions or down on North Twenty-fourth Street that he was interested in a job with the band. The addition of George would be for our fourth sax position. George jumped at the offer of joining, especially after I told him that we were going to record and that I would try to get Johnny to record him on a ballad or a blues ballad, which Johnny was very adept at writing. George wasn't a blues singer.

I left word with my wife Betty to keep trying to locate Eddie Eugene, and if she found him, or if he called, she was to ship him on to us wherever we were playing. The last night at St. Cloud arrived and the gig was finished. We still had no word of Eddie. Phil Thomas told me that he knew countless good blues singers in Chicago who would be happy to get the chance to record. We had to go near Chicago, so why not stop there and let him try to look up one of the blues singers he knew? He spoke especially glowingly of a blues singer there named Joe Williams who was making quite a reputation for himself.

The Flex shuddered a few times with the same old push-rod trouble we had corrected, but otherwise she hurtled through the night and morning as I told Red to put the gas to her and get us to Chicago as early as possible. In Chicago, we decided to spend the day and most of the night, and then take off for Cincinnati in time to get there early Monday morning. This would give us time to look for a blues singer and to take in a show at the famous Club DeLisa. We arrived in Chicago at mid-morning, and Phil told us we could spend the time at his home. We could park the bus in front and some could lounge around in it and some in his mother's house where we could all have bathroom facilities available to us. Betty had joined me in St. Cloud to make the Cincinnati trip, and Phil's mother graciously gave us a room of our own for the day and evening. When we were settled, I called Johnny at the Manse Hotel in Cincinnati where I knew all black bands stayed. I had stayed there when I played with Basie and Millinder. Johnny instructed me to look for a blues singer if I wished, but not to concern myself unduly about it. He had just heard a young singer in Cleveland who could fly down the next day to record with us if necessary.

Phil didn't have any luck tracking down the singers he knew in Chicago, but finally that evening he located Joe Williams. He put Joe on the phone with me, and Joe informed me that he had just signed a contract with one of the big recording companies, but he would have been pleased to make my session. Joe Williams, of course, became a famous singer with Count Basie's band a few years later through a hit recording of "Every Day I Have the Blues" and other big recordings. Most of my band members went out on the town in Chicago that night to see the sights of the big city. Betty, Phil, Eli, and I went to the Club DeLisa to catch the fine floor show and the Red Saunders band. The night was especially enjoyable because I had the chance to see and hear my good friend, Porter Kilbert, who played first alto sax with Saunders. Eli and I both thrilled to Porter's lead work and his fine solos.

Late that night or early the next morning we met at Phil's house and took off for Cincinnati. The Flex gave us some anxious moments, but somehow Red took off the valve cover and worked with the push rods and kept us going. Finally, at 11:00 A.M., we arrived in Cincinnati and pulled up to the Manse Hotel. Johnny's big Aero Coach was parked in front, and we parked the smaller Flexible behind it. There, standing on the steps of the hotel to greet us, were Dude, Johnny, Earle Warren, and several other members of Johnny's band. We had made friends with all of Johnny's troupe on their two trips to Omaha to play the Dreamland in the last year. Dude and Earle hugged me and Betty warmly as we emerged from the bus, and Johnny stood by enjoying the scene. The members of the two bands mixed and shook hands. Those who were unacquainted with each other introduced themselves. Then Johnny and I withdrew to the side, and I informed him that we hadn't come up with a blues singer in Chicago. Johnny said, "No sweat, I have already alerted Charles in Cleveland, and he's standing by to catch a plane and come on here. He sounds just like Charles Brown, and his name is Charles Eckstein." Johnny and I were great fans of Charles Brown ever since his first hits with Johnny Moore and the Three Blazers. In fact, Johnny had been the drummer on the first of them, the great "Driftin' Blues."

The session was scheduled for four which left plenty of time for the singer to get there. We all checked in the Manse Hotel, and Dude, Earle Warren, Johnny, and I adjourned to the hotel's dining room to catch up on old times, as Red came to get his instructions about the bus. I told him to take it to the nearest Buick garage after unloading our equipment and to have the push rods fixed and a tuneup done. At two, Johnny said, "I have to get on out to 1540 Brewster, to King's studio, and work on some tunes for the singer. He's coming straight to the studio."

We then decided that Johnny's driver would take him and my men and our equipment out to King's studio early when Johnny went, and I would take a cab out in time for the session. I then went to my room and freshened up and changed clothes. At three, I called the hotel desk and requested that the clerk call me a cab. In a few minutes, the clerk called to inform me that my cab was there. As I came down the steps of the veranda around the hotel, I noticed an obviously blind man and another short, brown-skinned man standing at the curb near my cab. As I approached, the shorter man asked, "Man, do you mind if we share your cab? They said in the lobby that you're going out to King Records." I answered, "I don't mind, man, get in." The blind man was very reticent, but the other made conversation. He introduced himself to me and then introduced the blind man. "This is Ray Charles. I'm his manager, and he's between recording contracts, so we're going out to talk with Syd Nathan about maybe working something out with King." I don't know the details of why Ray Charles and King Records didn't get together, but the failure to land Ray Charles was probably the biggest loss in Syd Nathan's entire life. Little did I realize that this same young blind fellow would become one of the favorite artists of my lifetime, although I had heard and liked his first hit recording "Baby, Let Me Hold Your Hand."

Charles Eckstein, my men, Johnny, and the studio staff were all assembled when I arrived at King Records. Johnny was already humming backgrounds to my horn players for the first tune we would record. Johnny paused and called Eckstein and me together. First he introduced us and then said, "Pres, in case we got a hit, people would think the name Eckstein was a phony. They'd think we were trying to capitalize on the name Billy Eckstine, so I've decided to use the name Charles Maxwell." (My oldest brother, Sonny, was Johnny's good friend in Los Angeles, and Sonny's name was Maxwell.) The young singer assented, and we proceeded to record the first side, "Twilight Blues," which was a direct imitation of Charles Brown and of several tunes that he had recorded. Later in the session Maxwell also sang "Wonderin' Blues," another Johnny Otis composition styled after Charles Brown. With "Twilight Blues" out of the way, Johnny said "Pres, you guys go ahead and get that tune together that you said you wanted to do. Show Charles how it goes."

We had been doing the song every night with Eddie Eugene singing it, so all of my men were familiar with it. I took "Maxwell" into the little isolation booth they had set up for singers and told my musicians to strike up "Unconscious Blues." We sounded like a young version of Basie. Apparently, this influenced my interpretation of the song to sound like a poor man's Jimmy Rushing, because after a few attempts to show Charles how Eddie Eugene did the tune and how we wanted it to sound, I was doing the whole tune through from the words which were written down on a piece of paper for Maxwell's benefit.

Pretty soon we let Maxwell run through the tune with the band, and Ralph Bass clicked on the speaker in the studio from his seat in the control room and announced, "Preston, Why don't you sing this one?"

I protested, "Man, I can't sing. Don't worry, Charles will get it after a few more tries."

Both Ralph and the engineer who was working the recording board assured me that I was doing fine, and Ralph insisted, "No, you go ahead and do it, Preston. All right, strike up the band. . . . "

We did one take, and there it was done. I, with my sad voice, was on record as a singer. I was embarrassed, but everyone said I sounded like Jimmy Rushing, and I was somewhat reassured.

Charles Maxwell had done two fine Charles Brown–style tunes on the session, and I had done one. Then I called Johnny aside and told him about Big George's beautiful voice and how well George could probably do on a ballad if Johnny had one. He went through his briefcase and came out with a number that he had written some time before. When he ran it through with Big George, he became very enthusiastic about the possibility of recording the ballad. The tune was titled "Voodoo." Johnny thought about it pensively for a moment and said, "Let's do it. Who knows, it's got just as much chance of selling some records as anything else."

Now Big George was on record as a vocalist. He did a beautiful job on Johnny's pretty ballad, "Voodoo. "While we were recording this last of the four sides on the session, I noticed a short and very fat man with thick glasses enter the control room. He leaned over, looking through the glass partition separating the control room from the sound studio, and stared intently. Then he entered into some heated conversation with Ralph Bass and the engineer. Johnny was in the studio with us directing the session, and when he too noticed the little man in the control room, he said, "Oh, there's Syd Nathan. I'll take you in to meet him when we finish this one."

When Johnny and I finally went to the control room, he shouted spirit-edly, "Hey, Syd, how're you doin'? I want you to meet Preston Love."

Syd Nathan half scowled, "Hi, Johnny," and coolly acknowledged my introduction. Syd then belched "What's going on here? I think I'm getting a small blues group that's going to sell me some records, and you've got Duke Ellington's band here."

Syd's words were directed at Johnny and Ralph Bass, but they were embarrassed for me, and with the engineer's aid both of them set out to convince Syd Nathan that we had some hit material in the four sides we had made. Syd exploded, "And who is going to buy that last thing you were making when I came in? You might as well bring Kate Smith in here and try to sell her records to our rhythm and blues fans. And how much are all these pieces going to cost me?"

Syd listened to "Twilight Blues" and "Wonderin' Blues" by Charles Maxwell on the roll of tape, and he was somewhat placated. We stayed over in Cincinnati that night and caught a couple of good bands and singers playing in clubs. The next evening we were off for our next gig in the corn belt, with visions of hit records in our heads. Before we left, Syd Nathan had given each of us union scale for the session in cash.

As our popularity and strong drawing power grew and grew, Royce Stoenner continued to stuff my datebook with fat bookings, but I began to fall behind in paying his commissions. With the bus breaking down constantly, the entire profit from engagements began to go for repairs or toward renting cars or buses to get to a gig when the bus had broken down and the repair took too long to enable us to get there. I was always determined to get to the gig by some means or other, but every now and then we would break down at the most inopportune time and place, and in spite of all my efforts, we couldn't make it. This was always a major catastrophe to me, because I wanted my reputation for reliability to be spotless.

Occasionally, I had to owe the band members for a day or two, but I managed never to default on one penny of their wages. By August, I had taken all I could, so I resolved to get back to Brookings and pick up the Green Hornet. We had stopped in Brookings several times to check on it, and there it sat on a parking lot at the college, apparently causing no one any concern. With a fraction of what I had spent on the Flex, I could bring the school bus up to top shape. Certain repairs on the little bus were less than half of what they cost on the bigger one.

In the second week of August, we were in the midst of a seventeen-day tour of lake pavilions in northern Minnesota and the summer dance pavilions in northern North Dakota when the Flex began to require at least two quarts of oil every sixty or seventy miles. On a particular Sunday in August, we were booked for our second time that summer at the Maple Lake Pavilion in Mentor, Minnesota. Maple Lake was a cheap, filler-type engagement, but we were happy to play it for $150 because there weren't too many Sunday spots in that area. It was operated by an ex-bandleader from that area, Wen Schu, and his wife. There were several nice hotels in Crookston, Minnesota, which was a large town for that area and near Mentor. We always checked in at the Hotel Crookston and drove over to Maple Lake for the dance and back to sleep at the hotel. I told Wen Schu about my bus trouble, and he recommended a garage in Crookston that had taken care of his buses when he operated his band. The next morning, Red was waiting at the door of the garage when the mechanics arrived for work, and after a cursory examination of the motor the garage's manager assured Red they could remedy the oil loss and tune up the motor by noon and have us on our way to our engagement for the night. The garage was run by two young brothers who had recently taken it over from their dad when he retired. Both brothers worked as mechanics and doubled as managers of the business. The brothers kept their word to the letter, and by noon we were on our way to North Dakota. We had only about 180 miles to go to the next gig, which was a pavilion near a tiny North Dakota town almost straight west of Crookston.

The repair on the bus was one hundred dollars, but I was consoled by the fact that it should easily get us through this series of dates, and then I would get us back into the Green Hornet. We were riding nonchalantly west on Highway 2 about ninety miles west of Crookston and a short distance into North Dakota when there was a sizzling sound in the rear, and black smoke poured out of the ventilators on each side of the rear luggage compartment. Red threw on the brakes, and we rushed back and opened up the cowl to the motor. There, piercing the motor wall, lay three rods. The end of that motor had come.

There was a small town within sight ahead, and soon a farmer in a pickup came by and drove Red and me up to the town. I made arrangements for a filling-station owner to drive his tractor down and pull the bus into the town's only garage, and then I phoned the garage back in Crookston and told them what had happened. The brothers were sympathetic, and they felt duty-bound to help us since they had torn my motor down to fix it that morning. The older brother told me that he and a helper would be there within a few hours with a rebuilt Buick motor exactly like the one in the bus. They would make an adjustment, but I would have to pay some difference. I agreed, and then I set out frantically to try to find a means of transporting the band the remaining ninety miles to the gig. Finally, I was steered to a man in the country who owned a school bus, and he would take us to the job for sixty dollars and his gas. By the time the man arrived with the school bus, it was nearly dark, but we didn't ever start until ten at the North Dakota dances, which gave us enough time if we hurried. My fellows made the transfer of equipment quickly to the yellow school bus, and we were off for the engagement. The last few miles of the trip were on rough side roads as only North Dakota in that era could produce, which slowed us down, but we arrived at the dance pavilion a few minutes before starting time. The pavilion manager was a nervous wreck and lit into me with all kinds of accusations about my negligence, and about how he never hired colored bands for this and other reasons. No matter how hard I tried to explain our predicament and my determined effort to get there, he wasn't to be placated. I also tried to impress on him that there was no way to call him to tell him earlier, because I had tried when we first broke down.

My fellows and I were adept at setting up quickly in emergency situations like this, so at ten-fifteen we were ready to hit. Crowds in North Dakota never came to the dances until nearly midnight. As usual, we played the first hour and a half to an empty ballroom, but just before midnight the pavilion filled to capacity. It was four-thirty when we returned to the little town and our crippled bus. The garage manager from Crookston and his young helper had just arrived in a pickup with a motor in the rear. The manager and I closeted for a discussion of terms, and he agreed that he and his brother owed me some consideration, but he would have to have a balance of $360 to install the motor. I agreed to these terms, but I didn't have the cash. He asked what collateral I could give, and I offered as security the title to the Green Hornet, which I assured him was in good running order, parked on the lot of South Dakota State in Brookings. He accepted the school bus as security and proceeded to make arrangements with the owner to use his facilities to install the motor.

There was no way the mechanics could get the motor in the bus and ready to go in time for us to leave for our next engagement. We had nearly four hundred miles to go to western South Dakota, and then several days split between the Dakotas and Minnesota before returning to Omaha for a short break and some dates in the Omaha vicinity. Red Thompson took the owner of the rented school bus aside and convinced him that we would take good care of his bus if he would rent it to us to make the next few gigs. The owner was reluctant, but after all one of us had to bring his bus back to pick up the Flex. Red assured him that he would return his school bus in perfect condition or we would pay for any damage or mechanical deterioration caused by the trip. The school bus owner relented, and we agreed upon a rental price of fifty dollars per day. At around nine that morning we took off for western South Dakota. Three days later, our gig was as close as we would get again to the town where the Flex was, so Red deposited us at the hotel in the town of that night's gig before he departed to pick up the Flex. Before Red left, I gave him the $150 to pay the renter and enough money for gas up and to come back to pick us up, a round trip of 425 miles. Of course, the gas mileage on the Flex was barely half that of the school bus.

Red was a workhorse. He was powerfully built and tireless. He would happily do all of this driving with only the few hours' sleep he had gotten when I relieved him coming to that day's town. As I counted out the much-needed money for the rental and gas, Red still was able to forget his own fatigue and looked at me sympathetically.

"Count, if that big mother——ker breaks down again, I'm gonna put a bomb up under its ass."

I laughed dryly while trying to appear carefree. "You'd better not, because my insurance on that turkey lapsed a month ago."

In the midst of our best bookings and biggest weekly grosses, I arrived back in Omaha with just enough money to pay our most pressing household expenses. Betty was disappointed, but as always she continued to be optimistic and to encourage her downhearted husband. Most of our bills were mounting. I was incurring a rather large debt to the Internal Revenue Service for various taxes, and weeks were going by without my paying Royce his agent's commissions. Royce and Betty were forbearing, but the IRS was beginning to make life very miserable. Hardly a day passed that I didn't receive some harshly worded letter from them or a summons to appear at their office. The Internal Revenue harassment was something I was to live with for the next seven years. They are America's gestapo.

For the next few weeks, the Flex performed fairly well in that the breakdowns and repairs were relatively small and minor. I had it checked so often and had so many preventive minor repairs done that the band members kidded me by calling me a garage freak. They said neither the Flex nor I could pass a filling station or garage without stopping. I retorted that the Flex had me gun-shy.

In mid-November we had a series of dates that included black promotions in Denver and Wichita. By now, our band enjoyed great popularity and drawing power in these two cities. Since we had many friends in Wichita and friends and Betty's relatives in Denver, Betty usually accompanied me on trips that included these towns. On this trip some of the dates required a show, so I took along a fire-eater act and an exotic girl dancer who would play all of the engagements. We played a very successful show in Denver, and after spending several days on Colorado gigs we embarked on our trip for a four-hundred-dollar Saturday gig at the Officers Club at Fort Leavenworth, Kansas. The Friday night job was near the eastern border of Colorado, and when we finished that night we took off for Fort Leavenworth, which was quite a distance. The Flex was humming through the night down the highway in western Kansas when there was a clanking noise in the rear of the bus. Red quickly slowed the bus and crept along until we came to the first town, which turned out to be Osborne, Kansas. We found the one all-night truck stop, and the night attendant was also a mechanic. He jacked up the rear wheels of the Flex and had us run the motor with the bus in gear. After listening a while, he announced, "Mister, it sounds like your rear-end pinion gear is shot."

I asked, "How big a job is that?"

His reply was, "Oh . . . we could probably get it out by tomorrow evening."

We had hundreds of miles to travel to Leavenworth, which necessitated finding an alternate means of getting to the gig. Luckily, there was a train scheduled to come through Osborne in a few minutes that would take us right into Leavenworth, arriving there around noon. The mechanic said it would be all right to drive the bus slowly over to the little railroad station, and we arrived there just in time to purchase tickets and to board the train, a fine modern streamlined train. After buying the sixteen tickets for the band, Betty, and the two show people, I had enough left to leave $250 with Red to bail out the Flex after repairs. The mechanic could not estimate the repair cost, but I gave Red all I could anyway.

Upon our arrival in Leavenworth, I called the club officer to explain our predicament. He said Red had already called to tell me the bus would be ready by three that afternoon, and the bill should be $220. We took cabs to the Officers Club, which wiped out my last money. All the men had been paid for every gig, so I was able to borrow a few dollars from John Burke, the trombonist who had replaced Donnie Kelly ten months before. The club manager made us welcome to lounge around the club as long as we were in an area that didn't interfere with his afternoon customer traffic. Our band and the show were going over terrifically when just before intermission, at eleven-thirty, Red appeared at the side of the bandstand. He was smiling through the space left by the long-ago loss of one of his middle front teeth. The second that intermission was announced we all rushed over, surrounding Red. He was shaking his head and smiling, "Man, that big rascal is running like a top now."

Red handed me a handful of gas receipts, the repair bill, eleven dollars, and some pennies, which was my change from $250. We were all pretty tired after the gig, but Wichita was one of our favorite towns and not too far away. Thus we decided to head for Wichita. I drove the bus to allow Red to sleep a while. An early arrival in Wichita would give us the chance to check in the Water Street Hotel and get a whole day of rest before gig time. I drove all night, making several stops to refresh myself with coffee and snacks. By mid-morning I was approaching McPherson, Kansas, which was fifty-five miles north of Wichita, when I heard a whirring noise in the rear end. The noise grew steadily louder and by the time I managed to reach a truck garage in McPherson I feared driving the bus another block. Again the noise sounded like rear-end trouble, but it was Sunday and the garages all were closed.

I called Perkins Nicholson, one of the promoters in Wichita, and he laughed,

"Boy, is that bus still breaking down at every tree? "Don't worry; I'll send more cars up there to get you all." He asked, "Did you bring Betty with you this time? When I answered yes, he insisted that Betty and I stay at his house. He, his wife Gladys, and Betty and I had become good friends since I had played several very big dances for him and his partner, Ray Overton, over the past year or so. An hour and a half later, Perkins arrived with three cars, one pulling a rental trailer. I must have had a premonition because I instructed all of the band members to take everything out of the bus and not to leave any of their personal possessions. We pulled the bus around to the service entrance and parked it, blocking the door of the truck garage. Red taped a note inside the windshield instructing the garage men to check the rear-end noise and leaving Perkins's Wichita phone number with instructions to phone the verdict to me in there in the morning. Red stayed with the bus.

As usual, we had a fabulous turnout in Wichita. I had a $325 guaranteed contract with no percentage privilege, so all we received was the guarantee and a great ego salve from the huge crowd and their demonstrative appreciation for our music. Eddie Eugene's blues and the band's show-manship broke it up. I tried not to think about the bus. Everyone who knew about the problem tried to cheer me up, but the thought of our predicament weighed heavily on my mind. There were the usual festivities during the dance, with drinks flowing at the tables, and Perkins had a small after-party at his home for Betty and me. But I couldn't even drown my inner despondency with rum sours (which was my favorite drink). I did a pretty good job of cloaking my preoccupation outwardly, but inside, I was actually mourning.

The next morning, Monday, we were sound asleep when Perkins's wife, Gladys, knocked on the door and called, "Preston, there's a long-distance call for you."

With my heart in my mouth, I hurried to the phone and answered it. On the other end, Red cleared his throat. He stretched his words slowly and cryptically, "Well . . . the bus is finished. Do you want the bad news?"

My heart was thumping, and I was actually trembling by now. All I could muster to answer was, "Yeah."

It seemed that Red was forcing himself to go on as he said painfully, "You have a practically new rear-end overhaul. The bill is $557.60."

Somehow, I felt relieved and calm. I said, "Listen, Red, that garage just *bought* themselves a Flexible bus. I'll wire you the money for your fare to Omaha, and I'll see you there next Sunday when we get in."

In Wichita, Perkins got us a rental on a newer carryall Chevy to make our upcoming gigs for the week ahead. Six days later we were in Omaha. The Saturday-night gig was a good one and only a short distance from Omaha, enabling us to get home early Sunday morning. Our gig for Sunday night was close to Omaha, and we would be off Monday and Tuesday at home. This was a break, because it would be easier to rent cars to make the Sunday gig.

Red lived on Decatur Street, five and a half blocks from our housing-project apartment, and after dropping off my other colleagues I went directly to Red's apartment and woke him and his wife. I gave Red enough money for gas to Wichita and his fare back after he returned the carryall to the rental company there. Then I asked him to drop me by our apartment. He said he would see that all the individual luggage was distributed before he took off for Wichita even if he had to go around to each one's place. On the way to my place, I was pensive, and Red tried to make conversation.

"What's the plan, Count? I don't see how you can take much more, man."

I refused to retreat into despair and paranoid self-pity as I replied, "Hah, I bet we'll see something now. I'm going to have you pick up the

Green Hornet in Brookings when you get back from Wichita. We're going to get that sweet little mother——ker fixed up in top shape, and now you cats are goin' to see me get myself straight."

Red rocked back and forth in agreement. "Man, where would you be now if you had done that a long time ago like you shoulda?"

I was very tired when Red dropped me off at home at ten-thirty in the morning, but I had to get busy arranging for two cars and a trailer to make that night's gig. The first person I called was my brother Norman, and I told him of all the events. He had advised me many times about the error of my "fooling with that damn Flex," but he sympathized. His reaction to my bad news was almost predictable, "Don't worry about a thing. You can take my car, and I'll get you J. C. Stewart's or Ed Lee Underwood's car for the other one you need."

With this problem out of the way, I called the phone number of the junior-class president who had hired us when we played the prom at South Dakota State. When the young student came to the phone at his dorm at the college, I greeted him, "Hi, Tom, this is Preston Love in Omaha."

He was cordial, "Hi there, Preston. We haven't seen you around here for some time. How's that great bunch of fellows of yours?"

"Fine, Tom. Say, Tom, would you do me a favor and first thing tomorrow have the Chevrolet garage there come over and take our bus into their shop and check it over just enough so that my driver can pick it up in a few days and limp the 230 miles to Omaha?"

The young man thought a minute, and then rather excitedly he said, "Gee, Preston, nearly a month ago a guy came here with a title for your bus. He had to work on the bus a little, then he took off with it for some place in Minnesota."

Betty had told me that a bill for $360 had come and that I had received long-distance calls from Crookston, always when I was out on the road, and the caller never completed the call when he learned I was not home. In the heat of all the problems with the Flex, I simply never followed through on the Crookston matter. Furthermore, I never had an extra dollar to pay on the mechanic's lien on the Green Hornet anyway. Norm came through with the two cars, and we made the gig that night and returned to Omaha Monday morning to spend Monday and Tuesday off in Omaha before the next booking. Realizing that I now had no transportation nor any means of getting any, I knew those two days would be busy ones for me, arranging for rental cars and a trailer to carry our equipment at a cost I could survive.

Being an inveterate late sleeper, getting up in the morning always struck terror in my heart; but I was up early Monday although I had been in bed only since 5:00 A.M., since we had returned from the gig at four. My first act was to call Royce and apprise him of all the developments. Royce was grim but as helpful as possible. He had some other disquieting news that he saved for last. Until the law was abrogated a few years ago, there was a regulation in the musicians' union that traveling orchestras paid a tax of 10 percent of the union scale of each local whose jurisdiction the band played in. In sparsely populated areas of states like North Dakota, Wyoming, and Montana, the closest union local to the little towns we played might be several hundred miles away, but every county was assigned to some union local, and the booking agent was required by union law to file a contract with an officer of the union local for every town we were booked in. No booking agent took the chance of cheating on this, because it was the duty of the officer of each union local to check every inch of his territory. These union officials knew all of the places that gave dances in their assigned jurisdiction, so it was easy for them to keep up with engagements in each area by subscribing to the little weekly newspapers in each county that advertised the dances. If a booking agent or band was caught playing affairs without filing contracts, the agent or band would be warned or fined or suspended from the union. Union tax for my ten-piece contract would be as low as six dollars in a union local where the scale was low enough, but it would run as high as thirteen dollars a night in certain locals. My median average union tax was eight dollars per night. Eight dollars might not seem like much, but that made my weekly average about fifty dollars. When you went weeks on end without paying any tax, this could accumulate to big money. In the bigger towns we played, such as Fargo, Wichita, and Denver, the union official would usually come in person to pick up the tax, but 95 percent of the time the tax had to be mailed to the union locals. This incurred another expense of stamps and money orders to mail in the taxes. I discontinued paying the taxes by check because our checking account stayed overdrawn in those days.

Royce's news was that he was receiving letter after letter from union locals about my mounting debt and that my union local in Omaha had called him to tell him that I would be suspended from union membership if I didn't send three hundred dollars to the national headquarters in Newark. Several of the locals in the Midwest had turned me in to the national body for nonpayment of taxes. Royce counseled me to attend to the union bill first. He had only one other band besides mine, and he needed a payment from me on his account, too. But he had advance deposits on several upcoming gigs that I authorized him to keep. This would whittle down our debt to him some. Then, too, I knew Royce had a fifteen-hundred-dollar contract for the New Year's event at the country club in Wichita, Kansas, with a five-hundred-dollar deposit in hand. But even after he kept that money and I paid off the band, I still could count on several hundred dollars to pay off some of our most pressing bills. New Year's was over a month away, but it gave me something to plan on.

By nightfall I had found two of Norm's friends who graciously agreed to rent one their cars for as long as I needed them. They were hustlers—gamblers—around the Omaha ghetto, and a few dollars was insignificant to them. They just wanted to help one of the Love brothers, and since they both had several other cars at their disposal, I was in business with two cars. Our agreement was that I pay forty dollars a week for each car, and all repairs were my responsibility. One of the gamblers was also a pimp, and he added a condition, "Little brother, any time you play Lincoln or Des Moines or Sioux City for a cullud dance, I want to go with you cats and we'll have a ball. You never seen a sport like me when I get around some of those fine young broads. Everything will be on me."

I readily consented to his condition.

Red arrived from Wichita on the morning bus. He called my house and I picked him up in the 1948 Buick, which was the newer of the two rented cars. I filled him in on all the news and all of the problems confronting the band, and when we arrived at his apartment, he said, "Come on in a minute, man."

I had known Red's wife since we were young kids, and she made me welcome. Red didn't hesitate before he began, "Look, Preston, now that you don't have a bus, you won't need a driver. You can save that twelve a night you're paying me. Anyway, my wife here is getting tired of me being gone so much. Man, you've been great to work with, but I'm going on back to driving for Chesley Pierce at Ritz Cab."

I thanked my friend for all the help he had been and took off for the houses of my third trumpet man and third 'bone man. I was already in as sad a mood as possible, so I might as well get it over all at once. At each of the two men's houses I explained that I was forced to cut the band because we wouldn't have enough room in the two cars, and I also needed badly the twenty-four dollars I would save each night. All of the transportation problems and seeing me fighting the odds had lowered the band's morale some, so neither of the young musicians was too disturbed by being cut. I gave them the option of working out a notice, but neither elected to because they felt they were helping me. The same as with Red, both musicians assured me that they would be happy to work with the band again in the future if things got straightened out so I could use them again.

The next five weeks were the best we had had in months. I watched the oil, grease, and other things carefully on the two cars. We alternated pulling the trailer with the cars weekly, and since I did most of the driving anyway in the Buick, I made sure that the cars were never driven over fifty miles per hour, which puts a lot less strain on older vehicles. Most of my musicians could drive a car, and they pitched in freely to take turns with the driving. We even began to have fun around the clock while traveling.

I was able to make a substantial payment on the union tax bill, which had grown to over five hundred dollars, to the national headquarters, and I promised I would wipe out the balance after the New Year's Eve engagement. Country clubs were our meat. So long as we played a few polkas and waltzes interspersed with the two-beat corny dance music, they would gladly accept our hot things, which white audiences expected all black orchestras to play. The New Year's Eve gig at the country club in Wichita was typical. We broke it up. Feeling very proud and self-satisfied, I sought out the club manager to receive the one-thousand-dollar balance. The manager courteously ushered me into his office and complimented me on the wonderful job we did. He shuffled several papers around his desk top, and then he pulled a white sheet from under a pile of papers. Reading the sheet to me, he said, "Preston, a friend of yours was here from the Internal Revenue and picked up your check and left this receipt for you."

I could hardly believe my ears, but the paper was a statement from the Department of Internal Revenue of having received one thousand dollars from Preston Love. The club owner seemed very casual, but he explained, "I don't know how they knew you were playing here, but a deputy from the revenue office here called me today and told me that he would be out to see me about your money. I guess they have their ways of finding out these things."

This was the lowest point so far in the existence of my band. At least when things had been rough in the early days I didn't have the large indebtedness I was faced with now, and I had owned a bus. Now two of my debts were urgent and couldn't be ignored or postponed. Both my bill with the musicians' union and the Internal Revenue Service had to be attended to immediately if I was to operate any longer. The IRS had made arrangements with me earlier that year for weekly payments, but each time the bus broke down I had been unable to meet the payments, which were sizable.

Luckily, we had a pretty good New Year's Day engagement and a good weekend coming up after the New Year's Eve debacle, which would enable me to pay off the men and accumulate enough to pay for the two cars when we got back to Omaha. New Year's Eve was double pay for the men in the band, or twenty-four dollars each. After the IRS picked up all of that night's pay, I had to use all the cash I had on hand to pay the men. In fact, I had to owe them a few dollars each until we worked the New Year's Day engagement. This gig was in a small town up in Nebraska, and the first thing I did upon arriving was to check with the ballroom operator as to whether anyone had been there to ask about my money. The operator assured me that he hadn't heard from anyone. I repeated this ritual every night until we finished the week out and returned to Omaha, The IRS hadn't been to any of the other gigs. No one in history has ever been persecuted and harassed by the IRS more than Preston Love.

Monday morning we returned to Omaha for several off days. As soon as I dropped each man at his home, I went directly to Royce Stoenner's office and told him about the Wichita incident. He was visibly upset. Royce knew that I had reached the end of the line as far as being able to raise any money or to get any more credit in Omaha. He thought for a minute, then said, "Listen, Preston, you can't go on operating any longer as things are. Bookings this year during Lent are going very slowly anyway, and I don't think you could survive even after things pick up at Easter."

He could see that I was almost to a state of panic, but he continued, "Now, a year isn't very long. In fact, I had to take a year out once when I had my band. Preston, you take a year off from your band and work somewhere where you get steady wages and pay off your most pressing debts, and then we can start fresh next year and not make the mistakes you made this time. You can fill the few dates I have booked for you in January before the union closes you down, and I'll cancel everything from there on or transfer some of your dates to my other band."

I relayed the news to my fellows that we would be out of business as of February 1. I told them that I would understand if any of them found something sooner with another band and left me, but every man except Phil Thomas, the drummer, stayed until the last night of the band's existence. Phil heard from home in Chicago that there was a good jazz gig open for him, and he took off for Chicago after the first week that I gave notice of the band's dispersal. In Phil's absence, we used Otis Keyes, one of the finest natural drummers who ever lived but who never became famous. His son, Calvin Keyes, is a recognized jazz guitarist.

Ten days before my band was supposed to fold, Johnny called me and reminded me that King Records owed me four sides on my contract and that he would set it up for me to fly to Los Angeles immediately to cut them. King was having some contractual problems with their great alto-sax star, Earl Bostic, and Syd Nathan wanted me to attempt to imitate Bostic on the four sides. Johnny would have four tunes prepared when I got there. Enthusiastically, I arranged for a flight to Los Angeles the next day to coincide with the arrival of my fare and expense money from King Records via Western Union. Then I informed Royce Stoenner and my men that they would have to play the final week without me, as I would be in Los Angeles recording. I put Eli Wolinsky in charge, but Johnny "Brother" Phillips, one of the rental-car owners, also agreed to go along with the band and act as an unofficial manager and see that the band was on time and so on.

The money from King Records arrived that evening as Johnny Otis promised, and only a few hours later he called from Los Angeles to check with me about the money and my readiness to head out there. Johnny opened his conversation with, "Hey, Pres, did you get the money from King?"

I answered, "Yes, but man, they sent me more than twice my fare."

Johnny said, "Yes, that's the amount I instructed them to send you. Now here's what I want you to do. I need a tenor [sax] man, and all of these musicians out here are trying to get corny on me. They think I'm getting rich, which is a buncha' bullshit, and I can't get even one of these little no-playing tenor men to go on the road for a reasonable price. This will be a nice break for one of your cats; so just bring the best tenor man you can get around there and you and him take the train. You'll have enough money for your round-trip train fare and the tenor player's fare. Whatever is left over, put it in your pocket."

I knew that Big George Williams was very available, because he wasn't working much around Omaha. When I called Big George, he happily agreed to leave with me the next day to join Johnny. After a restful train trip to Los Angeles, George and I were met at the Los Angeles Union Station by Johnny and his drummer, Kansas City Bell. Johnny had more good news for us. He had recently signed Little Esther to King's Federal label, which was the same label that King released my recordings on. Since Johnny was still under contract to another label, I would be the orchestra leader of record and make double the union scale on all her future recordings on the Federal label if I was available when she would be recording. He had a session for Little Esther planned two days hence, and he would use both Big George and me on sax. I would also be the leader of record. Then the next day after that, we would cut the four sides of mine that King owed me on my contract.

Included on the date with Esther was the great Ben Webster on tenor. Ben was living in Los Angeles briefly and highly appreciated the chance to make the money for the session. He was a pure despotic asshole on the session. Ben took charge as though it was *his* session or *his* recording company. Although he had no official status, he growled angrily at other musicians, giving them orders. He acted pugnacious and superior to them, especially the other saxophone players, while giving us orders. The night before the session I wrote a song called "Aged and Mellow" and one called "Don't Tell Me Your Troubles." Johnny rewrote the tunes some, and Esther recorded them with Johnny and me listed as co-composers. "Aged and Mellow" was fairly successful after it was released. We used a nucleus of Johnny's band on both Esther's session and my own. I did four sides, "Wango Blues," "Like a Ship at Sea," "September Song," and "Strictly Cash." "September Song" was my closest imitation to Earl Bostic, but none of the sides was very successful.

CHAPTER SIX

Preston the Bandleader, Part 2

✳

Johnny insisted that I stay in Los Angeles and join his band, but I knew my presence would create a financial burden for him. I would be an extra, unneeded sax man, and naturally Johnny would feel obliged to pay me more than I would actually be worth to him. I did, however, travel with the troupe and play a few California dates with them, just for old times' sake for Johnny before I entrained for home. Dude was no longer traveling with Johnny, and Johnny missed his companionship sorely. Johnny and I did get together several times during my stay on the coast, however, with my precious, beloved brother, Dude.

With the sessions completed, I returned to Omaha. There, things hadn't improved any. Johnny Phillips and Eli Wolinsky informed me of all the problems they had during my absence. The fellows had been impossible to control as far as punctuality and other discipline was concerned, and the operators had docked them at nearly every gig because of my absence as the leader. My need for money was prodigious, but Johnny Phillips had salvaged less than enough even to pay Royce Stoenner's commissions. February, March, April, and May 1952 were nightmares. The harassment by the Internal Revenue Service and other creditors was incredible. My final union tax bill before I was suspended from membership was several hundred dollars. Even if there had been a location spot open to me in town, I would have been forbidden by the Omaha musicians' union local to play it. At that time, there were two union locals in every town where there was a sizable black population. There was the black local, which was designated as the "colored" local and always the white local, which was designated the "mother" local. In Omaha we had Local 70, the white "mother" local, and Local 558, the "colored" local. Johnny Otis referred to number 558 as the "Amos and Andy Local" because of its rickety building and the older and uneducated union officials who were strict on its black members but completely subservient and fawning to the white "mother" local.

Soon after it was learned that my band was defunct, Eli Wolinsky was contacted by several of the white bands of the area to play alto sax with them. Eli recommended me, and soon he and I were working as a team on weekends with several of the so-called Mickey Mouse bands around Omaha. Eli's idol and his obsession was Johnny Hodges, Duke Ellington's great alto-sax man, as Earle Warren was my idol. Eli's other idol was me. I was seven years older than Eli, and he had an almost filial deference toward me. When he was a young aspiring alto player of seventeen in 1945 he had seen me with Basie in New London, Connecticut, near his home at Willimantic. This was one of my earliest dates with Basie after I replaced Earle Warren, and Eli stood before me throughout the entire gig. He always remembered my every action and mannerism that night in 1945. Eli's formal education was superior to mine since he had attended the University of Connecticut and New York's City College. I was very much influenced by his suggestion of authors and books for me to read during his stay with my band and later while we were working with the territory bands. We were roommates as we had been with my band. Eli spent all of his free time at my house visiting with Betty and me, raving over the tasty Afro-American dishes that were standard in our home as in most black homes. His favorite was chitterlings with my corn bread.

In the white territory bands, as with my band, I was assigned to the first-alto chair, and Eli played third second alto. The first band we played a weekend with belonged to Jimmie White, a lovable piano player who attended the University of Nebraska at Omaha full-time. Jimmie advertised his band as a "Lombardo Styled Orchestra." We had four saxes, three trumpets, two 'bones, and rhythm. Jimmie traveled in a newer and larger school bus than the Green Hornet, and the band was one big ball. There was no more pleasant group of young fellows in the world to work with than these twelve people. They treated Eli and me like celebrities and Jimmie paid us eighteen dollars a night instead of the fifteen the others received. Jimmie White was very pleased with his sax section as we sang out on the ballads in his repertoire. One night, feeling in an especially good mood, I led out on a slow arrangement with the wide and wobbly vibrato à la the Guy Lombardo reed section. I syruped it up and corned it up, and Eli also added the third-sax part in an exaggerated version of the Lombardo style. We had done this many times for comic relief in my band, and the audiences didn't detect our hilarious convulsions of laughter as a put-on, nor did the audience this night at the Jimmie White dance consider it offensive. The audience in this small Nebraska town went wild with appreciation as we schmaltzed up the ballad. Lovable Jimmie White leaped from his piano stool and gleefully waved to Eli and me, "That's it. Give me more of the style."

The "style" automatically meant the Lombardo style or the Lawrence Welk style in that part of the country. After this, several of the other Omaha orchestras operating in the area sought out the Wolinsky-Love team and we were soon getting an occasional midweek engagement as well as weekend gigs.

In late May, placards were placed in the windows up and down North Twenty-fourth Street announcing that Johnny Otis, Little Esther, and their show would play the Dreamland in Omaha the first week in June. As always, upon their arrival in town Johnny had the bus come directly to our house in the projects and deposit him and his effects before proceeding to Mrs. Patton's rooming house–hotel where the others would stay. That night, their crowd at the Dreamland was down considerably from the sell-outs the troupe had experienced every visit since they caught the big hit "Double Crossin' Blues" in 1950. Johnny was concerned, but not extremely so. He said another big hit record would propel the troupe right back to top drawing power. Neither he, Esther, nor Mel Walker had caught a hit for several months now, after having had a succession of hit recordings in 1950 and 1951. After the dance at the Dreamland, Johnny took stock of my dire predicament and decreed that I leave with him the next day for their engagement in Junction City, Kansas, and then on to Denver and their home base, Los Angeles. Eli was with us and requested that he, too, be permitted to make the Los Angeles trip. Johnny's permission was automatic. Around noon the next day, Johnny's big Aero Coach pulled up to our apartment in the Omaha housing project, and Johnny, Eli, and I loaded our luggage on the bus with the help of Johnny's band valet. I bade Betty and our son, Sandy, good-bye, with instructions for them to dispose of all of our furniture, as I would have them join me in Los Angeles within a month.

At Junction City, Johnny's crowd was only mediocre. Again, Johnny was concerned as he confided to me, "Man, we had three times this many people in this auditorium when we played here earlier this year, and those spooks went crazy over our show. They sure were much cooler tonight. Well, that's all right. I just signed with a different record company, and we're going back to Los Angeles and get in that studio and grind out some more hits like last year."

The next night in Denver was much more sensational, and Johnny was reassured. Johnny was well known personally in Denver from the year he spent there when he and Phyllis were first married, eloping from Berkeley,

California, in 1941. Both nights I played with the band, and Eli watched from backstage. Johnny's rhythm and blues show was mostly antics and showmanship interspersed with some occasional good blues and swinging backbeat up-tempo rhythm and blues. I felt somewhat out of place, but I did my dance and played my part along with the rest of the group. From Denver to Los Angeles would be a full day's ride, and the members of Johnny's troupe were anxious to get home to their familiar surroundings after the long national tour. The next afternoon we were approaching Las Vegas when his bus began to mess up. Shades of the Flex! The driver pulled into the International Truck garage, and the prognosis was for an expensive repair and a delay of several hours. Most of the members of the troupe elected to take other means of transportation to Los Angeles from Las Vegas, and Johnny had the valet call a cab to take him, Eli, and me to the Union Pacific railroad depot, where we caught the first train for Los Angeles.

In Los Angeles, I, of course, moved in with Johnny and his family, which now consisted of Phyllis, Johnny, and two young daughters. Eli was placed with Johnny's tenor man, James Von Streeter, who was Johnny's old friend as well as mine from our Lloyd Hunter days. Big George had been gone some weeks. He was not happy playing rhythm and blues and felt awkward about the showmanship required in Johnny's band, so he had remained with the group only for a few months. It was obvious that Johnny's financial state was rather shaky. For this reason, and because I had no valid union status, I made no attempt to join his band. Thus, I elected to take a job outside of music. Two weeks later, both Eli and I were working at Douglas Aircraft in Santa Monica as assemblers after a quick one-week training course. After two more weeks, Betty had sold all of our furniture at a fraction of its worth as she was forced to do in order to dispose of it. She and our son arrived by train from Omaha. Two days before their arrival, I had managed to rent an apartment in the same house where my brother Dude roomed. Wonderful, lovable Dude was now forty-five years old.

Somehow I adjusted to the regimen of early night retiring and early morning arising, but Eli soon found the factory routine unbearable and quit in near panic after three weeks. There were times when I, too, felt like flipping, but Betty soon took a clerical job, and we began to show immediate progress financially. We were able to make payments on our indebtedness back in Omaha, and my Internal Revenue file had been transferred to the Los Angeles office, where the deputies were much more sympathetic and courteous than the cranky ones in Omaha had been. Soon, I was making payments on the IRS debt and at least keeping pace with the big interest and penalties assessed against me periodically.

Johnny was on the road most of the time, but we saw him occasionally. Any time he recorded, he would use me on the session if possible. He was now directing A&R of West Coast sessions for Peacock and Duke Records, which were Don Robey–owned labels in Houston, Texas. Willie Mae "Big Mama" Thornton was a member of Johnny's troupe at this time, and since she was under contract to Duke Records, Johnny directed a session for her in the fall of that year, on which the first recording of "Hound Dog" was made. I elected to pass up that session because of my job at Douglas Aircraft. Willie Mae's "Hound Dog" became the number-one rhythm and blues hit in the nation several years before Presley's version was recorded. In September, my friend Ernie Fields came through Los Angeles on tour, and through me he met Eli. A few days later, when Ernie arrived back home in Tulsa, Oklahoma, he contacted Eli and wired him the fare to join Ernie's orchestra in Tulsa. Eli was elated to get away from Los Angeles and back into the music, but both he and I were otherwise deeply saddened by his departure.

In December, I played two Christmas parties with Stanley Morgan's trio at a famous Hollywood restaurant. Stanley was also working at Douglas Aircraft, and he played guitar with his trio or other casual combos on weekends. These turned out to be the only gigs I played from July 1952 until June 1953. In fact, I seldom touched my sax or clarinet during this period. New Year's Eve of 1952–1953 was the first time I hadn't worked on a New Year's Eve since my career began in 1940. By April we were making plans to return to Omaha and to resume the operation of my band in the Midwest. Early in May, we were riding down Manchester Boulevard on a Sunday outing with some friends when I spotted an elongated Chevrolet car, the type used as an airport limousine. It was parked on a used-car lot with a for-sale sign on its windshield. I instructed the driver of our friend's car to pull onto the lot, and when the car salesman approached me, I asked him the sales data on the bus-limousine. The salesman quoted me a figure of four hundred dollars and offered to give me a test spin in the 1942 "stretch" job. These limousines were actually conventional sedans that were cut in half and a middle section added to stretch them into twelve-passenger buses or limousines. This one was done at Armbruster's in Fort Smith, Arkansas. Years later, I was able to visit Armbruster's when playing in Fort Smith and see how the whole process was accomplished. The old stretch job drove perfectly on the test spin, and I checked it out thoroughly. It had been very well cared for. I put a twenty dollar earnest-money deposit on the Chevy, and the following Tuesday all arrangements for financing it had been completed with a loan company near the Los Angeles duplex where we had now lived for several months. That afternoon, Dude picked up the car for me and proudly parked her in front of the duplex. Dude was temporarily unemployed, and when Betty, Sandy, and I arrived home that day at different times, Dude took each of us for a ride around the block. Dude was more jubilant with each demonstration of the bus.

Our plans for returning to Omaha were soon finalized. Betty and I would place our two weeks' notices at our jobs on May 15. Sandy would complete his school year the day before Memorial Day. Both of our employers would be distributing vacation pay to their employees, and we figured we would have about six hundred dollars in cash to head for Omaha the day after Memorial Day. We had purchased a few furniture items, which a used-furniture store bought at one-tenth of their value. This was no surprise; we anticipated it after our experience in Omaha the previous year. I used the seventy-five dollars from the furniture dealer to pay off the final installment of my debt to the musicians' union for the old 10 percent surtaxes. I would rejoin the "colored" local as soon as we reached Omaha.

My mother, who was now nearly seventy-three years old, had been in Los Angeles for more than a year, staying with my sister Laura, who rented one of three little houses on Johnny Otis's lot. Mama longed to see the four of her children still living in Omaha, so she decided to take the trip

Marshall Royal, Preston Love, Betty Love, and Count Basie, Denver, Colorado, 1953.

back with Sandy, Betty, and me in the stretch job. The day after Memorial Day 1953, we packed our utensils, linen, and some other household items in the old limousine and headed up to Johnny's house, which was only three blocks from the duplex. Mama, Laura, Dude, and my oldest brother, Sonny, who had lived in Los Angeles since 1929, were waiting for us. Evening was approaching when Mama, Betty, Sandy, our pet dog, and I were loaded in and ready to embark on our return trip to Omaha. Johnny was out of town, but Phyllis and their two little daughters joined the group standing at the curb waving as we pulled away. Dude waved with his usual dramatic flourish. This was the last time I saw Dude alive. The next time I would behold his person would be in his coffin when his body arrived back in Omaha for burial on March 11, 1959. Oh, how did I ever survive his death?

The trip back to Omaha was pleasurable, with all the beautiful mountain scenery and the love and warmth we all felt for each other coupled with our anticipation of seeing relatives and friends back in Omaha. The old Chevy performed flawlessly for all of the 1700 miles, much of which was up and down steep mountain passes. I did all of the driving, with only short stops for maps, refueling, and eating. On June 3, 1953, we pulled up in front of Norm's house. Home at last! Later that evening, there was a mammoth reunion with Betty's mother and other relatives from her side and my side of the family alike.

A few days later, we rented a furnished apartment. I had already booked several quickie gigs, the first of which was only two weeks away. I didn't even have any musicians lined up, but that would be no problem. Furthermore, I had resolved to keep the size of my band small from now on — maybe seven, or at most eight, pieces. Eli and I corresponded regularly, and as soon as I informed him of our presence in Omaha and about my plans, he gave notice to Ernie Fields. Two weeks after we arrived in Omaha, Eli arrived and checked in with Cliff and Eileen Dudley, with whom he had roomed before leaving Omaha. Soon we had put together a fine eight-piece group. Donnie Kelly was out of the army now, and he joined the new group. Harry Lewis played our first few bookings on tenor, but Harry was back in Omaha only temporarily from Washington, D.C., where he had lived the past year with his dad, an ex-Omaha policeman. Our instrumentation was then two alto saxes, tenor sax, trombone, drums, piano, and electric bass. We condensed all of my big-band library to fit this instrumentation and bought several stock orchestrations of new pop tunes and older standards. Several Omaha arrangers began to write orchestrations especially for our new instrumentation, which could be voiced to sound like either a brass or reed section if orchestrated properly. We used several different male vocalists the first weeks of our operation before Lawrence "Streamline" McNeal joined as our permanent vocalist. Streamline had trouble with meter, but he had much of the true Afro-American feeling that I loved so well, and I stuck with him even when several other good singers petitioned for the vocal job with us.

The stretch limousine performed miraculously, and by mid-fall we hadn't had one breakdown. We used the first three seats for passengers and packed the rear seat with equipment. The rest of the equipment was strapped to the roof luggage rack under a tarpaulin. By July 1, with the help of one of Omaha's veteran musicians, Sam Grievious, bookings were coming in pretty well. Most of them were close to Omaha, but we were able to tap my band's former popularity for some good dates at distant points. Bookings were adequate for our survival, but in the Midwest bands were judged largely by the booking agent that represented them. The volume of a band's work was determined largely by the prestige of its agency affiliation. Therefore, our volume of bookings was rather inconsistent. The band did go over well at most places we played, especially at the country clubs, fraternal clubs, and the few bigger ballrooms that Grievious and I were able to book. We began to make ripples in the territory again. One day in early October I received a call from Royce Stoenner, who wasted no time getting to the point.

"Hey, Preston, how has it been going? I heard you were back in town and operating again."

I gave Royce an undoctored account of the band's status, and Royce said, "Well, Pres, you know I still have a contract on you and an investment in you. Come on out to see me, and let's talk it over." Before we hung up, Royce added, "By the way, are you booked for Christmas and New Year's Eve yet? I have some good dates kicking around for that time."

Two days later, Royce and I were back together, and my datebook was soon swelling again.

I wasted no time in contacting Phil Thomas, our drummer from the first band, and he joined us from Chicago before the month was out. Phil and I had been hunting and fishing partners, and the band members jokingly named us the Preston Love Safari. Now with Phil back, the good times would roll again. During Lent of 1954, when the after-Easter booking campaign began for the year, Royce Stoenner summoned me to his office to inform me that his agency was going to merge with National Orchestra Service (NOS), which was the biggest booking agency in Omaha history. They had booked Royce's orchestra when he operated it, as well as most of the other top territory bands at one time or other. NOS was now the agent for about fifteen bands, all of which were top area groups ranging in size from small combos to sixteen pieces. They also booked acts. I was happy at the thought of becoming a National Orchestra Service band. The agency was a big operation and operated like the big-time eastern agencies. Their system was similar to Royce's system at Music Management Service, but even more efficient. Most NOS bands operated sleeper buses like Nat Towles had featured and Lloyd Hunter had operated for a while. With NOS my band began to play even more prestigious ballrooms and clubs, and our average weekly grosses improved over what they had been with Royce. Our geographical area of operation also increased dramatically. We began to play engagements as far away as Florida, Georgia, and South Carolina, mostly for the military clubs. In late 1954, I bought a slightly newer Chevy stretch job that had also been elongated at Armbruster's in Fort Smith, and it also performed beautifully for mile after mile for a whole year.

About this same time, Streamline McNeal was forced to leave the band because of family considerations, and we hired Gladys "Sumac" Price, a young singer from Denver. Gladys was influenced by the great Dinah Washington and I have always considered it tragic that this fine young singer never recorded and never became a famous singing star. Gladys was the first of a string of five girl singers I hired over the next seven years as the female singer became a necessary fixture in our band. In the summer of 1955, I purchased a 1947 Chevy school bus in Phillipsburg, Kansas, and outfitted it with comfortable seats. It cost me only seven hundred dollars, but it, too, performed beautifully through mile after mile of economical and relatively trouble-free travel.

On New Year's Eve of 1955–1956, NOS booked us in the Officers Club at Webb Air Force Base in Big Spring, Texas, for $1200. The night before was for $450 at the Non-Commissioned Officers Club. Phil Thomas, Eli Wolinsky, Donnie Kelly, and I were the only four members who had been with the band on that dark day in August 1950 when we experienced the debacle here in this same Big Spring, Texas. Now, all of my musicians had been on weekly salaries for more than a year. Donnie was buying a brand-new 1955 Pontiac, and Eli had recently purchased a brand-new top-name alto sax with cash. Now, we would receive $1200 for one night instead of $100 as on that 1950 night for Walter Green.

When my band was at its top in the fifties, we enjoyed great popularity in the St. Cloud, Minnesota, area. In fact, from 1951 until about 1960, we were probably the biggest drawing card at the two ballrooms in St. Cloud and at several ballrooms in the small towns all around the immediate area. We were also a favorite at one of the colleges in St. Cloud for their proms, so during these years I spent quite a number of nights at hotels and motels in St. Cloud. In 1956, at the height of my popularity in the area, I decided one day to go around to the old Merchants Hotel and see if there was anything about it and the management that I would recognize. Much to my surprise, the hotel looked quite the same as it had sixteen years earlier. It still had the same owners. The tavern directly across the street was still there and looked much the same also. When we stayed at the hotel in 1940, the owners were a couple in their mid-thirties, and their three or four children were quite small; but now it seemed so strange to see instead a man and woman about fifty years old and several teenagers. Of course, I was a man in his early thirties instead of the nineteen-year-old boy they had known in 1940, but they readily remembered me and all the members of the band that had stayed there in 1940, so we had a wonderful, nostalgic visit. I went back to see them several times over the next few years, and upon one of my returns I was most surprised to learn that the owner and his two sons were operating a concession in a carnival. They had bought several big pieces of equipment that were parked on the lot next to the hotel, and each summer they traveled through Minnesota and the Dakotas operating their concessions at county fairs and other celebrations with a carnival. They did well at this enterprise.

Roswell, New Mexico, became one of the key towns of my band's operation. When I think of Roswell, a most humorous incident involving a very dear woman there flashes across my memory. The first time I was ever in Roswell was in early 1954 when we were first booked at Walker Air Force Base on the outskirts of town. At Walker, we were booked for two nights, one at the Non-Commissioned Officers Club and one night at the Officers Club. This necessitated our finding rooms for the two nights. Roswell wasn't a southern city geographically, but we always regarded it as part of our southern tours. It was a borderline city so far as racial politics were concerned, and a small percentage of the white restaurants and the white motels had only recently begun to serve black people because of pressure from the black personnel at Walker Air Force Base. Roswell was neither southern nor northern, but a little of each. Nat Towles was operating a six-piece combo that was booked by National Orchestra Service, the same agency that was booking my band. Towles's combo had just preceded us to Roswell at Walker Air Force Base, and Nat had left word with the people at the agency to tell me that the place to stay in Roswell was at Mrs. Collins' guest house. The rates were very reasonable, and Mrs. Collins had the nicest "colored" rooming house in town. When we arrived in Roswell for the early 1954 engagement at Walker, we sought out the black neighborhood, which was usually easy to find in each town by being near the railroad tracks, but in Roswell this wasn't the case. However, we found the ghetto easily enough. A man in front of the Sunset Café directed us to Mrs.

Collins's hotel, which was about five blocks straight down from the corner near the Sunset. In a few minutes our vintage bus pulled into the vacant lot beside Mrs. Collins's guest house.

It was mid-winter, but in Roswell it was a pleasantly warm night with the sweet, warm zephyrs so typical of that part of the country and the deep South. If I ever write a song about the South, something in the first line will have to attempt to describe those romantic southern zephyrs that I learned to love so much. The Collins hotel was an elongated house whose size had been accomplished by augmenting the length of a regular-sized house. On one side of the hallway there were five doorways leading into medium-sized bedrooms. Mrs. Collins occupied the second bedroom back from the front, and her daughter Lillian and her son-in-law Paul occupied the room next to her. On the other side of the hallway at the rear of the house was one large room with two double beds and contiguous to it were two more medium-sized bedrooms. Then, on that side, came the kitchen, the bathroom, and a combination foyer and living room into which the front door served as the main entrance. There were a total of five rental rooms; since all bands of the era doubled up, and since the big bedroom could sleep as many as four, Mrs. Collins could take care of a pretty large troupe. The front stoop was the usual small platform with several comfortable chairs, which was standard for homes in that area.

Mrs. Collins was a stocky, brown-skinned woman who appeared to be about sixty-five years old, and she was visibly pleased to see us musicians, although she tried to appear unconcerned. She welcomed us at the front door and ushered us into the neat little front parlor. There were pictures of all of the orchestras that had stayed there with her all around the room, and several pictures of Earl Hines's orchestra. It didn't take long for us to learn that she was the widowed mother of Booker T. Collins, once a well-known string bass player for some years with Earl Hines and other big bands. Booker T. now lived in Chicago but had traveled with a number of bands in the Southwest, which was one of the main reasons Mrs. Collins had enlarged her home to accommodate "Negroes" who might be traveling in the area and finding it difficult to get sleeping accommodations.

We soon discovered that Mrs. Collins was a religious woman but not unwise to a mundane existence such as ours. She feigned a slight sternness, but there was always a rather sly and wise glint in Mrs. Collins's eyes and in her manner. In other words, Mrs. Mary Collins was an older woman but not unhip. I was always clowning it up when I felt it necessary to relax new acquaintances, and I showed an inordinate interest in her talk about her son, Booker T. I also took a great interest in the various pictures of him around the room with different bands, so I perceived that Mrs. Collins

Preston Love and His Orchestra, South Dakota State University, Brookings, South Dakota, 1955. Left to right: Eli Wolinsky, Donnie Kelly, George Miles, Sweetpea Rogers, Jordan Leavy, Kim Robinson; Vocalist, Dee Robinson.

took an immediate liking to me. She seemed to develop quickly a maternal feeling toward me that lasted throughout our acquaintance. Lillian and her husband Paul also made us feel at home, and they, too, seemed so happy to have some strangers from distant places as guests, especially musicians.

The NCO clubs on military bases had been integrated only a few years prior to this time, and they were usually run by club managers or club secretaries who catered mainly to the taste of the white noncommissioned officers and their wives. Many of these were lovers of hillbilly music, Lawrence Welk–style corn, and Western music. What they called good music in the fifties was something by Bill Haley, Elvis Presley, or one of the other corny groups of the time. We were one of the very few black orchestras playing the military circuit perennially at that time, and the black personnel at the bases looked forward anxiously to our appearances at the clubs. When a Negro orchestra played one of the clubs, the black personnel and their wives and guests turned out in large numbers, and it was rather like "their night."

Nevertheless, the NCO secretary in charge of the club invariably made it clear to me that we shouldn't play too much "jazz," which really meant for me not to play too much of any of the kinds of music that appealed to the black people who would be in the club. Even if we had an overwhelming majority of black clientele in the club, I knew that I wouldn't be hired back as often—or maybe not at all—if a few of the white NCOs or their wives went to the secretary and complained that "the Preston Love band played too much colored music." In their privacy with the club secretary, I knew they probably referred to it as "nigger music."

Our first engagement at the Walker AFB NCO club was a mild sensation because I mixed up the music, playing the latest popular songs and danceable ballads for the whites and playing rhythm and blues standards for the black people. This was the beginning of a most fruitful relationship for my band in Roswell, New Mexico. Within a few weeks my agency was swamped with bids for our band all over the town and also found the buyers at Walker very anxious to book us there. In fact, each January for the next few years my agency would set our bookings at Walker (and several other military bases) for the coming year. We would often be in Roswell for as long as a week. We were subsequently booked at the NCO Club, the Officers Club, and the base theater, and we played regularly at the Elks Club, two local country clubs, and a ballroom in Roswell. We had several other towns like this, from Fargo, North Dakota, to Wichita Falls, Texas, where we had several accounts in the town. Our arrival in those places and in Roswell soon became a pretty big occasion. In the towns with a few thousand black residents, we were the same as at home.

The first time we returned to play Roswell was later in 1954, and we were shocked that in the time we had been gone, Mrs. Collins's son-in-law Paul had died. She and Paul's wife Lillian still seemed in a state of shock. I never knew the details of Paul's sudden death, but he had died shortly after our first stay there. Paul couldn't have been much past forty years old, and since he had been so congenial to us, his death came as quite a shock. Lillian was now a widow, and she and Mrs. Collins now lived in the guest house alone. From 1954 until mid-1956 we stayed at Mrs. Collins's so often that I lost track of the times. Mrs. Collins seemed to love several of us in the band the same as if we were her blood sons. When we first moved in, however, she had laid down one strict rule: there would be *no women* visitors in our rooms at any time unless it was one of our wives who might join us there or who might be traveling with us. If some young lady wanted to come by to see one of us, she was welcome to sit in the parlor and visit, but that's where her visit would end in Mrs. Collins's house. Some of the fellows in the band were rather unhappy about the no-women ruling, but they complied. Whenever they scored in Roswell, they made other arrangements for bedding down.

In the late summer of 1956 we played three days at Fort Bliss near El Paso, Texas, which is just slightly more than a hundred miles from Roswell. While at Fort Bliss, one of our fellows in the band connected up with a very pretty girl who was a member of the Women's Army Corps (WAC) stationed at Ft. Bliss. The two young people became quite enamored of each other, and since we were going next to Roswell for five days, they decided that the WAC would take a leave and travel to Roswell with us and spend the five days with my young sideman. However, there was the problem of Mrs. Collins's rule about no girls. She would know that the couple wasn't married because the sideman's wife had been in Roswell with him several times and stayed at the Collins guest house. Thus, the young musician was forced to devise a plan, and the rest of us agreed to help him with it.

The WAC rode with us in our bus to Roswell, and when we arrived there we dropped her off at the Greyhound bus station downtown, where she waited at least an hour to give us time to check in at Mrs. Collins's. Then, she took a cab and arrived at the guest house with some well-rehearsed story about just passing through Roswell and at the last minute deciding to stop there and spend a few days visiting some friend of hers stationed at Walker AFB. To make sure that there would be a room available for her our sideman insisted on taking the second bed in a big room with two other men in the band. He explained the decision to triple up to Mrs. Collins as a choice motivated by economy, because we saved a dollar per night whenever three or four took the two double beds in the big room. Everything went off without a hitch, and within an hour or so we were all ensconced at the Collins guest house. The only room left when the WAC arrived was the room farthest from the room occupied by Mrs. Collins, which was the perfect arrangement as far as the two paramours were concerned. We were very cooperative in aiding the two conspirators, and we were very careful not to appear to know the WAC and careful that she never left the house nor arrived at the exact same time that we did. We stopped each night after work and ate some of the delicious food at the ramshackle Sunset Café before going to our rooms. The Sunset also served as the only after-hours spot in the small ghetto; so we hung out with our local friends and had a few drinks. By the time those going home in our bus to the guest house arrived, Mrs. Collins was always sound asleep, and it was an easy matter for the band member to slip into the WAC's room and spend most of the night before stealthily slipping back to his room before it was time for Mrs. Collins to arise for the day. All in all, the two young people had a very enjoyable five-day visit, made even more so by the intrigue of outsmarting Mrs. Collins. On the day we were leaving after completing five days at the base, the WAC made arrangements to take the Greyhound bus to El Paso a few hours before our scheduled time of departure to our next gig, so she calmly gathered up her bags and took her leave. Mrs. Collins bade her a courteous farewell, and we felt very smug and clever about the whole deception. I felt the most relieved, because I had been afraid that Mrs. Collins and Lillian would catch on, and as leader of the band and as their favorite in the band, I knew I would have to be the one to pacify Mrs. Collins if they discovered the ruse.

Shortly after noon that day, we began to load our equipment and our luggage into the back compartment of our bus while Mrs. Collins sat quietly on the porch, shaded from the afternoon sun and heat. She calmly watched us loading as she always did each time we left. I had remarked once to the band members that every time we departed from Mrs. Collins's she watched us like a mother who might be afraid that this was the last time we would see each other for some reason or other. Finally, we were loaded and the band members began to board the bus. I was standing by the door of the bus waiting for the last person to enter, since I was going to start out driving. When the last member got on the bus, Mrs. Collins called softly, "Preston, may I see you for a moment?"

The first thing that crossed my mind was that one of the fellows hadn't paid his rent, or that someone had taken one of Mrs. Collins's towels, which had happened a time or two previously, at which time I always mailed her whatever was owed once I found out about it. Since the bus was parked on the lot not far from the porch, I took a couple of long strides and jauntily hopped up on the little porch beside Mrs. Collins. She said, "Sit down here next to me, son."

I still had no idea of what was coming when she quietly continued, "Now, son, you didn't think that I didn't know that girl was with you all, did you?"

I sputtered and stammered for something to say, and I felt like a little boy caught with his hand in the cookie jar. She went on, "That boy ought to be ashamed of himself bringing that girl here. You all know I don't allow that—and him with that nice wife up there in Omaha. And I'm ashamed of *you* helping him to try to fool me. The only reason I didn't make him and that girl leave my house is because I didn't actually catch them in anything, but I knew what was going on."

I still tried feebly to insist that none of us knew the WAC, but my protestations were halfhearted, so Mrs. Collins said, "That's all right. You go ahead now, but you all know better than to bring any stray women into my house."

She seemed more hurt than angry, and I felt ashamed. I bade good-bye until our next return and boarded the bus. I seated myself at the wheel, cranked up the bus, and backed out of the yard and headed for Clovis, New Mexico, our next engagement. When I got on the bus, I could see that everyone was curious about what Mrs. Collins had to say to me, but I decided to let them sweat a while before revealing her conversation to them. I acted nonchalant and noncommittal. Finally, after we had gone a few blocks toward the highway, our burly drummer hollered from the rear, "Hey, Preston, what did old lady Collins have to say?"

I figured they had suffered long enough, and I had enjoyed the humor of their sweating long enough, so I recounted the conversation to them. A couple of them howled with laughter that we had been unmasked, and my roommate, Eli, said between guffaws, "Uh-huh, you cats didn't think Mother Collins was sharp enough to catch on to what was happening."

But some of them began to grumble and to berate Mrs. Collins in absentia. Our drummer took the position of spokesman and asked me, "Preston, when are we going to stop staying at that old house with that old lady? We have come up in the music world the past couple of years; so why don't we start staying at one of the white hotels here? I heard that Hotel Roswell and some of those fine motels on the highway have opened up to colored people."

There was a chorus of agreement from most of the guys, so I answered, "Man, you know I'm for anything that makes you cats happy. If you want to, we'll make it to one of those ofay hotels next time we're here."

Our next booking in Roswell wasn't far off, and a few weeks later we were back for a three-day stay. We all rather looked forward to checking in a plush hotel with private baths, television, and the other luxuries. The Hotel Roswell was an old-style hotel built in an elaborate and plush style of a past era. It was quite a large building in the heart of downtown, and although it was old, it was kept in a state of good repair. One by one we trooped into the lobby to check in. Sure enough, the desk clerk politely began to distribute registration cards to each of us. Most of the people in the lobby of the hotel were older people and were staid, conservative

Stretch job number 1 in Minnesota, 1954.

types. They seemed to go with the furniture, which was in the style of luxury hotels of previous eras. The prices were quite reasonable, and we signed in and went to our respective rooms, which were large and plush but also rather old-fashioned. After taking a bath and changing clothes, I sauntered down to the lobby by way of the ornate stairway and headed for the hotel's coffee shop. Several of my band members were already down from their rooms and in the lobby. I could see that their presence was causing quite a sensation among the old whites. I moved to an inconspicuous place in the lobby and watched the guarded stares of the white guests, who were trying with all their might to act as though black people had been staying at white hotels in Roswell for a hundred years instead of for the one year or so it had really been.

By mid-afternoon, several of our fellows had acquired their bottles of "relaxin' oil" (liquor) and gathered in one of the rooms to play tonk and to have a few drinks and laughs. In a couple of the other rooms occupied by the band, two of the other band members had taken out their horns and were practicing. As usual, I was lying down for an afternoon nap to be fresh for the gig that night. I had just dozed off and was having some pleasant dream about my band making it to the big time when the phone by my bed began to ring. I picked up the phone, and the desk clerk pleaded, "Mr. Love, some of your boys are creating a big fuss in room 306. It sounds like they're having a wild party, and some of them are blowing horns on the next floor. My phone here on the desk is just about to ring off of the desk with guests complaining that your boys are disturbing them. Mr. Love, we just can't have this."

I assured the clerk that I would attend to it and got up and put my robe and house slippers on and went around to room 306 where the tonk game was in session. Four of the guys were playing tonk and drinking as well as having a jolly time. They were glad to see me, because I nearly always joined in the tonk games and the party spirit that always went with them. I implored them to be a little quieter, which was like asking the wind not to blow when the "juice" was flowing, but they were understanding of my situation, and they muted the conversation and the laughter. I then went down to the next floor where the two members were practicing, and although they weren't playing excessively loudly you could still hear the horns for quite some distance from their rooms. I explained to them that the desk clerk was very unhappy with their practicing, and they put their horns back in the cases without protesting. I then returned to my room and my nap. I hadn't been back to sleep for more than a few minutes when my phone rang again. It was the desk clerk with the same story all over again about noise in room 306. I pacified him as best I could and repeated my trip around to 306. I knew it would be futile to try to suppress the party unless I stayed there, so I pulled up a chair and joined in the tonk game and had a few drinks myself. The reveling didn't stop entirely, but with my presence they held it down to a minimum until it was time for us to get ready for the gig.

That night after the gig, most of us stayed away from the hotel until very late, so when we came in we went quietly to our rooms and to bed. We thus made our debut at our first white lodging establishment in Roswell, New Mexico. The next day I arose at about eleven in the morning, which was very early for me, and I called the two motels that I had heard about catering to black people. One of them had some cabins with kitchen facilities, and their rates were quite reasonable, so I made reservations for our party of nine people. Then I had the desk clerk call each member of our group, and I explained that we would move out to the motel where we would have more privacy, since we would have cabins with private entrances and each cabin was slightly removed from the others. Within an hour or so we were all in the lobby of the hotel and checked out. We quickly loaded our bus and headed out to the highway. The bus pulled up in front of the motel after a few minutes' ride and we parked at the motel's office as the band members trooped in to select their accommodations. The managers were a man and wife who both had deep southern or southwestern accents. Many people indigenous to states such as

Kansas, Missouri, and Arizona have accents similar to people from the deep South, so sometimes it was difficult to distinguish between a southern accent and just a plain countrified drawl. The couple was quite congenial, however, and within a few minutes we were all checked in and on our way to our respective cabins. Most of us doubled up, but now with the anticipated deluge of female companionship, a couple of the guys took single cabins. Eli Wolinsky and I were roommates, and we selected a cabin with cooking facilities because I would always cook up a big pot whenever we stayed where there was a kitchen. In fact, I would always cook a pot or two whenever we stayed at Mrs. Collins's for several days. We kept a box full of utensils and spices in the bus at all times for these contingencies.

Since there wasn't time to stock up on groceries and to cook before gig time, we decided to run across the highway to a café that was located directly across from our motel. Several of us had the same idea at the same time, so we met as we headed over there. When we entered the neat little restaurant, there was a well-dressed white woman seating the parties as they entered. She appeared to be in her late forties or early fifties, and she seated each group with a great flurry of politeness as they entered. When she saw us enter, she busied herself nervously at the farthest point in the cafe from the entrance where we were standing. Whenever a party of white people came in and stood there by us awaiting a table or a booth, she quickly beckoned to them and seated them. Several of the parties who came in after us had been seated, until finally we got the message. I called the woman and angrily told her about her seating people who had come in long after we had, and she became very nervous, as we had the look of people who were thoroughly tired of this bullshit. In a shaky voice she said, "Oh, I'm so sorry, sir, but if you don't have a reservation I can't seat you."

She then spurted to another area of the café and busied herself with arranging the napkins or something on the tables. The cashier behind the counter near us was also a middle-aged woman, and she, too, suddenly got very busy arranging packages of gum and packages of cigarettes behind her, where she didn't have to face us.

That night, we played the NCO club and had our usual big turnout of our black following. With our new private quarters the fellows felt free to invite several friends to come out to our cabins for some drinks after the gig. We were off by midnight, so by one most of us were back at the motel as several carloads of our friends began to arrive for a night of festivities. Since Eli and I had taken a large cabin, the party was directed to where we were staying. Most of the band members had come in with our bus, but some of them had stayed back to ride with friends and to direct them to the party. As the cars arrived, I went to the door to welcome the first contingent of our guests. When I opened the door in response to their knocks, I noticed the motel manager and his wife pacing around nervously at the end of our row of cabins. Every now and then they would huddle and talk to each other in hushed tones while pointing towards our cabin with anxious stares.

By now, several cars had begun to arrive, and with the arrival of each one I could see the managers peer around the corner of the end cabin or walk nervously out into the driveway, sometimes nearly blocking it to the cars. Finally, the party was in full progress, but I had now lost most of my enthusiasm for it because I expected the phone to ring at any minute from the office or the manager to burst in and spoil the fun for our guests. Surprisingly, my phone never rang, nor did we hear from the managers. But when the gathering began to break up around three in the morning, as each party went to the parking area to their cars, both the man and the wife walked over near them and watched them, peering into the car as it pulled out. We spent the rest of our stay at the motel being stared at by the manager and his wife with their troubled expressions. The morning after our last night at the base we loaded our bus to take off for our next engagement. When we were all on the bus and ready to take off, I stood in front of the vehicle as Greyhound bus drivers do.

"Fellows," I said, "I've had enough of Roswell's integration bullshit, and the next time we come back here it's Mrs. Collins's for me. Any of you who wish to stay elsewhere are perfectly welcome to go there in the bus after you drop me off at Mrs. Collins's house." That was the last night we were ever in Roswell that any person in the Preston Love Orchestra ever stayed at any hotel or motel besides the Collins guest house, and from then in 1956 until 1961 we spent many nights there.

In 1955, we were on our way to Roswell, and since we had a day off in-between gigs, we were traveling leisurely. On our way, we went through Albuquerque, New Mexico, and we decided to stop and look over the black neighborhood to see if there was a restaurant with good soul food there. As I was driving the bus along one of the streets looking for the black section, I could see an old Hudson in my rearview mirror. It seemed to be following us. When the driver of the Hudson began to flail his arms out of his window as if to flag us down, I pulled over to the side and stopped. The Hudson pulled over in front of us, and out stepped Buster Coates, grinning from ear to ear! We embraced joyously. I hadn't seen Buster in about twelve years, since he left Omaha in 1943. Miss Georgia had died in that year, and Buster left Omaha shortly after with some group and never returned. There were several musicians in the car with Buster, and they, too, got out and began to get acquainted with the men in my band. After several minutes of the usual jolly talk when two groups of musicians meet, Buster directed us to follow him and his friends to the apartment where all of them stayed. They were working at a club in Albuquerque and shared an apartment where they could cook or practice or whatever else they felt like doing. Most combos on locations in towns usually rented an apartment for the whole group because it was economical and convenient to be all together. The usual bottles were procured, and we proceeded to have an old-time musicians' get-together. A few of the cats had some joints of pot, and those who wanted to turned on in a separate room in the apartment.

Buster filled me in on his movements of the past twelve years, most of which had been spent between Albuquerque, El Paso, and Amarillo, Texas, playing in combos in and around these areas. He had been playing electric Fender bass for a few years since the electric bass had come into prominence with small combos. We partied until mid-evening, and one of Buster's friends went out and brought back some delicious Mexican food, which we devoured greedily. I then lay down on their rickety couch and took a short nap so I would be prepared to drive when we continued to Roswell, and at about eleven o'clock I awoke. The party was still going on around me, but it hadn't disturbed me because I was quite drowsy from drinking and eating. The men in Buster's combo kept expressing their regrets that we had come through on their night off, because they were anxious for us to hear Buster play the Fender bass with them. Around that area he had become the ninth wonder of the world to musicians with his bass playing. Finally, around midnight, we took our leave of Buster and the cats and took off for the remainder of the trip to Roswell.

Several months after this we ran into Buster again in Artesia, New Mexico. He and some of the men from the Albuquerque group were in Artesia on a location, and my band had come to play the Elks or one of the fraternal clubs. Luckily, we got off earlier from our gig than Buster's combo, so we were able to get to his gig in time to hear Buster play a few sets. The electric bass, which resembled a big guitar with amplifier, was relatively new then, and only certain rhythm and blues combos were using them. Even some of the bigger names in the rock and roll and rhythm and blues fields still used the big upright bass violins. Buster, being a fine guitar player, had already mastered the Fender bass, which was more like a bass guitar than anything else, and although it has become the nearly universal bass instrument, I have neaver heard anyone play it with more authority and feeling than Buster Coates. I have since done innumerable recording sessions with studio electric-bass players who were earning fifty thousand dollars or more a year, and most of them would sound like amateurs beside

Buster. Yet a man like Buster might be living in Los Angeles and conceivably earning only a few dollars per week if he wasn't in the studio clique.

After Artesia, I didn't run across Buster Coates again until the summer of 1957, at which time we were booked for a whole week at Amarillo Air Force Base at the NCO club there. On the day of our opening at the air base, we pulled up to the Carter Brothers' Motel in Amarillo to check in for the week, and while we were checking in, up waddled dear old fat Buster Coates. He had a permanent cottage at the motel because he was now living in Amarillo and playing with Frank Hines's combo at the Black Elks Club. Frank Hines was a good alto-sax player, and he and I became good friends during our stay in Amarillo. Buster made me welcome to stay with him in his cottage at no cost, and he also made Eli welcome after I explained that it would cause a financial hardship for Eli if he had to pay a whole week's rent for a single. Eli and I moved in with Buster, and during the week we had old-home week, talking about Omaha and the St. Cloud days. Buster's steady girlfriend came over daily and concocted delicious southern food for us, and every day was one big round of laughs. Buster was a most jovial and likable man. He now controlled his sleeping sickness with some medication that he had a steady prescription for. Best of all, we got to hear Buster play the electric bass nightly during the week because we were finished at the Elks Club every night nearly two hours before their combo finished. My fellows sat in and jammed with Hines's combo most nights, and Frank urged me nightly to bring my alto and join in, but at that time my only interest was in playing lead in the section. I still had no interest in jamming as an instrumentalist, and Frank Hines played well enough in the jamming department for me. Buster played so much bass every night that he had all of us cheering him like a contestant in an athletic match.

After that wonderful week passed, we returned to Nebraska, Iowa, Minnesota, and the Dakotas for several weeks of bookings. In September of that same year, 1957, I returned home from one of our short trips. It was early in the morning on a Monday because we had played the Sunday night fairly close to Omaha. When Betty came to the door to help me in with my baggage, she said, "Pres, there's something for you on the dresser in the bedroom."

I knew Betty liked to give me pleasant little surprises, but I detected that there was no happiness in her manner. I still strode unsuspectingly over to the dresser in the bedroom where Betty had laid out an envelope for me. I picked it up and saw that it was from Amarillo, Texas, and was addressed to Mr. and Mrs. Preston Love. The envelope was already open, and as I attempted to pluck the letter from inside a small card fell on the dresser. I picked up the card and read "OBSEQUIES—CLAUDE COATES." The little card chronicled the details of Buster's funeral. In the letter, Buster's girlfriend explained how Buster and Frank Hines were killed about two weeks previously while on their way to pick up a new piano player for their combo in Albuquerque. It was late at night, and a few miles outside of Amarillo Buster and Frank hit a truck at very high speed, killing both of them outright. I was devastated.

Betty then proceeded to fill me in on all of the other events that had occurred during my absence, She had seen Donnie Kelly, and he was getting his affairs settled. He told her how much he missed the band. Donnie had left us a few months earlier to settle some business affairs in Omaha that couldn't be attended to properly if he was gone constantly, and I replaced him with a trumpet player, Dave "Duffy" Goodlow, who joined us from Minneapolis, supposedly for a few weeks until Donnie had attended to his affairs. Duffy purchased a valve trombone before he left Minneapolis to join us, and soon he became the dominant figure in the history of my band. Duffy played excellent trumpet, valve trombone, and occasionally accompaniment on the piano. He was also one of the finest, well-trained, and natural music arrangers I've ever known. Dave Goodlow kept us well stocked with orchestrations on new pop releases and wrote delectable arrangements of jazz numbers and standards. He was a one in a million find for me.

Nineteen fifty-seven was an especially good year for my band's operation. The bookings were very good, and things progressed very well generally. Toward the end of summer, I ran across a 1948 Pony Cruiser bus in Lincoln, Nebraska, and purchased it forthwith. Orchestra leaders in the Midwest had always spoken glowingly about "Ponies." They were comfortable, very attractive, medium sized, and could be outfitted with Chevrolet, Ford, or International Harvester motors. Ours came with the International. Pony Cruisers had a name among bandleaders for durability and economy. My musicians felt very proud of the Pony because it was a much more glamorous rig to pull into town with and more plush than the school bus. Even more important, I could afford to operate it. I treated myself to the luxury of a bed, which was a mattress, pillows, and blankets spread on the wide backseat that stretched the width of the bus. By now, our gigs were nearly 50 percent military. We played top military clubs all through the South, Southwest, and Midwest. We even found ourselves playing bases as far away as Sumter, South Carolina, Savannah, Georgia, Columbus, Ohio, and Miami, Florida. In 1958, National Orchestra Service informed all of its band leaders that the agency would be sending all of us to play for military clubs outside of the continental United States. The trips would be for one to three weeks at each foreign stop, and we would have a full-fledged stage show with us. The band members and I were excited at the thought of going out of the states to perform. Royce Stoenner was designated as the overseas salesman at NOS, and my first overseas bookings were scheduled in Bermuda in August and October of 1958. We were routed so that we had a few bookings going east to New York, where we took the plane to Bermuda from what was then Idlewild Airport.

Eli Wolinsky was no longer with the band. He probably would have been if he hadn't moved back to New York before NOS announced that we would be going overseas. Eli loved New York, and in April 1958 he could no longer resist the magnetism that New York City had for him. The first person I called when we arrived in New York en route to Bermuda was Eli, and he came to meet us immediately where we had parked our bus in front of the Alvin Hotel, directly across the street from the famous Birdland. We had only about twelve hours to spend in New York before flight time, and it was the first time in New York for some of my people—and the first time there since 1947 for me. When Eli first moved back home to New York he had made friends with Earle Warren, who used Eli on his gigs whenever he was bandleader and needed another sax man. After a few phone calls, Eli located Earle, who joined us at the Alvin Hotel café. I hadn't seen Earle since 1951 when he was road manager with Johnny Otis. He, Eli, and I spent an enjoyable night of nostalgia together before the time came for our band to head for the airport at three in the morning.

Peg Leg Bates joined us as our feature act in Bermuda after NOS booked him through an eastern agent. All of my band members and I fell in love with the beauty of this little island. On our next trip to Bermuda in October, I saw Eli again in New York, and also my dear friends Buddy Tate and Jimmy Rushing. I hadn't seen Tate since 1948, and Jimmy Rushing since 1953, when he played an Omaha club for a week, but I had corresponded regularly with them both. They had been out of town working in Toronto when I was in New York two months earlier. The second time in Bermuda, as before, we played all of the clubs at Ramey AFB and a couple of civilian clubs booked by NOS. Our show on the second trip consisted of a ventriloquist, a magician couple, and our usual drum-solo number done by the band and our clever drummer, Kenny McDougald. Our next trip outside the states was to Harmon AFB in Newfoundland, over Thanksgiving of 1958. We flew to Harmon from Montreal, Canada, via Nova Scotia. None of us cared for Newfoundland because of the daily blizzard conditions and overwhelming racial prejudice dominant in the town of Stephenville near the air base. In January 1959 we flew to Alaska from Seattle for two weeks, and a month later we flew to Puerto Rico from New

York. After the Puerto Rico junket, we didn't arrive back in Omaha until March 10. We had been gone from Omaha nearly four weeks.

When we crossed the bridge into Omaha from Council Bluffs, Iowa, we drove two blocks south to Harney Street and up to Sixteenth Street, where National Orchestra Service was located on the sixteenth floor of Omaha's City National Bank Building. I knew there would be a pile of mail there for the band since we had been gone so long. I parked the bus in front of the bank building and instructed Kenny McDougald to run up and pick up our mail at the agency. I remained at the wheel of the bus since we were parked in a city bus-stop zone. Little Kenny bounced out of the bus jauntily and within five minutes he was back with a handful of mail and a wide-eyed expression on his face. As he handed me the pile of letters he exclaimed, "Preston, they said up there that your brother passed."

I literally tumbled from the driver's seat to the front bus seat as I groaned, "Which one? Which one?"

Kenny replied, "They didn't say which one."

It was apparent that it pained him to be the bearer of this bad news. In stunned silence we all stared into space, and then George Miles, our bass player (father of rock star Buddy Miles) hurtled his 240 pounds forward into the driver's seat. Of her nine children, my mother had lost one, my brother Billy in the military service in 1944. Now I couldn't even speculate which of my precious four remaining brothers had died and how or why. George Miles drove as though he had a police escort, and in half the normal time we pulled up to my house. George half carried me as I stumbled towards our door, and as I leaned on the door he rang the bell. Soon Betty opened the doors as I repeated over and over, "Which one?"

When she could regain her composure, she answered, "Oh, I see you've heard. Dude! He had a heart attack two days ago."

Dude's body arrived two days later from Los Angeles for burial. He died at fifty-one. Naturally, Johnny flew back to Omaha immediately to be with us.

CHAPTER SEVEN

My Years with Motown

✳

Gigs in the early months of 1959 were average for that time of year, but spring and summer did not bring the usual sharp rise in the volume of our business. There was also a noticeable drop in the number of the big fat dates that I had grown to expect periodically. The sharpest drop was in the number of dates available for us on midweek nights. We referred to these as the bread-and-butter gigs because they enabled the leaders to meet their weekly payrolls while realizing more profit from the higher-paying week-end gigs. Every now and then we would run across one of the other NOS bands, and in my conversation with the leader he would invariably refer to the drop-off in the volume of the bookings. None expressed any extreme fears, but each was feeling the bite of less revenue, as was I.

There was certainly no panic when we went to Panama in September 1959 for a two-week tour of military bases. Panama was an interesting place. We enjoyed it more than anywhere the band had been outside of the United States except Bermuda. After the two weeks in Panama, we picked up our bus at the Miami airport and headed for Cocoa Beach, Florida, where we played one night at an air base located there, then headed for the Midwest. The last gig before we returned to Omaha was a Sunday night in a small town east of Des Moines. After we played the last note that night, all of us packed the bus hurriedly to head for Omaha to see our families and friends, since we had been gone nearly a month. I usually did all of the night driving, or at least started out first on leaving a gig, but this night Joe Adams, the piano player, said "That's O.K. I'll take it tonight, Preston," and we were off for Omaha. I was pretty tired because we hadn't checked into rooms for two or three nights, with all of these long distances we had to travel leaving Miami, and I had done a big share of the driving. There was the usual chatter for a while after we headed out Highway 6 toward Des Moines and Omaha, but soon everybody was asleep. I was thankful for my little improvised bed in the back of the Pony Cruiser as I dropped off to sleep to the rhythm of the bus's movement. The next thing I remembered was a sickening thud. When I came to my senses, I was lying face down against the back of the reclining seat located directly in front of my backseat bed. My face was numb, and I had to rub my left eye before the vision became clear in it. For a moment I thought I was blinded in the eye. Finally, when I was able to stand up. I could see that the inside of the bus was a shambles, Joe Adams was still seated in the driver's seat, but it was pushed backward, and two women were standing beside him checking him and the rest of the fellows over with a flashlight. Several of the bus seats were torn loose from their moorings and turned over on their occupants, who were beginning to dig out from under the debris and the seats. Then Joe began to call out the names of the band members one by one. As each answered, I was relieved. By now I had stumbled to the front of the bus, and the woman holding the flashlight checked my facial injuries. As fate would have it, she was a registered nurse. She felt my nose and forehead and took a facial tissue from her purse and wiped away the blood. She said, "You have a broken nose, Mister, but the rest isn't too bad."

I then stepped out of the bus and went to the rear to check the scene. There was a new '59 Plymouth sedan completely demolished. Sitting in the driver's seat was a young white boy holding his shattered arm. Another young boy identified himself as the driver's friend. The second kid's car was parked nearby with its lights on to light up the scene. He pointed to his car and mumbled, "We were playing 'chicken,' and when you guys came around that curve in the highway, Bill here was sitting in the middle of the road with his lights off."

Soon red-lighted cars and two ambulances approached with their sirens screaming and took three of us off to the hospital in Newton, Iowa, which was eight miles east from the scene of the accident, barely one mile outside Colfax, Iowa, a tiny town. Our injuries were attended to, and they kept us overnight before releasing us. All of those in our band who were not hurt took the bus to Omaha from Newton the next morning. The three of us who were injured—Donnie Kelly, tenor sax player Harry Vann, and I— took the first bus we could. In Omaha, I made arrangements for the sale of the Pony Cruiser to a salvage company. They paid me one hundred dollars after taking their tow truck over to Newton and towing the bus back to Omaha. My insurance on the Pony had lapsed, so NOS contacted their lawyer, George Kanouff, who contacted the insurance company in Iowa that had a policy on the '59 Plymouth. After a few phone calls from Kanouff, the Iowa insurance company agreed to settle with us for about $4500. Kanouff assured me that he would happily go to court and sue for more if I wished, but I needed the money immediately to get a bus, because renting cars was too expensive. Barely a week after the accident, the other two injured musicians and I met at George Kanouff's office with the insurance adjuster. They received $250 for their injuries, and I received the rest for the wrecked Pony Cruiser and my injuries. Ten days later, I found another Pony Cruiser for sale in South Dakota and purchased it for a thousand dollars cash. It was two years older than our other one.

Fall was approaching and although we were optimistic, bookings were becoming very spotty. Several salesmen left the agency, and as each left, his area or territory was divided among other salesmen who handled their own area and whatever part of the other territory was assigned to them. One day I stopped by the agency to chat with Royce Stoenner. The secretary informed me, "Mr. Stoenner is no longer with us, Mr. Love." I was incredulous. She asked, "Would you like to see Mr. Orr or Mr. Williams?"

I answered, "I'll see Claude Orr."

Orr was a piano player and had been a salesman with National Orchestra Service for twenty-four years. His territory was the Dakotas and Minnesota. He also had a few accounts in northern Iowa and northern Nebraska, with operators who insisted on dealing with Claude because he had dealt with them so squarely for many years. All of the other salesmen had to take one of the company cars out and visit their territory at regular intervals, but Claude made only two swings a year to his most distant accounts. He could handle his territory the rest of the year by phone and letters from the office. Neither Claude nor Lee Williams, the vice president of National Orchestra Service, seemed willing to give me any information about Royce's sudden departure, and that was the last time there was any discussion of Royce Stoenner between anyone at NOS and me.

By the end of 1959, nearly all of the NOS bands were experiencing pains in their finances and we openly discussed it with concern when one of the other band leaders and I saw each other. With big sleeper buses and ten or twelve people on guaranteed salaries, it doesn't take long to feel the crunch if the bookings fall off even moderately. I had nearly licked my Internal Revenue debt and my debt for back commissions owed to Royce since 1951. My indebtedness to Royce was transferred to National Orchestra Service as part of his assets when Royce merged with NOS in 1954, and I paid a small monthly installment on this when I became one of the NOS bands. But with the shortage of bookings and the sudden dramatic decrease in revenue, I began to miss payments to both the agency and the IRS. With the arrival of the new year of 1960, things began to look rather bleak, as bleak as in the early days of my band's inception or during the Flex era of my band's history. Shortly after New Year's, I went up to the NOS office on some business or other, and Claude Orr asked me if I would see him in his office after I finished my other business. His words were, "I want to see you when you finish with everyone else. Now, be sure and don't leave without coming to my office."

With my other business completed, I strode around to Claude's office. He quickly closed his door and began to talk quietly, "Did you know they gave us notice today that NOS is folding on February 1?"

At first, I thought he might be joking. Claude continued barely above a whisper, "Just think, I've been here, twenty-five years, and I'm nearly sixty. I don't know what I'll do."

Excited, I whispered, "But, what about all the dates they've booked on the bands?"

Claude said, "They will be giving two weeks' notice to all of the bands soon. We are all busy now canceling all of the dates in the books." He then half-opened a desk drawer and let me see a stack of contracts. "All of these are to be canceled. They won't let us salesmen transfer the dates directly to the bandleaders, but I think I can salvage all of your dates and line up some new ones for the spring if you're interested. In fact, I know I can salvage all of the spring proms and some of your better accounts."

I nervously assured him, "Oh, yes, go to it right away. "

Claude was emphatic. "Now, Preston, I'll do what I can to keep us in business, but I'm going to need my commissions just as bad as you need money, so let's understand that now."

When I arrived home, Betty, too, could hardly believe the news I brought about NOS. My band members were equally incredulous and also disturbed by the news. Betty and I had two new little ones now. Portia was three years old, and Norman one and a half. Betty was newly pregnant with our fourth child. She was naturally much concerned about my news. In a few days, all of the NOS bands received written notice that National Orchestra Service would cease to operate in two weeks. Some of the leaders who had been associated with NOS a long time simply folded. The others made a mad scramble to get connected with agencies in places such as Denver, Houston, and Atlanta.

Claude Orr did pretty well for us that spring and summer, but I was forced to put the men back on nightly salaries for the first time in five years. Claude was able to keep most of the accounts he had handled for NOS in the Dakotas, Montana, and Minnesota, but he didn't seem to be able to book many military bases in the South and Southwest, which had been our lifeline for the biggest part of every year since 1955. From the fall of 1960 on, however, things turned for the worse. Claude still put an average of six dates a month in the book, but I was thrown into the situation of booking myself most of the time. Most of my own bookings were cheap dates or percentage jobs. During particular periods the bookings were horrendous. It became very difficult to hold personnel, and there was a constant turnover of musicians and singers in the band. At times, I would have to take any caliber players I could find in order to show up with the eight called for in our contract. On occasion, we had to leave Omaha with only seven. Sometimes our employer would complain or dock for the person missing, but sometimes no mention would be made of it. Nevertheless, our sound or our program always suffered when we were down a musician or singer. Eddie Eugene had been back with us off and on since 1957, and he and Donnie Kelly were trying to stick it out with us. But by late 1961, things seemed hopeless. By now, I had fallen far in debt to the musicians' union again for the 10 percent taxes, and my debt to the Internal Revenue Service was mounting again. Finally, we began to arrive at engagements only to find that the IRS had attached our fee. It was always on the one gig in the week with a good guarantee, and my people and I would be pointing toward this money to get a little bankroll in our pockets to pay off some other pressing debt.

Luckily, the "new" little Pony Cruiser gave us a minimum of trouble. It was a 1946 model, slightly smaller than the first one and outfitted with a regular Chevrolet car motor that was even more economical. Eventually, I did have to have a new motor installed and to make other minor repairs, but this is to be expected of any bus. Once the little Pony was repaired, it ran mile after mile without breaking down again. Now, without a big agency behind us, our jumps between jobs averaged nearly twice as long as they had when the agency booked us and routed our tours to keep the mileage as low as possible between engagements. Hughes Chevrolet across the river in Council Bluffs serviced the little Pony regularly when we were at home. I had a monthly charge at Hughes, and they didn't hesitate to put a new motor in for me on credit when the old motor was worn out, but I put the bus up as security for the four-hundred-dollars charge. Somehow I was able to hang on through the winter months until Easter of 1962, but around the time that bookings would pick up, Hughes attached the Pony Cruiser for the three hundred dollars I still owed them. I had been able to make only two payments since they installed the new motor in the fall of 1961. I was almost relieved to turn the bus over to Hughes, since they had been so lenient and patient.

Johnny Otis called me often. His fortunes had taken a turn for the worse after another run of success brought on by "Willie and the Hand Jive" in 1958 and 1959, but he continued to urge me to forget about Omaha and move out to Los Angeles and be his partner in several ventures in

Johnny Otis and Preston Love in Los Angeles, 1962.

which he was involved. He and Phyllis lived in a huge mansion they bought in 1957, and he assured me that there would be more than enough space for Betty and me and our three little ones, Portia who was five, Norman who was three and a half, and Ritchie who was one and a half. Johnny and all of my friends in music and show business chided me for my determination to live in Omaha, but now Johnny berated me persistently in our friendly manner.

"You dumb motherf——er, what on earth would make you want to stay back there in that little burg? You know I like Omaha, too, but, man, we have to come out to places like Los Angeles and New York where there is safety in numbers, where everything in our business is happening."

I thought, "Johnny to the rescue again," and relented. "All right, get it all ready. We will leave for Los Angeles three weeks from today on May 16."

Claude had booked three weeks of good high-school and college proms in the Dakotas and Nebraska through May 15. The only nonschool dates we played were one at the Bismarck, North Dakota, country club, and one at the country club in Sioux Falls, South Dakota, and they were good money dates. The three weeks gave us time to accumulate some money for the Los Angeles move and to dispose of furniture and other effects not important enough to ship. Claude devised a system to circumvent the IRS for these three weeks, in case they intended to confiscate our money. Each buyer mailed him the check for each engagement when they signed and returned the contracts, and Claude passed the money on to me after the engagement was fulfilled. Only once did the tax department attempt to pick up the fee for an engagement, and it was far enough in advance that the school was able to call the nearest Internal Revenue office and get the check released with the explanation that they would be stuck for a band if I didn't get the money in advance. For the next weeks, we used my car, and I paid Donnie Kelly twenty-five dollars per day and expenses to use his car. We pulled a small trailer with my 1955 Chrysler. For the last three weeks, I used a singer, Clyde "Jay" Walker, who had worked with us briefly before. Eddie Eugene had a chance to work at a club in Des Moines, and I gave him my blessing to go. Jay and I became fine friends. We fished daily when possible, and I sympathized with his valiant attempt to stay in music and still support his wife and four small children. Jay Walker was the first avid fishing partner I had since Phil Thomas left the band.

Our old Chrysler was getting pretty worn out, and when we tried to sell it the top offer was around one hundred dollars, so I promised Claude Orr to leave the car with Donnie Kelly and Jay Walker, who would try as best they could to fill any future dates he might book. The last time I saw the old car was when Jay Walker drove her down Spaulding Street from our house the morning of May 16 after we arrived back from the last gig I would make. We had owned the old girl since she was beautiful and practically new. As Betty set out to dispose of utensils and other effects and to arrange for our latest exodus, she remarked, "Well, here we go again."

When I entered our house the morning we disposed of the car, Betty had everything all boxed and ready for the cross-country trucking company that would be there later that day to load it for transport to Los Angeles. Her mother and her mother's twin sister, Nirissa, had worked several days with her, packing dishes, linens, and small furniture items in addition to helping with cleaning our little house in order to have it ready for the people who were leasing it from us. Our train reservations were made for late that night. We had a compartment for me and Betty and our three little ones. Our oldest son, Preston (Sandy) was almost twenty now and attending Northwestern University on a football and track scholarship. Sandy wouldn't be back in Omaha for some time because he was going to attend summer school. Betty was busily feeding Portia, Norman, and Ritchie when I entered the house. After my usual affectionate greeting from the kids I retired to the bedroom for a quick nap. I knew our last day in Omaha would be a busy day for all of us once I awoke. I had been asleep for a couple of hours when I received a long-distance call from Johnny in Los Angeles. As soon as I answered, Johnny shouted in the phone, "Guess what? Do you remember my telling you that my friend Bill Griffith was working on a television show for us? Well, he came through. You're still leaving there tonight, aren't you?"

I answered yes, and Johnny continued, "Well, the day after you get here we film our first show. At last I've got another television show . . . back on television again, and your ass is going to be playing that first alto in the big band with a feature spot every week. Blik [Avant], Bardu [Ali], and I will meet you at the depot, Wednesday morning. So get your butts on that train and come on."

I had never played a note on television before this. Late that night we loaded our excited little kiddies into our compartment at Omaha's Union Station and bade a tearful good-bye to Betty's mother, aunt Nirissa, Norm, Donnie, Jay Walker, and a host of other relatives and friends. May 16, 1962, signaled the end of the band business as I had know it for those many years and the end as well for me as an itinerant full-time orchestra leader.

The next nine and a half years in Los Angeles brought me the biggest successes of my career in the music business, but they would be mostly in the rhythm and blues field and the pop field. Except for a seven-month stint with the Ray Charles big jazz band on first alto and an occasional gig with part-time and rehearsal bands in Los Angeles, my jazz big-band career had ended. Big bands on studio and recording dates usually meant something entirely different from the bands of the big-band era. Some few big-name orchestraters such as Quincy Jones were recording with feature big bands, but all of the big studio orchestras I played with on recordings and television shows were nothing more than enlarged groups engaged to back up singers and other performers. These orchestras seldom were even accorded a feature spot on the shows, although they were usually made up of the nation's finer musicians. As a leader or instrumentalist I also backed most of the biggest names in the pop and rhythm and blues fields, often traveling for limited periods with them. This required capable musicianship but nothing more, as the big orchestra was seldom featured or regarded as more than a necessary complement to the star performance. These nine and a half years in Los Angeles made possible the complete liquidation of my indebtedness to the Internal Revenue Service for the first time in seventeen years. Upon our arrival in Los Angeles in May 1962, Johnny vouched for my payment of my debt to the musicians' union through the Los Angeles union local. When I liquidated the old surtax debt, this signaled the end of my problems with the musicians' union for the first time in many years.

The day that I became the lead alto-sax man in the Basie band, June 6, 1945, was definitely the high point of my musical career, but most of my successes in music have come long since then because of my six years as head of the West Coast Motown Band and my years as a contractor for many recording dates and shows in Los Angeles. I don't wish to give the impression that Preston Love was any great cog or force in the Motown chain, but as the leader of the West Coast Motown Backup Band from 1966 until 1972, I did perform a reasonably significant service that most of the personal managers and the Detroit office of Motown considered essential. My relationship with the Los Angeles office of Motown was excellent. In the early years of my tenure nearly all the shots were called from the Detroit office of the company. There were times in those nearly seven years that I received as many as eight or nine calls a day from either Ms. Johnson, Maurice King, or one of the personal managers at the head office on Woodward Avenue in Detroit. Occasionally, I even heard from Mr. Ralph Seltzer, the head of Motown's legal department. Mr. Seltzer developed a particular liking for me and for the way I attended to the business of supplying backup music for the Motown artists when they were on the West Coast, and he began to extend a warm friendliness toward me after a couple of years. Mr. Seltzer is a man of apparent high quality.

Ben Barrett Musical Service was the contractor for all Motown recording dates and television shows that were done on the West Coast. Barrett often used fifty pieces for their recording sessions and only rarely hired me as a woodwind player. As I recall, he used me on one album with the Four Tops in 1968, one album with Brenda Holloway on which we recorded her composition "You've Made Me So Very Happy," one album with singer Chris Clark, and as first woodwinds on the "Smokey Robinson Motown Television Special" in 1970.

The genesis of my relations with Motown occurred early in January 1966. I was at our rented house in Los Angeles preparing to take off for the Santa Anita Racetrack, which was my daily haunt (along with any other racetrack in the area that happened to be running at the time). I received a call from the Grant Music Center and its owner Henry Grant, who acted as an unofficial clearinghouse for helping less fortunate black musicians to gain employment in the Los Angeles area. Grant said, "Preston, can you rush right out to the Trip Club on Sunset Boulevard and just take your alto sax?" I didn't dream what this entailed, but I simply answered yes—avidly. Henry Grant replied, "Hurry. They are waiting for you." I grabbed my alto and ran out. Cranking up the old Love Dodge station wagon, I headed for the Trip Club, which was about twenty minutes away. When I arrived at the club, there were six or seven saxophone-player friends of mine sitting around the east wall of the club at the side of the bandstand. Cornelius Grant, the guitar player and conductor for the Temptations, was standing impatiently on stage awaiting my arrival, as were Bill Upchurch, their bass player, and their young drummer genius. Frankly, at the time I had never heard of the Temptations or of Motown.

I took my saxophone from the case hurriedly and joined the Temps' rhythm section and three horn players who had been awaiting my arrival. There was one tenor sax player, Melvin "Tank" Jernigan, and two trumpet players: Mac Johnson and former Jimmy Lunceford and Louis Jordan band member Bob Mitchell. Cornelius quickly signaled to Upchurch, and he began that very recognizable bass introduction to "My Girl." Grant pointed to my first alto part, which he had laid out on my music stand before I arrived. About two thirds of the way into the arrangement of "My Girl" there is a very beautiful repetitious figure for the lead alto sax. It is written in the key of A-concert or six sharps for the alto sax (the key of F-sharp), which seems to make the melody more strident and rich. Grant threw his head back in his droll manner and signaled for the band to stop. He turned to the other saxophone players sitting around the wall and said, "We have our man." Until then, I wasn't aware that all of them had already auditioned for the gig that I learned was to be for eleven days, backing the Temptations at the beautiful, popular Trip Club. After the rehearsal of the entire repertoire, Cornelius Grant and Bill Upchurch cornered me. Grant said, "Man, have you ever played this music before?" Of course, I said no, and they said, half to me and half to each other, "We have had this music, especially "My Girl," played by alto men all over the country, but nobody ever played it as quickly as you and with all that soulful phrasing." Bill said, "Wait 'til Melvin [Melvin Franklin, bass singer of the Temptations] and them hear this dude."

When I first came back to Los Angeles in 1962, I had played a one-nighter at the Long Beach Auditorium backing Marvin Gaye with the Johnny Otis band, but I was oblivious to his Motown connection and generally unaware and unexposed to the new "soul" music that was so popular at the time. Thus, the 1966 location at the Trip was actually the beginning of my Motown experience and awareness. Frankly, I was so steeped in the Ellington, Basie, Billie Holiday, Charlie Parker music era that I had never heard of the Temptations and knew very little about Motown. Consequently, I viewed the upcoming eleven days with little interest except for the badly needed (at the Love household) $220 we would receive for the gig. Their first-alto book was somewhat challenging, but I thought rather arrogantly of the whole thing as below the dignity of one

Preston Love and Aretha Franklin, Los Angeles Forum, 1968.

who had known the thrill of hearing and playing with the wonderful Count Basie of the previous era. But, oh, what a revelation! How could I ever have been so wrong, so off base? We did two shows each night and three shows on weekends to frenzied and very demonstrative fans. The fan reaction and the stupendous performances by the Temps were all so very infectious, and we musicians were also drawn into the spirit of this wonderful ambience. By the end of the first night, I was a Temptations addict. My saxophone book seemed to become a part of my actual fabric. From that night in January on, I was hooked on the Temptations and that great soul or rhythm and blues.

On the fourth day of the Trip engagement, I received a call to do a paid rehearsal for an album by someone named Frank Zappa. I was to play flute. At the rehearsal, trombonist Fred Murrell asked me if I received the call from Ray Charles about joining his band as first-alto player for their annual tour which would begin in three weeks. I said no, but Fred said, "Don't worry, you will," and I did. Of course, we know that Frank Zappa made that album, his first, and went on to become famous with his Mothers of Invention. Frank had been a boyhood idolizer of my friend Johnny Otis, so he knew all about the history of Johnny and me, and he acted very excited about meeting Preston Love, a rather obscure musician whom he never expected to meet in person. Two weeks after the Temptations location, I got a call from Carl Greenberg, owner of the Trip, to play lead alto with Motown's Martha and the Vandellas, who would play the club for eleven days, same as the Temps had done. Carl Greenberg was a prince, a lovable and friendly man who took a liking to me while I was doing the engagement there with the Temps. The timing was perfect. By now, I had been rehearsing with the Ray Charles Orchestra for several days, and we embarked on my first road trip with him the day after the Martha and the Vandellas gig ended. The $220 would be a blessing, since I could leave my family enough money to tide them over before my first week's payday with Ray. The Los Angeles musicians' union did give Carl Greenberg a bit of a hard time for not using a contractor to hire the musicians and not attending such matters as union assessments, pension-fund payments, and so on—a union rule. Martha and the Vandellas were also a most enjoyable act to play behind. They weren't quite as sensational as the Temps, but the crowds at the Trip were excellent and responsive, and Martha's repertoire (lead-alto book) was quite pleasing for the old Count Basie war-horse to play.

I left with Ray Charles on his airplane at the end of January, and it wasn't long before his management and I began to have financial differences. Playing the lead alto book with Ray Charles was nearly as rewarding musically as playing the Count Basie book some twenty years earlier had been, and there is no question that Ray Charles is one of the most magnificent artists that the music world has ever known. On some nights, he would literally bring us musicians to tears with his plaintive vocals and bluesy piano solos. However, it soon became obvious that there was no future for me with his organization financially. This in spite of the fact that we were able to supplement our weekly salaries with an occasional recording date, and we also did quite well monetarily with the Coca-Cola commercials we recorded with Ray in mid-1966.

I decided to call Carl Greenberg about possibly playing some dates at the Trip. One day when we were in Dayton, Ohio, I phoned Carl in Hollywood to tell him I wanted to stay in Los Angeles and that I hoped he might have something for me at the club. Before I had a chance to tell him the purpose of my call, he said with much concern, "Preston, aren't they treating you right out there?" I then told him of my desire to return home, and he assured me that whatever he had coming to the Trip would be mine as woodwind player or contractor. With this in mind, I checked out of the Ray Charles organization in early July.

Fortunately, just days after my return to Los Angeles, the Temptations were scheduled to appear at the 54 Ballroom, a famous dance hall in the middle of the Los Angeles black community at Fifty-fourth and Broadway. Bass player–singer Joe Swift was handling the backup band, and he called me to play the lead-alto chair. The three days at the 54 Ballroom were relatively lucrative, and we had a couple more horns than the four we were limited to at the Trip Club. After that engagement we were booked for three one-nighters in the San Francisco Bay area. The first night was in Monterey, and when we arrived there the next morning we learned that Mr. Sullivan, the venerated owner of the 54 Ballroom, had been found shot to death some time after our last show the night before. I don't think they ever learned who killed Mr. Sullivan.

After the July dates with the Temps, there was hardly any Motown action in Los Angeles until October when Stevie Wonder was booked for an eleven-day location at the Trip. Again, Carl Greenberg called me personally and told me that Joe Swift would be the bandleader of record, but I would automatically be the lead sax player. On opening night of the Stevie Wonder stand, many members of the Motown hierarchy came for the two shows. These included one of Berry Gordy's sisters, plus composers and producers who were now becoming famous. Stevie's musical director was saxophonist Billy Mitchell, a Detroit native, whom I had known quite well when he played briefly with Nat Towles in Omaha and later when he was with the Count Basie band of the 1950s. Stevie's eleven days were sensational, but apparently the Motown people were dissatisfied with the orchestra management and with the way Billy Mitchell and Joe Swift handled things during the engagement. Immediately after the show closed, I received a call from Motown's Director of Music Control, Maurice King. He was calling from his office in Detroit, and obviously Ms. Gordy or one of the other Motown officials had telephoned him early that morning and gave him a report on their dissatisfaction with the way things had gone with the orchestra at the Trip. I had known Maurice King since 1944 when I met him backstage at the Apollo Theater in Harlem when playing a week there with Lucky Millinder. Maurice was himself an alto-saxophone player, and he was then traveling with the International Sweethearts of Rhythm as their musical director and arranger. He had come backstage to tell me that he liked my lead alto, which he heard from his front-row seat during our show.

Maurice King's surprise call was the beginning of a most important chapter of my musical career. In his very gentlemanly mien, Maurice explained to me that he and Motown were considering setting up a band-leader-contractor on the West Coast to handle all of the backup music for

Motown artists when they played concerts and nightclub engagements in the West. He addressed me as "Mister Love," and explained that Motown had such a setup on the East Coast with saxophonist Teddy McRae as its head. Somehow, my name had come up, probably from Carl Greenberg, and hence, the call from Detroit. I assured Maurice that I would strictly take care of business, and a few days later, I received a very official-looking correspondence from Motown attorney Ralph Seltzer in which he outlined my responsibilities and empowered me to represent Motown in any way related to the backup horn sections for Motown artists when they appeared in the western part of the United States. The artists brought their own rhythm sections and conductors, but occasionally I had to contact a drummer or a bass player for them as well.

In December 1966, Motown instructed me to put together seven horns to back Marvin Gaye on a two day minitour that had Gaye sharing the billing with Otis Redding. Redding was independent of Motown and had his own sixteen-piece orchestra traveling with him. The tour was scheduled to begin at a venue in the San Francisco Bay area and culminate on Christmas Eve at the Sports Arena in Los Angeles. Neither Marvin nor Otis was a hot item at the moment, but each of them had recent hits, so good attendance at the two dates was anticipated. The engagement in the Bay Area did well, and I was tremendously impressed with the unique and very African-American style of Otis Redding. I had heard very little of his music previously, but from that point on I became an avid fan of his pure genius. He had a fine big orchestra that stressed pure Memphis "soul" along with a tinge of jazz inflection.

Being my mother's son, I was always a rather frugal and thrifty type. I noticed that Redding's big charter bus was half empty even with the seventeen or so people in his retinue. Motown paid airfares for my musicians and me, but I realized that I could save them my airfare by riding back to Los Angeles in the bus provided for Redding's musicians. It would also be more convenient for me when we got back to Los Angeles to have them drop me off at my home rather than having to get transportation back from the distant Los Angeles airport. Consequently, I approached Redding and asked if he would mind if I rode to Los Angeles in the bus with his troupe. He answered readily, "Yes, brother, and any of your men are also welcome to join my musicians in the bus if they wish." Otis himself was traveling back to Los Angeles by plane. My musicians all declined to ride on the bus and took the return flight back, but I boarded the chartered bus with the Redding musicians. They were most congenial and hospitable to me throughout the trip, and they dropped me off at our home at 2035 West Twenty-ninth Place in Los Angeles. At my house, I bade them farewell and expressed my eagerness to see and hear them that night at the Sports Arena.

When we arrived at the gig, it was obvious that there would be a small turnout for the concert, something to which all performers and promoters are sensitive. In the case of the performers, their egos suffer, but for the promoter it is a simple matter of economics. Marvin Gaye and our Motown orchestra were scheduled to appear on stage first, and we started at exactly the scheduled time to a small crowd of about fifteen hundred fans who made the large arena look very empty. Marvin did his usual inspiring ninety-minute show, and after a twenty-minute intermission Otis Redding's big orchestra assembled onstage and launched into one of the most heartwarming programs of expressive and rhythmic black music that I have ever heard. I stood in an area of the backstage corridor between the dressing rooms and the path to the stage reacting excitedly to the Redding orchestra when I noticed the three young promoters scurrying about with very worried expressions on their faces. Surely the package of Marvin Gaye and Otis Redding should have attracted at least five or six thousand paying customers, which was the number the promoters needed to make a profit. Near the end of the orchestra's time on stage, Otis Redding moved quietly into the little alcove close to where I was standing, and he watched his band pensively as they performed with animation and spirit despite the small crowd. After some minutes, the three promoters and one of Redding's managers rushed up to him, and as they conferred with the star and his manager continued to shake their heads from side to side. The promoters left for a few minutes and returned to speak with Redding, but the answer to their questions was still no. It seems that Redding's booking agency had received the usual 50 percent deposit when they signed the contract for the date. Redding and his road manager were to receive the remaining 50 percent in cash before Otis went onstage to perform. When the promoters were unable to remit the balance called for in the contract, Otis Redding refused to perform on the advice of his manager. The promoters had prevailed upon Redding to have his orchestra do the opening introduction to the show to give them time to try and raise the money in time for Redding to perform.

Finally, it became apparent that the promoters would not be able to pay the balance of the contract, and everyone in the alcove concerned themselves with who would be the one to have to announce to the fans that Otis Redding would not be going onstage. It was well known in the promotion business that sometimes the customers got violent and rioted in situations like this, so no one wanted to accept the responsibility of going out and announcing the cancellation. One of the men said, "Let's ask Mr. Love of

Motown over there to make the announcement." I agreed to do so and walked rapidly to the stage where Redding's musicians were preparing to leave. I announced succinctly that Otis Redding would not be performing due to circumstances beyond the control of the management. Surprisingly, there wasn't the slightest note of protest or violent reaction from the audience, which filed peaceably from the arena.

Despite this unusual occurrence, I learned to love Otis Redding's music and to admire his very friendly and calm demeanor. How sad I was just one year later in December 1967 when I heard the news of his tragic death and saw the very graphic picture of his frozen body strapped in his airplane seat as it was lifted by a crane from the lake where his plane crashed. As for my band's fee for the aborted Otis Redding–Marvin Gaye gig at the Sports Arena, I was contracted by the Motown office, so we weren't the least concerned about the inability of the promoters to pay Redding. We knew that in a few days I would receive a check from Motown and Marvin Gaye with the entire fee paid in full. Motown hadn't reached the level of power in 1966 that they would enjoy a few years later, but operators or promoters nonetheless didn't make a practice of "shorting" or defaulting on payments to the giant of the black music business.

Soon I was receiving several calls per day from Detroit or from the local Motown office in Hollywood as a proliferation of popular Motown groups began to come west for locations or one-nighters. In February 1967, Motown's local office called me and instructed me to meet with Elmer Valentine, owner of the Whiskey A Go Go in West Los Angeles. Smokey Robinson and the Miracles and Tammi Terrell were opening there for an eleven-day stand, and I was to work out the financial details and other particulars for the six horn players that would back Smokey. Virtually all of the locations in Los Angeles and Hollywood nightclubs were for eleven days so the artists could open on a Thursday and close on Sunday of the second week. This was adhered to by the Trip, the Whiskey A Go Go, Ciro's, PJ's, Dick Barnett's Guys and Dolls, and most of the other major venues. The Whiskey A Go Go gig with Smokey and Tammy Terrell went smoothly, and Motown engaged me to take the horn section to San Francisco for two weeks to back the same show. This marked the first time of many that I would take bands to various cities in the West to back the Motown artists. We found ourselves traveling to Seattle, Oakland, San Francisco, San Diego, Phoenix, Denver, Portland, and various other towns. Sometimes the locations would be for weeks and others for only one day. We traveled to Las Vegas so often with the groups that my band members referred to Vegas as home.

In March 1967, the Detroit office asked me to put together a big band

Form 1099—U.S. INFORMATION RETURN FOR CALENDAR YEAR 1968							Copy B For Payee
18—79808-1	(Please keep this copy—Do not attach to your income tax return)						
	INTEREST						7. Commissions, fees, prizes and awards, etc., to nonemployees, and foreign items. (No Form W-2 Items)
1. Gross dividends and other distributions on stock	2. Earnings from savings and loan associations, credit unions, etc.	3. Other interest. Do not include amounts reportable in column 2	4. Patronage dividends and certain other distributions by cooperatives	5. Rents and royalties	6. Annuities, pensions, and other fixed or determinable income		
							$2,750.00

Type or print taxpayer identifying number ———▶

Preston Love
2035 W. 29th Place
Los Angeles, Calif., 90018

Diana Ross & Mary Wilson
2457 Woodward Ave.
Detroit, Mich., 48201

TO WHOM PAID If the identifying number is not shown above or is incorrectly shown, please furnish the correct number for this account to the payer   (OVER)

BY WHOM PAID (Name, address (include ZIP code), and identifying number)
U.S. Treasury Department, Internal Revenue Service

IRS Form 1099: Record of payment of work for Diana Ross and the Supremes.

replete with a fifteen-piece string section to play on April 23 at the Hollywood Bowl for a show featuring Diana Ross and the Supremes, the Fifth Dimension, Johnny Rivers, and Brenda Holloway. This undertaking seemed a bit too large for me at the time, so I called their West Coast recording contractor, Ben Barrett, to actually contract and manage the band for the engagement. I also played first woodwinds this time, which in itself, was quite a chore. The Supremes had changed their name to Diana Ross and the Supremes only weeks earlier, thus precipitating the acrimonious departure of Florence Ballard. The Hollywood Bowl engagement would be one of Cindy Birdsong's first with the group as Ballard's replacement. The concert was a sellout, attracting over nineteen thousand fans. I met Gil Askey, the Supremes' conductor, for the first time, and we went on to become good friends. That April 23 night turned out very cold in Hollywood, and all the players found it nearly impossible to keep their horns in tune with the strings. When a trumpet player, trombone player, or reed player had some bars of rests, their instrument went nearly a half tone flat, so when they came back in after the bars out the instrument was in an entirely different key until it warmed up. It was especially bad for us woodwind players. Our flutes, clarinets, or piccolos would be in their stands for long periods while we played saxophones, and when we picked up the cold horns, they would be miserably out of tune, actually a full tone flat in some cases.

Nevertheless, the Hollywood Bowl gig established the reputation of the West Coast Motown Band as a force in the Los Angeles area, since the concert received rave reviews and was a huge financial success. I soon began to receive calls for engagements with non-Motown artists and for nightclub and social-club engagements with my "West Coast Motown

Orchestra." My groups were soon very busy at such venues as the International Hotel, the Palladium, the Century Plaza, the Shrine Auditorium, the Sports Arena, and at various schools and other types of venues. Elmer Valentine made me the house-band leader for the Whiskey A Go Go, while PJ's, Ciro's, and the Trip would contract me to provide the backup bands for all their black attractions. I was also called to be the contractor and first sax (woodwinds) player for countless recording sessions at Columbia, Victor, Capitol, Liberty, and various other recording labels. In addition, I contracted recording sessions for nonunion productions (called "scab dates"). As first woodwind player and contractor for the dates, my fees were usually quite large, plus I got the reputation for being very liberal in the fees I negotiated for the musicians. My regulars included Bob Mitchell, Melvin Moore, Cat Anderson, Marshall Hunt, and Joe Mitchell on trumpets; Don Cook, Fred Murrell, and "Streamline" Ewing on trombones; Bill Carter on baritone sax; Eddie Synigal, Tank Jernigan, and Wallace Brodis on tenor sax; and two fine alto sax and woodwind players, Joe Epps and Ed Pleasants. On occasion, I would use one or more of the top studio players that were referred to in Hollywood as "heavies," because they received most of the prime, "class" work in the studios. I used a large number of Los Angeles musicians because I sometimes had as many as three bands going at once with Motown and non-Motown artists in town doing concerts and nightclub dates simultaneously while using me as the leader/contractor. The Los Angeles musicians' union began to refer black promoters and agents to my Motown bands, so nearly every black touring pop artist used me as their leader/contractor when they appeared in the Los Angeles area. As our reputation spread, I also began to hear regularly from black artists and presenters all over the country when they needed musical accompaniment in Los Angeles or anywhere on the West Coast.

In January 1968, promoter Hal Zeigler called me to put together a group of fifteen strings and thirteen horns to back Aretha Franklin at the Fabulous Forum in Inglewood. This was the first musical presentation in the history of the new arena, and the first of many times I handled backup music for concerts there. We also went to San Francisco for two concerts with Ms. Franklin, and I was to have the horn or string section with her several times in the next few years when she appeared in Los Angeles.

Those who used my bands for accompaniment when appearing on the West Coast included Sam and Dave, Tyrone Davis, Isaac Hayes, Sonny and Cher, Curtis Mayfield and the Impressions, Jackie Wilson, Freda Payne, Redd Foxx, and, naturally, all Motown artists. On one occasion in about 1970 I contracted a series of recordings made for Bill Cosby's Cosil Productions that we did at the old Nashville West Studio on Santa Monica

Boulevard. Our horn section got some weeks of much-needed employment out of it, and Bill Cosby was a gracious and generous host. He came to the sessions most days and sat around, socializing with the musicians and his producer-arranger before sending out for lunch and refreshments for everyone at his expense. The sessions paid union scale, but Cosby was very liberal in paying what actually amounted to considerably more than just bare minimum union scales. Since Cosby has gone on to such greater heights and financial reward, I often wonder if he remembers those recordings we did for him. I remember it only vaguely, but I think it was his intention to *sing* on those tracks we made.

Beginning in about 1968, when Motown controlled or owned most of the biggest drawing names in black show business, I saw amazing feats of how essential power can be in the business world. Politicians and other officials protest loudly that their purpose is to serve, but I have observed that pure raw *power* is the purpose or motivation for most endeavors by human beings. I became even more convinced of this when I observed Motown as *the* power in the field of black music. Around 1969, Ms. Johnson of the Motown office called me from Detroit to tell me that my nine horns would be backing Gladys Knight and the Pips for two or three days at Disneyland and for me to make all arrangements for the rehearsal and for the other details of our stint at the popular and powerful amusement park. When I called the proper authorities at Disneyland, they politely informed me that they wouldn't be needing the services of the Preston Love Motown Band because they had their own house band led by one Jack Eskew. They were polite, but I detected a note of adamance in the persons I talked to. I called Ms. Johnson in Detroit and told her, "Disneyland said they won't be using the Motown Band for the Gladys Knight engagement." Ms. Johnson said, "Oh, yes they will. Just hang up, Mr. Love. I'll speak with Mr. King and get back to you." About twenty minutes later, Ms. Johnson called me back and announced, "Mr. Love, you and your band *will* rehearse with Gladys's conductor and rhythm section at Disneyland on the afternoon of the first night of the engagement. Have a good three days." Maurice King later told me that the powers at Disneyland weren't very happy about bringing our backup musicians in, paying us, and giving us name tags for all privileges on the grounds, but that the Motown juggernaut had spoken.

On another occasion, a new club in the black community in Los Angeles hired Motown's budding new singer, Brenda Holloway, for a four-day weekend. Big things were expected for Brenda in the company, so Shellie Berger, the head of the Los Angeles office of Motown, instructed me to put a nine-piece band behind Brenda and to back the rest of the lineup of

Preston Love and his string section, backing Aretha Franklin, 1968. Guitarist is Bobby Womack. (Photo © Earl Fowler)

the show. The club would pay our fee for the rehearsal and the four days, per their agreement with the Motown office. After the last show of the four-day stand, I went up to the office of the young club owner and requested the fee for my, most of whom waited outside his office to get their money. I was always very impatient to get the money and pay the fellows because they were tired and anxious to get home, plus some of them might need their money rather urgently. When I told the young club owner that I had come for my money, he asked me rather menacingly, "Why should I pay you all this money? We had poor crowds, and I am losing money on the show." After a few minutes of bickering, I asked to use his phone and called Shellie Berger at his home where he was in bed for the night. Shellie said, "Give the phone to the owner, Preston." I handed it over, and all I could see was his head bobbing up and down as he nervously said, "Yes. Mr. Berger, yes, Mr. Berger, I understand," as perspiration popped out in his forehead. He could hardly wait to hang up the phone and begin counting out my money, every penny of it. My nine musicians were happy to receive their pay when I came out onto the balcony, but some of them had observed the whole thing and were doubled over laughing at the smart upstart club owner who they said seemed to be ready to attack me with a letter opener that he had taken from his desk drawer at one point in our "discussion" about my money.

On at least two occasions, one in Tucson, Arizona, and the other in Bakersfield, California, the Four Tops arrived for a concert and shortly before show time decided that they would not sing because one of them was not feeling up to performing. They got back in their limousine or chartered bus and told me, "We'll see you tomorrow night at the next town." The promoters raved and ranted, but they still paid me the money readily if the contract for the engagement was written that way. The raving and ranting stopped with the road manager or with me because they would be fearful of complaining too vocally to the Motown office for fear of the possibility of a boycott of them by Motown. The company always compensated them for their outlay for such things as advertising and engaging the hall or arena, but the promoters did not raise any hell with Motown, the giant of the trade. With any other agency or management group, those promoters would probably have scorched them or threatened a lawsuit, but I don't think that any of them ever crossed swords with the powerful colossus from Detroit in those days.

By 1968, nearly all of the hit television variety shows, such as Glen Campbell, Flip Wilson, and the Smothers Brothers, were having one of the Motown groups or single artists as a guest on their weekly broadcasts. Usually they would fly Maurice King in from Detroit to write an arrangement or two for the Motown guests or to conduct the big network orchestra behind them. Maurice's aged mother and his sister Sadaisy lived in Los Angeles as well, so I saw him at regular intervals. He spent all of his leisure time with me and my wife as we played poker or tonk nightly after he had finished his duties at the television studio or at his hotel where he would have to closet himself for long hours while writing the orchestrations for the big studio orchestra. When Maurice was not in town, I often drove his mother to get her groceries or did other errands for her. When I was too busy, saxophonist friend Eddie Synigal took care of Mrs. King's immediate needs such as shopping and other chores. On several occasions, Maurice was flown out to conduct a big concert at the Forum or some other venue when I had the orchestra with one of the Motown groups or artists such as Marvin Gaye. He was also sent out to conduct Eddie Kendrick's first solo engagement at the Greek Theatre for several days in 1970. The contractor, Phil Candreva, hired me to play baritone sax and bass clarinet for the three or four nights, and Maurice and I "entertained" the house musicians at the Greek Theatre with some good poker games before the show each night.

Diana Ross was generally accepted as "the class of the field," although no Motown group or artist could outdraw the Temptations' crowds while

Backing Marvin Gaye at Ciro's in Hollywood, 1967.

I backed the Motown people, nor did any of the Motown artists have
more hit recordings than the Temps during my Motown years. Miss Ross
was never very cordial and never seemed that aware of us as musicians, but
she was a most enthralling and classy performer when onstage. I doubt if
the name Preston Love would mean anything to Diana Ross if someone
mentioned it to her; she probably isn't aware that such an individual ever
existed, although I handled the backup band for her and the Supremes on
numerous occasions from 1967 to 1971. I still have in my possession several
tax statements signed by Diana Ross and Mary Wilson for the sum paid me

and my band each year. We never had less than a full horn section of four trumpets, four trombones, and five saxophones when backing them, and of all the Motown groups the Supremes paid us the highest salaries. When we toured with them Motown chartered the finest Trailways Golden Eagle bus for us, and we rode in splendor en route to such towns as Spokane and Seattle. Over the years they had some fine road managers including Sy McArthur and Dick Scott, both of whom were quite friendly with my musicians and me. Their conductor, Gil Askey, was a former trumpet player and arranger for big bands such as Buddy Johnson's, so he was like a rabbit in the briar patch when we toured with the big horn section that evoked the sounds of Ellington and Basie to Gil. He would bring his trumpet along some nights and play a solo with the band before the stars came on stage.

There is no question that the Temptations in their original lineup were possibly the most dynamic vocal group in history. Their young fans, especially the females, became so frenzied that we feared for the bodily safety of all onstage. Their choreography and their song materials simply drove audiences into paroxysms of madness, and we never played to less than capacity crowds at whatever arena or venue we appeared with the Temptations. In 1969, we were booked with them at the Wintergarden Ballroom in San Francisco when the Temps were at the zenith of their popularity. When my musicians and I arrived at the entrance to the old building, we discovered that the promoters had continued to sell tickets after the room was filled beyond its official capacity. Young fans were screaming and pushing to get in to see the show. The pandemonium reached such a high pitch that several of them began to tear strips of wood off the old building in an attempt to get inside. My musicians and I feared for our safety as we found it very difficult to part the wild fans so that we could get in to play our concert. My relationship with the Temps and their managers was excellent. Paul Williams and I had an especially good relationship, as we were both big jokers and pranksters. My band backed them at the Fabulous Forum in 1969 on Dennis Edwards's first night with the group after the firing of David Ruffin some days earlier back east. Edwards was very nervous and some fans booed him for having replaced the very popular Ruffin, but Edwards soon became quite an important member of the Temps to many of their fans.

The Four Tops were the best of the pop and soul groups so far as group harmonizing was concerned. They were capable of singing complex and "serious" songs in four-part harmony à la singing groups like the Four Freshman, the Hi Los, and the better jazz vocal ensembles. Yet the Tops could also turn it on with those "soulful" types of songs long associated with black blues and ballad singers. Levi Stubbs undoubtedly would have been one of the famous solo singers had he decided to leave the Tops and perform as a single, but this is something he never did. The Four Tops were as much a brotherhood as a singing group. In October 1966, I was asked to put seven horns behind the Tops for the usual eleven days at NBA star Dick Barnett's Guys and Dolls Club in the black community in Los Angeles. This was my first time backing the Four Tops. They hadn't had a hit recording for a while, so our opening on Thursday had fairly good, but not sensational, attendance. On the Saturday after the opening, Maurice King called the Four Tops' road manager and instructed him to schedule a special (paid) rehearsal for my band on Monday. He was rushing out the music for a recent Four Tops recording so we could rehearse it and begin playing it immediately. The music he was sending was for the tune "Reach Out," which was skyrocketing to the top of the soul hit charts. We practiced the new arrangement thoroughly, and that night it was put into the show's lineup. "Reach Out" was received enthusiastically by the moderate-sized crowd. Its arranger and orchestrater, Wade Marcus, had written a most unique and innovative arrangement, and our musicians played the music with much élan. By the weekend, "Reach Out" had soared to the very top of the charts and both shows were packed to capacity each night. With screams and applause, the audience demanded that we play "Reach Out" more than once. This experience only convinced me all the more that in music we are the slaves of the hit recording. Without a hit, the musician or performer is nobody, regardless of how much talent or ability he or she might have. With the hit recording, you suddenly become a hero, or at least someone very worthy in the eyes of the public. Great artists should be judged only by their talents and ability, not their propensity for catching hit recordings or by their failure to get hits.

I first met Stevie Wonder in June 1966 when the Ray Charles troupe played a star-studded concert at Yankee Stadium in New York City. The bill included the Beach Boys, the Marvelettes, Stevie Wonder, and Ray Charles. Of course, on all such shows, Ray Charles insisted that he close the show and be regarded as the star attraction. Our people were given a section of the Yankees' locker room as our dressing and lounging facility. Right next to us was the area being used by Stevie Wonder, who had just become famous with the hit recording "Uptight" and some other successful recordings on Motown Records. The young singer was doodling on his harmonica or constantly humming, and several of our musicians made friends with him. I showed an interest in Stevie, and he seemed to take a liking to me. He was fascinated by being on the same show with the great Ray Charles, who had been an idol of his. Ray Charles was given another, more private section of the locker room, so young Stevie was a bit disappointed that he couldn't meet with Ray. After a while, Stevie asked me if I would go to Ray Charles and ask him if he would let Stevie do a number with him at some time in our performance. Happily, I went to Ray's dressing room to relay Stevie's request. Ray's manager, Joe Adams, made it very difficult for members of the band to meet with Ray. In fact, you could get in to visit the U.S. mint easier than you could meet with Ray Charles unless you had some pressing business. I had known Joe Adams since 1945, when he was the first black disc jockey on a major radio station in Los Angeles, but he listened to my request rather impatiently and relayed it to Charles. Adams returned and curtly told me, "Negative." Young Stevie was quite disappointed.

When I became the bandleader for Motown on the West Coast later in that same year, I could hardly wait to remind Stevie Wonder of the Yankee Stadium incident. I finally had my chance in the spring of 1967 when I had my first opportunity to back Stevie with a horn section for a series of dates in the Los Angeles area. I hadn't spoke much to Stevie during an October date at the Trip when Joe Swift was the bandleader and I was a sideman, but as leader I now had more access to the artists. On several occasions, I barbecued at my home for Stevie, his conductor Gene Kee, and others in his entourage. They came to our rented home in mid–Los Angeles, and we had quite a convivial time. It seems that the stars were seldom entertained in the homes of ordinary people when they were in a city performing, so Stevie and his people had a wonderful time with my family. My younger children, Ritchie, Norman, and Portia, and the neighborhood kids were very excited about being in the presence of the great young singer, and Stevie responded with total congeniality.

Stevie Wonder could probably have been a great jazz artist if he had so chosen. On every show we did with him he played the song "Alfie" on his harmonica. Conductor Gene Kee took the tempo so slowly that we could hardly follow the cadence. There was a most beautiful lead-alto part in the reed section, and with Stevie's unique and incredibly beautiful harmonica ideas I sometimes found it difficult to restrain myself when the combination of Stevie's harmonica genius and the saxophone background struck a responsive chord in me.

Stevie was always rather hyper. He was a bundle of energy and movement. This caused quite a scare when we were doing an eleven-day stand at Marty's on the Hill in Los Angeles in 1968. Marty's on the Hill was located in front of an adjoining motel that was about one hundred feet behind the back door of the nightclub. Stevie, his guide, and Gene Kee entered the back door from a room in the motel that they used as a dressing room for

Stevie. The back door opened right onto the stage. It was all nice and convenient because we would be onstage "cooking" with Stevie's overture "Uptight" when Gene Kee led Stevie to the microphone, and the show got to rolling. One night we were onstage "smokin'" with "Uptight" while awaiting Stevie's introduction and arrival through the back door. But there was no Stevie. I finally got up from my chair in the reed section and went through the back door to see what was detaining him. Between the motel and the back of the club there was a large swimming pool for the guests. There was Stevie standing by the pool, soaking wet, with his guide and Gene Kee hovering over him frantically. With his erratic and hyper movements, Stevie had fallen into the pool en route to the back door of Marty's in a split second when the guide wasn't watching him closely. It was all a big lark to the laughing and jovial Stevie Wonder, but it was no joke to Gene and the guide. If Motown had heard about Stevie falling into the pool, his wet tuxedo, and the carelessness of his helpers, I'm sure there would have been some summary dismissals or reprimands. Gene and the guide hurriedly returned Stevie to the motel and re-dressed him while our band played a couple of the popular rhythm and blues tunes, so no harm was done.

Gladys Knight and the Pips was a most enjoyable act to accompany. They always seemed to be enjoying their work and they seemed more inspired and animated with each show. There is hardly any room for controversy that Gladys is one of the greatest female singers of her era. Her vocal ability transcends that of just a "soul" or pop singer. She was also the most sincere, warm, and congenial of the Motown people that I backed. When Maurice King was in Los Angeles at the same time as Gladys, the three of us played poker for long hours, either at their hotel (usually the Century Plaza) or at my house. When they came to our house, I prepared some tasty snacks and we had lots of laughs. At the Century Plaza, Gladys sent down to room service and treated us. On several occasions when I took my wife Betty and my three younger children along with me, Gladys treated us all to expensive desserts and snacks ordered from room service. On the other hand, Gladys didn't have any mercy on Maurice King or anyone else when it came to raising a pot or turning out the winning hand in poker.

In my personal and subjective appraisal, Marvin Gaye was the finest male singer of the so-called soul era of the music business. Marvin could have been the most versatile all-around singer of his times, since he was equally adept at singing any style, from blues and jazz to the most commercial youthful pop tunes. His warmth and gift of feeling touched the hearts of people of all ages or musical tastes. His ballads "Born Free" and "You've Changed" reminded me of such wonderful singers from the past as Dan Grissom and Pha Terrell. When we did a two-week engagement with him at Ciro's in 1967, Marvin had Maurice King come out from Detroit to conduct the big band, and in those shows Marvin sang the widest range of musical idioms and styles that I have ever heard sung by any singer, and he did them all equally perfectly. Of course, Maurice King was the ideal conductor for the rather classical-style arrangements that Marvin sang on songs such as "People" and "Born Free." That band at Ciro's, incidentally, was one of the finest I had ever organized for any artist, since things were very slow at the time for black musicians in Los Angeles. I had my pick of the finer musicians at my disposal, such as drummer Paul Humphrey, who later became so busy in the studios that one had to call ahead three or four months in advance to hire him for a recording session, television show, or live engagement. Marvin was a bit of a musician himself, so he deferred to good players and gave them more respect than many of the other vocal stars did. He actually seemed flattered to have the former Ellington, Basie, and other big-band alumni playing behind him when I hired them and he recognized their names.

On April 2, 1969, we were to begin a short tour with Marvin beginning at San Diego State University. Motown arranged for transportation to take my horn section the one hundred miles to San Diego early enough for afternoon rehearsal. Marvin flew down from Los Angeles on an evening flight, and when he arrived my fellows and I were in the locker room of the university arena preparing for the concert. Even before he greeted us as he usually did, Marvin began to pace up and down the room with his head down and a concerned expression on his face. I asked solicitously, "What's the matter, Marvin?"

He moaned, "Oh, just think, I'm *thirty* years old today." The fellows burst out in laughter, but Marvin was dead serious.

I told him, "If you think thirty is all that bad, try for the forty-five that I will be in twenty-four days." The tragic nature of Marvin's death still pains me when I think of the waste of that great talent and genius.

Like Marvin Gaye and the Temptations, Smokey Robinson was a big matinee idol with the young females. His high and fragile voice along with the message of his songs simply drove them into hysteria. There were several times that the curtain was rung down on the show and the concert aborted because security couldn't stem the hysteria of the fans and consequently feared for the safety of the audience and the artists. Bobby, Pete, and Ron—the Miracles—were adequate window dressing for Smokey and complemented his singing some with their dancing pirouettes and singing backgrounds, but the whole show actually centered around William "Smokey" Robinson. I always approached Smokey with a

Backing Smokey Robinson and the Miracles at the Whiskey A Go Go, Los Angeles, 1967.

certain attitude of awe whenever I had to discuss business or something with him. Ron represented the group in most of the business aspect of the troupe, but occasionally I would have to go to Smokey's dressing room to discuss something. Smokey was totally immersed in the musical aspect of the appearances, so I avoided bothering him with other matters as much as possible. Realizing what a giant he was among composers and how big a part he played within Motown, I always felt rather uncomfortable in his presence for fear that something might endanger my situation with the company. I also detected that Smokey took measures to put me at ease when I approached him awkwardly and reluctantly. He was a very quiet and apparently gentle man, and I never saw any egotism in him, in spite of his stature in the music business and in the world of Motown. We did various one-nighters and club dates in West Coast cities and other trips with Smokey and the Miracles, but I never saw Smokey doing the womanizing thing like most of the other male stars that we backed.

Martha Reeves probably received less recognition than she deserved as a singer-performer because of the presence at Motown of Diana Ross and Gladys Knight. Martha's chances for greater stardom and wealth were also, no doubt, lessened by the presence of Motown's great male singers, Marvin Gaye, Smokey Robinson, and Stevie Wonder: a fact that I'm sure

Martha was quite aware of and frustrated by. The Vandellas were much like the Miracles were with Smokey: an adequate complement but totally overshadowed by the star lead singer. Martha's show was actually all Martha Reeves in the final analysis. She was a whirlwind of a stage performer, and her recordings did quite well, but she never overcame the disadvantage of being at the same agency and recording label as so many other star singers. Martha and I enjoyed a certain degree of friendship since I sympathized with her situation at Motown and often cut the price of my musicians whenever the cost of the backup band was charged to her budget—something she expressed great appreciation for when I took seven horns to San Francisco to play two weeks at the Jazz A Go Go and found that our fee consumed most of her profit from the location. Naturally, I reduced the band's fee drastically out of concern for her unenviable situation. It is gratifying for me to see that Martha Reeves has had something of a renaissance in the past few years and is finally receiving some degree of recognition for her important contribution to Motown. Ironically and fatefully, just as I completed writing the previous sentence, a local radio station began to play Martha's "Dancing in the Street" on the office radio where I am writing this. "Dancing in the Street" was a piece of music that we played at every show when backing Martha and the Vandellas.

In August 1971, my family and I decided to move back to Omaha. Many of my friends and associates considered this a very foolish move on my part, but we were determined to return home, since we always considered Omaha to be our roots. On August 28, we arrived back in Omaha after two and a half days of driving from Los Angeles. We had considerable savings and our debts were all cleared, so we felt secure in making the move. Unfortunately, Omaha was no longer the town we had known all our lives. It had changed, especially so far as the music business was concerned, and all for the worse. Except for the tours of Europe I have made over the years and the school residencies I have performed in Iowa and Nebraska, my involvement in the world of music hasn't been very rewarding since our return. Even teaching courses ("Black Music in Social Perspective," "The History of Jazz") at Omaha's University of Nebraska campus for seventeen years was a disappointment, since only a small number of students in this day are interested in jazz and its factual history. Nor is there much interest in black music among the students, except for the music by the very latest stars. One can hardly blame today's youth for this because their tastes and views on music have been manipulated by those who control the music business. This is true of the whole country, but in larger cities there ought to be enough students to have a sizable minority that is sincerely interested in our music's history.

Backing Tammi Terrell at the Whiskey A Go Go, Los Angeles, 1967.

I last saw the Temptations in person when I played first woodwinds at a concert they played at our Omaha Orpheum Theatre in 1985. They were touring in a package with the Four Tops, with Gil Askey as their conductor. The Temps, the Tops, and Askey seemed very happy to see me, and they treated me like visiting royalty or the returned long-lost prodigal son, Melvin and Otis from the Temptations expressed incredulity that I moved back to Omaha from Los Angeles. They told me that the local promoter-contractor had called Gil in L.A. to ask him, "How unhappy would you be if I didn't hire Preston Love to play the first-alto chair for the Orpheum concert?" They indicated that they thought this Omaha promoter must have been out of his mind to imagine that there could be a first-alto sax player comparable to Preston Love in Omaha, especially one who could play the Motown style of lead alto sax. Gil Askey indicated that he detected local politics and petty local jealousies in this conversation. My last time backing the Four Tops was in about 1986 when they played two shows at a beautiful new club in Omaha named Cleopatra's. I was engaged to put seven horns behind the Tops, who were simply wonderful as usual. It was a grand evening for me, as Levi, Obie, Lawrence, and Duke constantly lauded me before my hometown people and called me from my seat in the sax section to play solos and take bows. I had dinner with Levi and the rest of their entourage in the club's lower dining room as we chatted about the good old days in Los Angeles and on the West Coast.

About the same time, Gladys Knight and the Pips were booked at the Auditorium in Omaha and for the next night one hundred and forty miles away in Des Moines, Iowa. I received a call asking me to play lead sax for both concerts from the very individual who had called Gil Askey about the possibility of using another sax man for the Temps' appearance in Omaha. Of course, typical of local music politics and practices, I was the *only* black in the horn section. The young conductor who accompanied Gladys Knight had heard a lot about Preston Love from Motown people in Los Angeles, so he seemed quite surprised at my presence in Omaha when I introduced myself to him. At the afternoon rehearsal he treated me with such deference that I was embarrassed for the others in the five-man reed section. It was fun playing Gladys's repertoire again after so many years, doing the old things I had played with her earlier and the newer things that had been hit recordings for her in the intervening years.

Shortly after the rehearsal, I went down to Gladys's dressing room in the auditorium's backstage. I rapped on the door, and her maid answered. I told her that my name was Preston Love and that I would like to speak with Miss Knight. The maid disappeared, and seconds later Gladys swept to the door and greeted me with hugs and warm greetings. The Pips were nearby in their adjoining room, and they too rocketed over to greet me. Each one nearly stumbled over the other's question, "What are you doing here in Omaha?" I explained that I had moved back in 1971, and that I would be playing first woodwinds on the show that night and in Des Moines the next night. My career and my self-confidence were at a rather low ebb at this time, so their warmth and congeniality buoyed my spirits immeasurably. I assured Gladys that Betty would be down to see her when she came to the concert later, and when Betty arrived the warm reunion scene was repeated. Gladys had seen our daughter Portia in the Los Angeles airport some weeks earlier and kept saying, "Oh Betty, Portia sure resembles you now. When she was a girl, I thought she only favored Preston." Gladys and her entourage took a different means of transportation to Des Moines than our horn section did, but backstage at the Veterans' Auditorium there, Gladys and the Pips and I had a few moments to reminisce before and after the concert. They are quality people and so unlike some of the stars of show business.

During my days as the West Coast bandleader, neither the Marvelettes or the Spinners came to the West Coast to tour. However, in the late 1970s, the Spinners came to Omaha on a bill with Chaka Khan and Rufus and some other opening acts. The Detroit office engaged me to put together thirteen horns to back the show, so I contracted twelve of Omaha's best musicians while playing lead myself in the reed section. Maurice King came to conduct for the Spinners, and we had two wonderful days together. I cooked one of my better soul-food dinners for my old friend, and Betty convened an all-night poker game with her friends. Maurice was the center of attention and enjoyed our reunion. His death in 1992 left me with a deep sadness.

In referring to America's contribution to the world of music, I often say such things as, "There will never be another Duke Ellington." I stretch this to include various others such as Count Basie, Charlie Parker, and Earle Warren. I must also add, "There will never be another Motown—that is, the Motown of the 1960s through the early 1980s. The recordings of Motown artists during those years are probably the last important pure and unspoiled or undiluted black music that will occur in the history of this country. Earlier in this century there were various eras and categories of African-American musical art such as jazz, blues, and rhythm and blues, but in the 1980s black music became more and more bastardized and commercial and less and less artistic and representative of true African-American culture. Motown embodied all that black music had been in the previous eras, while still presenting it in a more modern and diverse package.

One has only to listen to the musical backgrounds of the Motown hits of the era I spoke of and to the rhythms of the Detroit Motown rhythm section with Benny Benjamin or "Pistol" Allen on drums and James Jamerson on bass. These sounds, along with the unique horn figures, were within themselves enough reason to buy nearly all or any of the Motown releases. One might review or trace the recordings of such Motown stars as Marvin Gaye, the Four Tops, the Temptations, Smokey Robinson, the Supremes, Gladys Knight, Martha and the Vandellas, the Marvelettes, Stevie Wonder, the Jacksons, and Mary Wells for the inspiring and fitting musical accompaniment of the Motown rhythm section and horn-string sections. Even the most commercial of those Motown recordings retained a high degree of traditional and characteristic African-American feeling and expression. To a large degree, this has disappeared from the black music of the 1980s and 1990s. In fact, much of today's funk and jazz are an insult to the term "black music" and to the memory of our great and creative black musicians and singers of previous history. Today's black hit recordings are often without warmth, depth of expression, or at all related to the roots of black American history. They are often performed by individuals without any great gift for blues, jazz, or any of the musical styles that black artists originated in previous years. The only motivation of current music is to get hits and make stars of sometimes most undeserving "artists," and this is usually done by marketing and hype, which amount to a form of brainwashing of uninformed and misguided young buyers of today's music. There is hardly any vestige of real African-American musical art or tradition in most of today's popular black music. There will never be another Motown.

CHAPTER EIGHT

Basie Revisited

✳

Early in 1983, Buddy Tate began to correspond with me about a proposed tour of Europe for a group of the original and early members of the Basie orchestra. The tour was tentatively planned for later that year. Tate and Sweets Edison were working on the plans with Jean-Pierre Vignola of Feelings Music in Paris. Buddy and Sweets felt that there were enough of the earlier Basie alumni remaining to capture the essence of the original Basie "thing." By the summer of 1983, a three-week tour had been "blue-printed" for late October and early November of that year. The side-men would be a mixture of very early players and musicians who had worked with Basie quite recently. There had already been various Basie alumni bands that had toured Europe in recent years, but some people felt that these weren't representative of the purist Basie sound and tradition. Our saxes would be Earle Warren, C. Q. Price, Paul Quinichette, Buddy Tate, and myself. Earle and I were to play altos, Tate and Quinichette tenors, and C. Q. would play baritone. Scheduled on trombones were Dicky Wells, Al Grey, Eddie Durham, and Curtis Fuller. The trumpets would be Ed Lewis—the original lead trumpet player for the early Basie band of the thirties—Harry "Sweets" Edison, Joe Newman, and Snooky Young. Nat Pierce was to play piano, with Gus Johnson on drums, Freddie Green on guitar, and Ed Jones on bass.

Most of us were very excited and enthused about the upcoming tour, especially all of us in the reed section. Not all of us had worked together with Basie, but each of us had worked with the other at some time in various other bands, and we had had a great rapport. Furthermore, some of the individuals such as C. Q. Price and Ed Lewis had never been to Europe before, so it would be a novel experience for them. With this personnel, it certainly promised to be a magnificent representation of the true Count Basie style and an overall fine band. I was already booked for two weeks at

Preston Love and Count Basie, Paxton Hotel Lobby, 1975.

the end of the big-band tour as the featured attraction at the Meridien Hotel Jazz Club in Paris, so I would be in Europe for a total of five weeks. This would be my fourth tour of Europe. I did three weeks with the Eddie "Cleanhead" Vinson troupe earlier in the year, and we had played one night at the Meridien Hotel Jazz Club.

It seems fate plays strange tricks at times. Only a few months before the Basie tour was to begin, both C. Q. Price and Paul Quinichette died quite suddenly. They were replaced by Heywood Henry and Skippy Williams respectively. Heywood was renowned for his great years as baritone sax and clarinet player with the Erskine Hawkins Band of the thirties and forties. He never worked with any of the Count Basie orchestras, but Heywood was completely familiar with what the Count Basie "thing" was all about. Skippy Williams worked quite briefly with the Basie band in early 1939 when Herschel Evans died suddenly. Skippy was the interim replacement until Buddy Tate joined the band. Shortly before the tour was to start, Snooky Young canceled for business reasons. This was a big loss to the band because lead-trumpet players of his caliber are quite rare. Plus, Ed Lewis hadn't played his horn for many years, and he was now reaching an advanced age. Snooky was replaced by Al Aarons, who had played with Basie bands during the fifties and sixties. The tour's trumpet section would be made up of three fine soloists and Ed Lewis, and each player agreed to pitch in and play as much first trumpet as their lip stamina would permit. Buck Clayton would lead the band but not play his horn. Aside from leading the band, Buck was to bring arrangements that he had done of various older classic Count Basie recordings such as "It's Sand, Man," "Blue and Sentimental," "Down for Double," "Doggin' Around," "Tickle Toe," "Jive at Five," "One O'Clock Jump," "Jumpin' at the Woodside," and "920 Special."

Although Buck didn't play, his presence brought together the original trumpet section of the early Basie successes beginning in late 1937. Buck, Harry Edison, and Ed Lewis comprised the Basie trumpet section when I first saw them in 1938 at Omaha's Dreamland Ballroom. As I write this, I can look across the street from my desk at the *Omaha Star* and see the site of the Dreamland Ballroom in the Jewell Building. The old structure was renovated in 1985 and opened as an office building. My small combo played for its grand-opening ceremonies in September of that year. Unfortunately, during its renovation, nothing was left to indicate that there was ever a ballroom in the building. Yet I had seen most of the greats of black music on the ballroom's stage in the thirties, forties, fifties, and sixties.

Trombonists Al Grey and Dicky Wells were also forced to cancel the European tour on short notice. Grey had other commitments, and Dicky's health forced him to cancel. Grey was replaced by Mel Wanzo, who had played with the Basie band of the fifties and sixties. Gus Johnson also canceled, and he was replaced by Frankie Capp. Capp and Nat Pierce jointly owned a band in Los Angeles called the Juggernauts, so Pierce recommended Capp when Johnson bowed out. Johnson had been the drummer with the original Jay McShann Orchestra of the forties. He then played with Basie for some years in the 1950s. As a drummer, Johnson was the essence of the Kansas City–style swing; he would have been the ideal drummer for the tour. Freddie Green took three weeks off from the then-current Basie orchestra to be with us. He is essential and indispensable to any band aiming to play the "real" Count Basie style. Freddie Green's guitar has always been the quintessential embodiment and sound of what we refer to as the Count Basie style. Even in cases where Basie had drummers and bass players who didn't fit his style all that well, Freddie Green still gave them some semblance of the traditional Count Basie rhythm-section sound. Of course, the rhythm-section of Walter Page, Jo Jones, Green, and Basie was without equal in the annals of swing or jazz. That rhythm section was largely responsible for all of the successes that Count Basie had. Some later bass players and drummers with Basie were reluctant to admit this, but I think it is axiomatic.

On the afternoon of October 22, 1983, I enplaned from Omaha's Eppley Airfield for Chicago, where I took a later plane directly to Paris, and then to Brussels. In Brussels, Jean-Pierre Vignola met me, and we exchanged warm greetings. Jean-Pierre had also been the producer of the tour I had made six months earlier with the Cleanhead Vinson group. He took me upstairs in the Brussels airport, and there were most of the fellows who would be with the Countsmen, the name that was selected for the Count Basie reunion group. I hadn't seen Buddy Tate, my most precious friend, in about three years, not since he had visited with me at Kennedy Airport in New York while I was en route to Sweden in 1980, but he and I had corresponded regularly by letter and talked on the telephone frequently. Sweets Edison and I had been together earlier that year. I was with the Cleanhead Vinson group, and Sweets's group with Benny Carter had shared several dates with the Cleanhead group in France. Joe Newman and I are absolute contemporaries, with our birth dates only a few weeks apart. Joe and I were very good friends as youths when we worked with Basie in 1943 and then intermittently from 1945 to 1947 when I rejoined Basie to replace Earle Warren. I hadn't seen Joe Newman since 1959 when my eight-piece band spent the night in Wichita, Kansas, at a hotel just around the corner from the one where the Basie band was staying. Naturally, ours was a warm and emotional reunion. I never knew Eddie Durham personally, but I had seen him in Omaha at the Dreamland Ballroom with Don Redman's band in 1936 and with Basie in 1938 and 1939. This great individual and I struck it off well from the first moment of our introduction to each other, and we became good friends on the tour. How strange it was to see the man now at nearly eighty years old after having first seen him when he was a handsome young man in his early thirties!

Freddie Green had come to Omaha quite often since my return there in 1971, so it probably had been only a few months or weeks since I had seen him, but being with Freddie again was a pleasure because we have always had a fine rapport. Buddy Tate introduced me to Mel Wanzo, Al Aarons, Skippy Williams, Heywood Henry, Nat Pierce, Ed Jones, Frankie Capp, and Curtis Fuller. I had seen all of these people at one time or other except for Frankie Capp, either with Basie or some other band, but I didn't know any of them very well except Mel Wanzo. Mel had become friends with my youngest son, Ritchie, when Mel was in Omaha with Basie during the seventies. Mel encouraged Ritchie to become a professional musician.

Preston Love during tour with the Countsmen, 1983.

I knew that Ed Lewis was to be on the tour, so I asked Buddy where he was. Just at that moment, a black man and woman approached the gathering of us musicians, and Buddy said, "There's Rags." Rags was Ed's cognomen in the Basie band. I hadn't seen Ed Lewis since January 1948, shortly after I left the Basie band in Los Angeles. It was now some thirty five and a half years since we had seen each other, and some forty-five years since the first time I saw him on the stage of the Dreamland Ballroom on a summer night in 1938. Ed, of course, would have been a man of about twenty-eight then, and I was a kid of seventeen. Ed was with his second wife, Frankie, a nice woman whom he had married a few years earlier after the death of her husband and the death of Ed's first wife, May Lou. I would never have known Ed, nor did he recognize me. In fact, it was hard for each of us to be convinced of the other's identity. After such a long time, age had changed us both very much. Here I was, now sixty-two, and when Ed had last seen me, I was twenty-six. Ed was much smaller than I remembered him, and his complexion was considerably darker than before. I later learned that this was due to some illness that he had suffered because of his work as a motorman in New York's subways for nearly thirty years after he left the Basie band in 1948. On this tour a friendship between Ed Lewis and I bloomed, one that I shall always cherish.

Conspicuous by his absence was my longtime idol, Earle Warren. I hadn't seen Earle since 1958 when we saw each other in New York City when I was en route to Bermuda with my eight-piece group, but I had talked to him long-distance a few times since. When I inquired about Earle and Buck Clayton, Jean-Pierre explained that they had gone on to Nancy, France, where we would open the tour that night. All in all, the reunion in the Brussels airport was a wonderful experience. It was like a family reunion, and emotions ran high.

Our plane for Nancy left in mid-afternoon, and within a couple of hours we were at our hotel in the town. As we poured into the hotel's lobby, I could see Buck Clayton and Earle Warren as they were hugging everyone and greeting them. In the twenty-five intervening years, Earle had changed drastically. I had seen Buck only a year or so earlier when he came to Omaha to bury his sister, Margie, who lived in town, so there was little change for me in the great trumpet player's appearance from when I had last seen him. My reunion with Earle was something special: teacher and pupil, idol and idolizer, and so on. I looked forward to the coming three weeks and to hearing the man whom I consider to be the greatest lead alto player of them all, at least to my personal taste: Earle Warren, whom all of the original Basie guys called "Smiley." There was only a short time before the concert, so we had less than two hours to rehearse the whole repertoire that we would be playing on the tour. Chairs and music stands were hastily set up in the lobby of the charming little hotel, and Buck Clayton passed out the orchestrations he had prepared. The only tune from more recent Basie orchestras was "Shiny Stockings." Nat Pierce had made an arrangement of the tune especially for this tour, and he passed it out. My music stand had only second alto sax parts, which we musicians always referred to as third alto, because it was set a third below the first alto part. Earle, of course, would play the lead-alto chair.

Upon examination of the various tunes such as "Down for Double," "It's Sand, Man," and "920 Special," Buddy Tate, Earle Warren, Sweets Edison, and I noticed that Buck Clayton had changed the arrangements of all but a couple of the old Basie classics. They were in higher keys and with very different figures than had been on the original recordings. Also, the solos were put on different parts, or "chairs," from the originals. On most of these, I noticed that Earle's lead parts were written away up in the air so that he was playing high shrill notes most of the time. The fingerings on some of these would be simply murderous. Everyone was rushing to get the rehearsal started so we could get to our respective rooms and get cleaned up in time for the evening concert. Buck quickly kicked off the first number, "Down for Double." Several of the fellows in each section had mentioned that they hadn't done any reading of music or big-band playing for quite some time. In the reeds, Skippy Williams and Earle Warren had said that they were rusty from not having done any of this kind of playing for many months, or years even. Of course, Ed Lewis hadn't even touched his trumpet for years until he began to practice for the tour. The brass section sounded good for the opening notes of the rehearsal in spite of the fact that there wasn't a lead trumpet specialist on the tour. The rhythm section also was quite acceptable in spite of the fact that I couldn't appreciate an amplifier on the bass violin of a Count Basie rhythm section. The reeds, however, were an immediate disaster.

With the very first bars of the arrangement it was apparent that we were going to have big trouble putting together a section that wouldn't be an embarrassment to the Count Basie name. It was also apparent from the first few bars that Earle Warren would never play lead or first alto sax again in any big band. The beautiful tone that I had worshiped so much was no longer there, and it was hard to recognize any semblance of the sound he once had. Furthermore, Earle played so far behind the beat that it was impossible for the rest of the reeds to follow him. Time was growing very short and Sweets Edison and Nat Pierce began to make wisecracks and playful snide remarks to the reed section like musicians had done in the days of traveling bands. But most of their remarks were directed to Earle Warren and Skippy Williams. Of course, Skippy hadn't done any playing, especially reading music, for many years, and I would later learn what had caused Earle's loss of tone. Freddie Green just sat looking at the section with a sorrowful expression on his face. Occasionally, he shook his head in disbelief.

There wasn't time to clean up each arrangement, so we just did a cursory run-through of each number, leaving mistakes and all to chance. Soon we got to Nat Pierce's "Shiny Stockings." It was apparent immediately that Earle would never be able to come close to articulating the figures that Nat had written, so I volunteered to take the lead-alto part off of Earle. Players such as Mel Wanzo, Curtis Fuller, Joe Newman, and Al Aarons had played this number with Basie when it was first recorded, so for them it was duck soup, but none of us in the reeds knew it. However, I had done a considerable amount of studio playing, big-band playing, and various shows that came to Omaha, so I never got out of practice doing lead alto work and sight reading. Naturally, I had an advantage over those who hadn't had the opportunity to do any of this kind of playing for a long time. "Shiny Stockings" posed no big problem for me, and we were able to get the arrangement together reasonably well without too much laboring over it. I was happy for this, because Nat Pierce was standing over the sax section, gesticulating in a rage until we were able to clean up the rather tricky bebop figures he had written for the sax section. The time for the concert was fast approaching, so we had to cut short the rehearsal. I could foresee the night's concert in Nancy being a total disaster. My fears didn't altogether materialize, but the reeds certainly did not play well. And many of the biggest problems came from confusion within the rhythm section on the faster numbers. It was apparent that it would take some time for Frankie Capp and Eddie Jones to achieve good communication between their instruments.

All in all, the concert was a great success, as all of the concerts on the tour were. Our enthusiasm and the band's dynamism were so exciting that the audiences went mad over the Countsmen in every city. We all seemed to be having so much fun and enjoying ourselves so much that it was infectious to the audiences. Furthermore, the names Buddy Tate, Buck Clayton, Earle Warren, Eddie Durham, Freddie Green, Ed Lewis, and the others have special meaning to European jazz fans. Whatever the band lacked in precision and other technical perfections, it more than made up for in enthusiasm. It had that flavor and attitude of the early Count Basie style, what I would refer to as the "real" Count Basie. European audiences are not concerned with technical proficiency and precision where black music is concerned, so they appreciated that "raw" expressive thing that Count Basie first took to New York from Kansas City in 1936. The Countsmen of 1983 were literally a sensation during those three weeks in Europe. After Nancy, we went to Paris. We participated individually in a jam session one evening at the Meridien Hotel Jazz Club. Then the full band played concerts, first at Maxim's of Paris, and next in the main ballroom of the Meridien.

The sax section still remained a big problem. It just couldn't hold together, even on the simpler arrangements. Freddie Green and Sweets Edison began to urge me to take the first lead book from Earle. Nat Pierce joined the chorus of those who were constantly expressing frustration with the reed section. Probably the most vocal of all was bass player Ed Jones. Jones didn't seem to have much admiration for the early Basie bands the and rhythm sections of the Walter Page–Jo Jones era. His idea of the greatest Count Basie reed sections included *only* Marshall Royal as their lead man. Ed Jones constantly made remarks to me that brought me to realize that he was no fan of the pre–Marshall Royal Basie bands. Of course, this put us in opposite camps.

After Paris, we flew to Madrid, and upon our arrival at our hotel there,

Paris, November 1983. From left to right: Jo Jones, Preston Love, and Michael De Silva. (Photo © François Perol)

Freddie Green said, "Love, take the lead book. *Take the lead book,* and get those guys together for a rehearsal." I said, "Aw, Freddie, I couldn't do that and embarrass Earle like that." Freddie knew of my great worship of Earle Warren, as did all of the older members of Basie's band, and he understood how it would hurt me to do this to Smiley. So Freddie said, "Listen, Preston, nobody in the audience will know who is playing first alto. Smiley shouldn't give a damn who's playing lead so long as you can get that section together and sounding like a real reed section." At Freddie's insistence, I went to Buck Clayton's room, and he gave me all five of the saxophone books. There were still about three hours before the concert in Madrid, so I called the rooms of all the sax players and told them to come as quickly as possible to my room for a rehearsal. Shortly afterward, the saxes gathered in my room, and we carefully rehearsed each piece of music with myself on lead and Earle on second alto. Freddie Green came to listen to the rehearsal and constantly nodded his approval as we were able to clean up the parts. The reeds were never perfect, nor were any of the other sections, but at least we were able to get it together.

I was very careful to give Earle Warren at least three of the arrangements to play lead on. They were "One O'Clock Jump," "Doggin' Around," and "Tickle Toe." These were things that he could lead on and we could bolster him enough to prevent his falling far behind the tempo, which had become some kind of mental hazard with this great lead-alto man. The hour and a half rehearsal was invaluable to our sax section, and we all felt better about getting onstage for the Madrid concert. Onstage that night, a crestfallen Earle Warren came up to me and said, "Thank you so much, Buddy, for not making it embarrassing for me. Since you are playing lead, you might as well sit in this chair," and he pointed to his lead chair in the center of the section. I said, "Are you kidding? That chair in *any* Count Basie orchestra will always belong to Earle Warren. Furthermore, I would rather sit over there to your right between you and Buddy Tate so I can talk stuff to both of my great friends."

There is no question that in the Basie environment I strove to be Earle's alter ego, so we were able to throw back fairly closely to the Basie reeds sound of the thirties and forties. With Earle and me on the altos and Buddy Tate on tenor, the unison parts of "Tickle Toe," "One O'Clock Jump," and the other Basie standards sounded very similar to the original recordings of those tunes. For me, this was a moment of utopia, since to me the real "Basie" ended with the breakup of Basie's big bands of the thirties and forties. His orchestras of the "renaissance Basie" period beginning in 1951 were often very good bands, sometimes even great bands, but with the passing of each day they became less and less like what I consider the pure Count Basie sound. When Basie built his style in the Kansas City days of his early bands, he apparently had a particular thing in mind for the band's purpose and intent. This was carried over rather religiously into the bands he took to the big time of New York City in 1936 and 1937. His bands of the thirties and forties retained that particularly unique Basie flavor, but in the fifties the pure Basie "thing" steadily changed to something different, with a different meaning and purpose. From the fifties on, the Count Basie orchestras ceased to tear at my heartstrings as they did in the days of Lester Young, Earle Warren, and Sweets Edison.

After Madrid, we did a series of concerts in France. Jean-Pierre chartered a fine big bus. Everything was done to make us comfortable. The bus was well stocked with fine liquors, beer, and snacks. Various times, as we went through quaint little French villages, Jean-Pierre had the driver stop and find the town's finest café at which Jean-Pierre bought our lunch, breakfast, or dinner. Without exception, the food and the wines in these small cafés was exquisite. In spite of the division of opinion among some of the older Basie men and some of the members of he renaissance Basie era, we were one big happy family, and there was an aura of love and brotherhood that was tangible.

Nat Pierce brought along his collection of the earlier and later Count Basie recordings. Our group was about equally divided between players who were on the earlier things and those who were on the later ones. Pierce played the recordings around the clock over the bus's speaker system, so Buck, Sweets, Buddy, Ed Lewis, Ed Durham, Freddie Green, and Earle listened to themselves on those classic Basie masterpieces of the early band. Nat even had a couple of recordings on which I played lead, such as "Queer Street," "Blues Skies," and "Robin's Nest." Late at night, when the laughter and kidding around died down in the bus, there was usually an awkward silence as Nat Pierce carefully selected recordings from each era of Basie history. As the different recordings came over the speaker system, each faction knew what the other was thinking without one word being spoken. Pierce was a devoted admirer of both the old and new Basie, and he straddled the fence as to his main loyalties in this regard. I perceived that he loved the feeling and spontaneity of the early Basie bands, while as a successful arranger-orchestrater, he appreciated the greater emphasis placed on precision and balance in more recent Basie bands.

There was no question that Pierce had a purpose in playing the recordings. I think he rather enjoyed the little unspoken division or difference of opinions about the comparative merits of newer and older Basie bands. He was completely aware of my sentiments on the subject. On one of the first nights of the tour, after drinking quite a bit, Pierce roared, "This is the worst reed section I have ever heard in my life." Most of his comments were directed at Earle Warren and Skippy Williams. Skippy was a big, happy-go-lucky guy, the most good-natured person on the whole tour. In the rear of the bus, he just roared with laughter and good-natured comedic quips. Earle Warren sat right in back of Nat Pierce's seat, which was directly across from my seat. Buddy Tate sat right behind me, and as Pierce continued to berate the reed section, Buddy nudged me between the opening in my seat. It was late at night, but there was enough light that I could see Earle Warren's misery as I glanced over and back to his seat. Pierce was very inebriated by now, so I didn't address my remarks to him. I didn't want to be responsible for a big melee all the way over in Europe, but I had reached the limits of my tolerance. Ed Lewis and his wife Frankie were seated directly behind Buddy Tate, and I didn't want my profanity to be heard by her, so I said it as quietly as possible to Buddy Tate, but really for Nat Pierce's ears. I said, "The next motherf——er who belittles or ridicules Earle Warren is going to have to kick my ass or taste my right hand. They can say whatever the hell they want about me, but not about that great man who helped make the Basie sound what it was." I went on, "Earle Warren is one of those most responsible for bringing stardom to the name Count Basie, and as far as I am concerned, all the other lead-alto men of the band's history put together don't make one Earle Warren." That was the last time Nat Pierce criticized Earle in my presence, except to say what a truly great genius Earle had been as the leader of the Basie reed section. Coincidentally, after that tour, Nat Pierce and I became fast friends before his death five years ago.

The next day I was returning to the bus as Sweets Edison laughingly announced from his seat in the rear section of the bus, "I told you all about cracking at Red Love's man, Smiley. That's Red Love's idol, and Red was a great prize-fighter when he was young. You keep on messing with Red's boy, Smiley, and you're goin' to have to taste Red's famous right hand and left hook." Sweets Edison is a very clever and humorous person, but there was much truth in his humorous jests. I was happy that Buddy Tate had told the other people on the bus about my respect for Earle, so I didn't have to contend with any more references to Earle's current failings as a lead-alto player.

A day or so before all this transpired, Earle Warren had told me the story about how he had lost his ability to apply proper pressure to the mouthpiece, which made it quite impossible for him to retain the magnificent sound he was known for on the alto sax. The loss of his best sound and the constant discomfort to his mouth while playing were the cause of his problems trying to play lead alto now. It had all happened a few years earlier, when Earle was living in New Jersey before he moved to Geneva, Switzerland, where he had resided for some six years at that time. He was driving home from playing golf, and he had the top down on his convertible. The hot sun caused him to pass out, and he had an accident. His car was demolished, and Earle's mouth and gums were severely injured, which necessitated his wearing partial dentures. At one time after the crash, Earle thought he would never be able to play his instruments again. This accident probably ended Earle Warren's days as a big-band lead alto player, although he was still able to function as a flutist, clarinet player, and alto sax player in smaller combo work.

One of the first stops in France after Madrid would be Mantes La Jolie, which is the home of Jean-Pierre Vignola. Jean-Pierre's parents lived in this beautiful little city some forty miles from Paris. I had played there earlier in the year on the Cleanhead Vinson tour, and there we shared the concert with the Sweets Edison–Benny Carter group, which included Oliver Jackson on drums, Jimmy Woode on bass, and pianist Gerald Wiggins. On any tour promoted by Jean-Pierre, he arranged it so that the troupe played his hometown, and while the group was in town his mother prepared a lavish dinner, replete with the finest wines and cocktails. On the Eddie Vinson tour, Mrs. Vignola entertained us royally. While at the Vignola dinner party, Benny Carter and I chatted for a long spell. Carter is a gentleman in all senses of the word. He was most surprised to see me playing rhythm and blues *tenor* sax almost entirely except for one number on alto. I had last seen Benny when we both played the Stockholm Jazz Festival in Sweden some three years earlier in July 1980. On the Countsmen tour, we were scheduled for two days in Mantes La Jolie, first an off-day and then we would do a concert on the second night. We arrived in Mantes La Jolie in the late afternoon of October 27 after a long bus ride from a city in southern France where we had played our first night after Madrid. Soon after we were all checked in our rooms at the wonderful little hotel, each room was called by the desk clerks to inform us that there would be a party at eight in the hotel's dining room near the lobby. We were cautioned not to eat anything before the party, because there would be many dishes served. Most of us were surprised to learn that the inevitable party would not be held at the home of Jean-Pierre's parents.

After freshening up, I strolled around a few blocks in the area of the hotel, and before long it was time to prepare myself for the party. Eight o'-clock seemed to arrive quickly, and I joined the rest of the troupe in the bright little dining room of the hotel. Also traveling with us throughout the entire trip were Mrs. Al Aarons and Nancy Elliott. Aarons and his wife are two very pleasant people, and we struck up a good relationship. They had spent a year and a half in Paris in the early 1980s when Al was there to play the show *Sophisticated Lady* with a small band from Los Angeles, so the Aaronses spoke French quite well. Albert Aarons is an excellent modern jazz-trumpet player whom I saw several times with the Basie band in Los Angeles and in Omaha during the seventies. I have always felt that he should have been a much more famous name among modern trumpet players. Nancy Elliott is a young photographer who came along as Buck Clayton's companion and associate. Nancy probably has many priceless photos that she took on the tour. I have only seen a few of them, but all of the pictures of that tour will probably be quite valuable some day. Soon we were all gathered in the hotel dining room. The foods and liquors were elegant. The little café was buzzing with conviviality and brotherly love as we converged upon the many exotic French dishes and fine wines. We were joined by various people from the town of Mantes La Jolie, including the family of Jean-Pierre Vignola. I sat at a table with Buddy Tate, the Aaronses, and Skippy Williams. All was laughter and contentment. Suddenly there was a collective gasp from those facing the doorway to the hotel lobby. I turned around quickly and could hardly believe my eyes. Jean-Pierre was pushing *Jo Jones* into the café in a wheelchair.

I think Jean-Pierre Vignola was experiencing one of the happiest moments of his forty-three years on earth. He was probably more pleased with himself for this than for any other deed of his life. Jean-Pierre had flown Jo over from New York City especially for this occasion so that he could be with his people: the Countsmen. Nearly everyone in the dining room rushed to greet Jo. He addressed the gathering briefly, constantly wiping tears from his eyes. It was a poignant and emotional moment, especially for those of us from the earlier Basie era. It was one of the happiest and most satisfying moments of my life and career. Jo was no stranger to Mantes La Jolie. He spent part of each year there with his "lady," Madame Therese. Jo and Madame Therese had lived together for a number of years in New York City. Upon her retirement from the nursing profession, Madame Therese moved back to live in her native city, Mantes La Jolie. She remained very loyal to Jo Jones, and he joined her in Mantes La Jolie for several weeks or months each year. Various French jazz devotees were his benefactors and paid for Jo's airfare for these trips. Of course, Madame Therese accompanied Jo to the party at our hotel. She informed me that she was having a small party at her apartment the next afternoon for the older members of the Basie family—Freddie Green, Buddy Tate, Buck Clayton, Harry Edison, Eddie Durham, Ed Lewis, Earle Warren, Joe Newman, and myself. The party was scheduled so as to give us plenty of time to prepare for the night's concert.

Joe Newman and Earle Warren didn't attend Madame Therese's little reception. I was bitterly disappointed that Smiley hadn't joined in, but I listened eagerly to the stories exchanged by the early members of the Count Basie Orchestra. Some of the things they talked about dated all the way back to 1937. Jo Jones sat in his personal easy chair while consuming rather large drafts of cognac. He was a most interesting and entertaining storyteller. I divided my attention between caressing Madame Therese's two enormous house cats and listening to the engrossing stories of these jazz giants. I think we all sensed that this might be the last time this group of compatriots would ever assemble and visit each other. Madame Therese outdid herself on the French cuisine she prepared. It was simply wonderful. I left the party with the others, filled with emotion. I promised myself to try some day to articulate my feelings of that moment. I had experienced a big moment of history here with those idols of my youth.

The concert that night at Mantes La Jolie could be described as lightning and thunder. Jean-Pierre booked us this time at a smaller venue than the hall we had played earlier in the year with the Eddie Vinson show. The ceiling was quite low on the stage, and the acoustics were very live. With all of the band's enthusiasms and inspiration, we sounded very loud. It was a loudness that warmed the heart, however. The little hall was packed to capacity, and the audience was in a frenzied state from the opening note of the concert. Midway in the first set, Jo Jones was wheeled from the wings of the stage to a place near the drummer, who was elevated to the right and rear of our reed section. Just before the number "Blue and Sentimental," Buck announced Jo Jones, and the audience went wild. Jo beckoned to some of the band members, and they lifted him from his wheelchair to the drum stool as Frankie Capp slid to the side. For all of his debilitated condition, Jo Jones still showed flashes of his great genius, even on the second number, "Jumpin' at the Woodside," which featured Buddy Tate's tenor sax solo. Jo could hardly hold the swift tempo, but it wasn't altogether a disaster or a fiasco.

At intermission, we retired to a room at the front of the hall that had been improvised as a dressing room. It was well stocked, as usual, with snacks and the finest cognac, beer, and other liquors. The fans literally stormed the two entrances to the dressing room, so we spent most of the intermission signing autographs. Many people brought jazz history books, album covers, and pictures of the different players for us to sign. I was surprised to see several people with copies of my new Swedish album, *Strictly Cash*, which had been released a few months earlier. I signed the album covers for them, and also signed copies of such books as Hugues Panassie's *Guide to Jazz* and Stanley Dance's *World of Count Basie* alongside my name in them. This is standard procedure whenever American musicians tour Europe.

The second half of the concert was even more inspired and animated than the first. Buck Clayton tried several times to soften the band down as he directed, but it simply was "happy time" for the group of enthusiastic players, and no one particular individual or section of the band was responsible. It was a spontaneous eruption of pure Count Basie. After the concert ended, I was at the back of the little bandstand packing my up horn as Eddie Jones was placing the cover on his bass violin. I was obviously in a happy and elated state of mind and anxious to join the rest of the troupe in the dressing room for a last cocktail and some back slapping.

Ed Jones summoned me for a moment and asked, "Well, Preston, what do you think of this band compared to the Basie band of the fifties and sixties now? That band wouldn't have played that loud, even in this small place."

My first impulse was to retaliate with something like, "Well, Eddie, an *amplified* bass didn't help the softness any" or to say something more sarcastic, but I simply said quietly, "The original Basie band and his later bands had two entirely different styles and entirely different purposes, Ed." I could have also added that the original Basie orchestra to me was the greatest single unit in the history of swing or jazz except for perhaps early Duke Ellington, but if you want to disagree, please be my guest.

The rest of the tour took us to Ireland, England, Switzerland, and Italy. In Chichester, England, the Count Basie Society treated us as gods. They presented us with gold-plated pens engraved with their logo. We often spent long hours on our charter bus, and I divided my time between conversations with most of my old friends and my newly made friends in the band. Curtis Fuller kept us all laughing most of the time. He and Nat Pierce went through some verbal comedy routines that should be recorded for sale. Aside from his trombone genius, Curtis Fuller has a most clever, quick, and humorous mind. Buddy Tate is one of my favorite people, so I felt privileged to have the opportunity to spend three whole weeks in the company of my long-standing friend.

A pleasant surprise was my new friendship with Ed Lewis. Ed and I had enjoyed a good enough relationship back in the forties when we were with Basie; in fact, Ed Lewis and Dicky Wells were probably the only members of the very early Basie personnel who extolled my lead alto playing as compared to Earle Warren's when I played with the band in 1943 and from 1945 to 1948. But now in 1983, Ed Lewis and I became almost a mutual admiration society. Ed, his wife Frankie, and I often chatted together for long periods during the tour. Although Ed looked very different, his voice was identical to the way I remembered it back in the thirties and forties. I first heard Ed's voice in 1938 when I stopped him in front of the Dreamland Ballroom in Omaha as he was arriving to play a dance on a summer night. I asked him for his autograph as several of us young Basie zealots gathered around him to ask him sophomoric questions. I was seventeen years old and had been playing alto only a few months or so. I had just been bitten by my Earle Warren lead alto fanaticism. I asked Ed Lewis that night when Earle Warren would be arriving for the gig, and Ed chuckled with the understanding and fatherly patience of a musician accustomed to seeing young fans go crazy over their idols in every town. Ed answered something about Smiley being along soon, signed his autographs, and continued on up the steps of the ballroom to get ready for the night's gig.

Another incident I recall about Ed Lewis happened in 1947 when we played most of that summer at the Paradise Club in Atlantic City, New Jersey. Every Wednesday at the Paradise was rehearsal day for the Basie band. On this particular Wednesday, we were to rehearse several new arrangements brought in by Buster Harding, the arranger who had written "920 Special," "Red Bank Boogie," and numerous other numbers that had been successful recordings for the Basie band. On one of the tunes, Buster, whom we called "Boot Whip," became irritated that I wasn't quite bending the notes in the sax work as he hummed them. My patience grew thin also, and I explained to Harding that a saxophone didn't have the capability of imitating his voice exactly as he envisioned the bends and scoops. In the background where the trumpets sat, I could hear Sweets Edison's squeaky voice saying, "S——t, Smiley would bend those notes any way you want them if he was here."

Ed Lewis immediately jumped to my defense, "Man, leave that boy alone. Smiley is great and all that, but that kid is covering the hell out of that chair." Sweets rejoined with some acerbic remark, but Ed had the last word, defusing a potentially volatile situation. Ed directed his words at the whole trumpet section, "I don't care what *anyone* says. I have heard all of the great first alto men, and that boy doesn't have to hide his head around *any* of them." My ego and my self-confidence always suffered terribly when I thought of the likes of Earle Warren and Willie Smith, so Ed's words were an unction to my young ears.

As the end of the Countsmen tour approached in early November 1983, I grew more and more melancholy. Jean-Pierre constantly promised to assemble practically the same personnel for another Basie tour, but I realized that it would never transpire. This would probably be the last time in our lives that most of us would ever play a note of music together or even see each other again. We played our last concert in Milan in November. Earle Warren's lady, Fabienne, had rejoined us after having spent the first few days of the tour with him and then returning to their home in Geneva, so Earle didn't hang out with us after the gig in Milan. He and Fabienne retired early without my having the chance to bid them farewell. Several of the troupe were going on to other places in Europe to perform, so they wouldn't be at the airport the next morning to leave for Paris and the U.S. I was going to Paris the next day to open for two weeks at the Meridien Hotel. The next morning we flew from Milan to Paris where we would bid our final good-byes. Absent from the group were Earle Warren and a couple of others who were headed for different destinations. At the De Gaulle Airport in Paris, we had a couple of hours to visit before the others' plane left for New York. Heywood Henry and Skippy Williams exchanged business cards with me, and we assured each other that we wouldn't let this be the last time we would perform together. Heywood and Skippy have both died recently. I learned of their deaths with tremendous sadness. I spent much of the time talking to Ed Lewis, and we promised to correspond

Jam session at Meridien Hotel Jazz Club, 1983. From left to right: Skippy Williams, Eddie Durham, Al Aarons, Heywood Henry, Earle Warren, Eddie Jones, Preston Love, Freddie Green, Nat Pierce. (Photo © François Perol)

regularly. Oh, how happy I was to have renewed my friendship with this fine person whom I hadn't seen in all those thirty-five long years! I had also learned to like his new wife, Frankie, very much. Shortly before the time for their plane's departure, Eddie Jones walked over to me and warmly shook my hand as he said, "Preston, you worked your butt off, man." I thanked him and wished him the best of luck in Hartford, Connecticut, where he has lived for several years while working in an executive position for a major national company. Jean-Pierre and I then took the bus provided for transportation to downtown Paris, where I spent the next two weeks at the Meridien Hotel Jazz Club, now the Lionel Hampton Room.

I opened there on November 12, 1983. The Meridien gig is a good one. The artist is provided a fine room in the hotel, and the house rhythm section is made up of fine players who do a very good job of backing up the featured soloist. An important fringe benefit is that each night when you arrive at the club the bartender gives the artist six tickets for any kind of liquor or cocktail you might desire. This is a key benefit because drinks at the club are very expensive, costing more than nine dollars each. Most of the artists save up their ticket allotment and use them to entertain friends or parties who come to the club. After my two-week stay at the Meridien, I had accumulated about fifteen tickets that I never used. The tickets were left in the top drawer of the combination desk-table in my room. A couple of days after I opened at the Meridien, I began to get calls from Jo Jones and Madame Therese from Mantes La Jolie. They were anxious to catch my performance, and I made arrangements for them to come early in the next week. I would have the necessary number of tickets for drinks to entertain them properly. The following Tuesday night I took the elevator down to the lobby where the jazz club is located, and there was Jo Jones in his wheelchair. With him were Madame Therese and Michael De Silva. De Silva is a drummer who played with a number of performers such as Sammy Davis, Jr., before Michael moved to live in Paris. For years now, Michael De Silva had been a very good friend of Jo Jones. I helped them find a table in the club and made arrangements for their rounds of cognac with my tickets. The featured artist at the Meridien only had three short sets of thirty-five minutes each, so I had lots of time to visit with Jo Jones and his party. Madame Therese told me that she and Jo knew I would be lonely away from home on America's Thanksgiving Day, which was only two days off, so they were going to prepare Thanksgiving dinner for Michael and me. Their party stayed for two of my sets; I acknowledged Jo Jones to the audience during each set, and the fans gave him standing ovations. The name Jo Jones is one of the important jazz names in France. The French regard him as the greatest of drummers, as do I.

It was during this stay in Paris that I also learned how important a figure jazz saxophonist Sidney Bechet was in that country. Sidney Bechet was something of a national hero to French people. The house bandleader and musical director at the Meridien was a large drummer called Moustache. He and I talked a lot during my stay. I had met Moustache on several previous trips to Paris, but I got to know him well this time. Early in his career, Moustache had played drums with the great Sidney Bechet for several years. This single credit has been the basis of Moustache's entire professional life. He was now well into his fifties, but the fact that he had once played with Bechet made him a national figure in French jazz and gave him the attendant financial security and independence that went with that stature. Unfortunately, Moustache was killed in a car crash in 1987.

On Thanksgiving Day, Michael De Silva and I caught one of the speedy French trains for the forty-mile trip to Mantes La Jolie. Michael knew Paris quite well from having lived there several years, so I simply followed him. We were able to take the train at one of the subway stations near the Meridien. The train made several stops at other substations, but we were in Mantes La Jolie nonetheless in less than one hour. We took a cab from the station to Madame Therese's apartment. She and Jo Jones were happy to see us. Madame Therese announced that she had tried hard to find a turkey, but there was none available in Mantes La Jolie, so she had instead prepared a chicken for the dinner. Jo sat in his easy chair all afternoon while Michael and I joined him in liquid refreshments. Jo still continued to drink large amounts of cognac in spite of his doctor's advice against it. Despite his halting speech brought on by serious mouth surgery, and despite Jo's weakened condition, he was still an absorbing person of great wit. He regaled us with interesting stories and humor while Madame Therese remained in the little kitchen most of the evening preparing what turned out to be a sumptuous Thanksgiving chicken dinner. Several times I fought back waves of melancholy at being away from my wife Betty for one of the very few Thanksgivings since we married in 1941. Here I was on Thanksgiving, thousands of miles away from home and family, and of all places, in Mantes La Jolie, France.

For more than ten years now, Jo Jones had planned a book titled *Me and Count Basie*. From the time I first moved back to Omaha in late 1971, he had been calling me from New York, Los Angeles, or wherever he was to discuss my putting his book down on paper. Jo had visited me in Omaha on at least two occasions in the seventies, and much of our time was spent discussing the manuscript for which I would be Jo's amanuensis. He felt that since I had known him since he came to Omaha to play with Lloyd Hunter's Band in 1931 and since I had followed the history of the Count Basie Orchestra avidly, I would be the ideal one to do his book for him. Then we could possibly have it edited or tightened up by someone like Stanley Dance or Frank Driggs. It was to be a prodigious undertaking and a challenge for me, but at Jo's insistence I agreed to do the manuscript with him. Several times on that day in Mantes La Jolie, Jo informed me that he'd made a grant proposal in New York or Washington to get the funds to enable us to do the book. He planned to come to Omaha and check in at the Airport Inn as he had done before, so I could spend a week or so taping his verbal information. Jo was pretty sure that the money from his grant proposal would be awarded. I was skeptical but hopeful that the project would come to fruition. What Jo Jones had to say about his association with Count Basie and about his own career should have been written down. It would have been interesting and edifying. After Thanksgiving dinner that evening, Michael De Silva and I caught a train back to Paris in time for me to rest a couple of hours before my first set at the Meridien, which was at ten-thirty each night. I never dreamed that I had seen Jo Jones for the last time, although I did talk to him several times on long-distance telephone calls after he returned to the United States.

Jean-Pierre Vignola booked the artists for the Meridien Jazz Club with the approval of Moustache, so Jean-Pierre came to the club most nights to see if everything was going well for both the artist and the club's management. When I arrived at the club that night for my first set, Jean-Pierre was there waiting for me. He announced, "Preston, I called your wife in Omaha to tell her that you miss her on Thanksgiving and that we will take good care of you. We won't let you be sad and unhappy." Jean-Pierre has had close associations with most of the big names in jazz because of his affiliation with jazz promoter George Wein and with the Meridien Hotel. He has been a great benefactor of American jazz musicians, and he is a very popular person with all of them. I last saw him in Nice in July 1985 when we played the Nice Jazz Festival with the Johnny Otis Group. Jean-Pierre was one of the assistants to George Wein in presenting the festival.

My very enjoyable and rewarding five weeks in Europe in 1983 made Omaha seem even more depressing to me than it had been before my arrival back home in late November. My hometown had once been an important center for black music and musicians, but now good jazz players are almost nonexistent, or at least very rare, in Omaha. Yet there are legions of musicians in the city calling themselves "jazz" players and there are various lounges and bars referring to the music they present as "jazz." Most depressing is the fact that the laypeople of the community have become so ignorant on the subject of jazz or black music. The uninformed or apathetic public of my hometown can hardly differentiate between the worst player and someone who might actually have the ability to play jazz. Consequently, hordes of totally inept musicians without the slightest concept or talent for jazz have become dominant in the jazz scene in Omaha. How this could have occurred seems quite incredible to me, but none of the local critics or newspaper columnists of the city are willing to point out the sad state of jazz in town. Of course, most of them are as uninformed about the music as the laypeople are, but there are at least one or two critics in the city who might recognize terribly poor jazz when they hear it.

Then, too, racism is rampant in Omaha's music business, so whatever jazz there is in the city is dominated by whites, no matter how mediocre or untalented they might be. The same is true of the pop and r&b fields in my hometown. It doesn't augur to get any better either, because most of the major organizations in town who have the power to improve these conditions are themselves tools of the local dominant musicians. They certainly are not at all interested in benefiting the city's black players and singers, except for extending some token patronage to one or two of their black lackeys or cronies. Unfortunately, many of the potential music fans of Omaha aren't aware of what is going on in the real music world except for the dross fed them on television, so when I speak out so openly and caustically, they feel that I am judging my hometown unfairly or that I either have some personal agenda or that it is an attempt to glorify myself. Of course, this is not my purpose. When I point out these injustices and irrefutable truths, I have in mind the next generation of young black musicians and performers who haven't had a chance at careers or recognition for their talents. I've *had* my career. I've *lived* my life. It would be so simple and easy, not to mention safer, for me to desert the black musicians and silence my protests, but I refuse to do this. I often suffer reprisals and retaliation for my outspokenness, while my own black compatriots desert me and bad-mouth me.

On December 7, 1983, I was in the town of Cascade, Iowa, in the first week of a two-week jazz residency at their high school. I was spending the first week staying at the home of one of the teachers and her husband. Early on the third day I was there, I was in the bathroom preparing myself to leave for the day at the school when the couple's baby-sitter called me to the telephone. When I arrived at the telephone, I recognized my wife Betty's voice on the other end. She had called to inform me that my mother, beloved Mexie, had died in her sleep at the nursing home where she had been since 1974. Mex had turned 103 on October 31 of that year. I had quite a difficult time traveling the two hundred and seventy-five miles back to Omaha from Cascade because the Greyhound buses were on strike, but after many hours and several long waits in depots of other bus lines, I was able to get back in time to arrange for Mama's funeral that weekend. On the following Monday I returned to Cascade to complete the two-week residency. The state of Iowa and its arts council in Des Moines had been my salvation, as Mex would say. The Iowa Arts Council had been generous and gracious to me beyond description since I became their first jazz artist in residence when that program was first funded by the National Endowment for the Arts in the early 1970s. I still cherish and zealously protect my relationship with that Iowa Arts Council.

Nineteen eighty-four started out quite uneventfully for me, especially with respect to the music scene in Omaha. I was in negotiations for a couple of European tours for the year, but neither seemed to gel. On my birthday, April 26, shortly before eight o'clock that morning, I answered the telephone. The voice on the other end of the line said, "Mr. Love, I am a reporter calling from Radio Station KFAB [Omaha's biggest]. I hope I am not breaking some bad news to you, but have you heard that *Count Basie died this morning?*" All I could think of to say was something like "wow" or "gee." The reporter asked if he could interview me on their station. I assented, and the interview began live. Before the day ended, I had been interviewed by nearly every radio and television station in Omaha. I actually became so hoarse by the end of the day that I could hardly speak. My relationship with Count Basie was widely known in Omaha because he had come to town several times since we moved back. Basie had always given me a plug from the stage of his concerts or in his interviews for radio and television in Omaha. Our pictures had appeared together in the local papers, and I wrote articles and reviews about the band when they appeared in Omaha. Basie had also asked me to introduce them on several occasions when they played such places as the Orpheum Theater and the Oar House in Omaha, so the local media had a field day interviewing me about Basie's death. Later, I heard of a few local petty and envious persons who accused me of getting mileage out of the news coverage of Basie's death. Jealousy abounds in my hometown, especially among its African Americans.

The name Count Basie symbolized all that music meant to me in my early life and my early career. Even today, the music of the early Count Basie bands remains the dominant force among my musical interests. This represents nearly all of my life, at least all of my *adult* life. Basie realized this probably more than anyone except perhaps my wife and my friend, Johnny Otis. Hence, Basie and I became very good friends over the years. On every occasion that I saw him around the country up until the last time in 1981, he tried to articulate the special place he had for me in his consideration. Countless musicians feel that they had a special relationship with Count Basie. I am certainly one of them.

When Basie first fell ill, and it seemed he might be moribund, I received a flood of calls and letters from musicians and other friends who asked, What will become of black musicians after Basie? They were referring to the fact that his was the last of the full-time big bands headed by a black person, and even Count Basie found it difficult to survive and to sustain a big band that was predominately black. Personally, I'm skeptical. I feel that the death of Count Basie signaled the end of certain African-American artistic music as we knew it in this country. This is a great loss to the world and to future generations of African Americans. The cynical and avaricious controllers of the music business are not at all interested in preserving art, or preserving history, or preserving authenticity. This is evidenced by the corruption and distortion of black music that has already been fostered by our music industry. Their failure to preserve black American music or to give honest recognition to the contribution of black musicians and singers reflects one of the worst forms of racism. Those of my generation and earlier generations of black music will soon conveniently be erased by old age and death, and the corrupters of history will have things all their way: a free hand to alter history and to erase even the memory of those great African-American creative giants who gave this country so much rich art. I regret to admit that not all of the corrupters of black music have been whites. The limited number of successful black performers and purveyors

Preston Love receives honorary Doctor of Music degree from Creighton University; daughter Portia Love receives master's degree. May 9, 1992.

of black music must share the guilt for what has happened to black music in this era of American show business. Black music, the same as all other styles of American music, has become an exercise in packaging and marketing without regard for its quality or purity. I am appalled to observe many of our black singers using all-white or nearly all-white backup musicians while performing musical idioms that were innovated and developed entirely by black Americans. In most cases, the white backup musicians are *competent* musicians technically, but very often they show no particular innate feeling or talent for black music. Thus, black music has become diluted, bastardized, and commercialized to the point that it is losing its distinctiveness. This, of course, makes the commercial purveyors of music very happy, since it eliminates the necessity for black musicians, black singers, black dancers, and black promoters. Today's black audiences have come to regard this synthetic or spurious black music as the real thing. Where will the next generation of Duke Ellingtons, Aretha Franklins, Ray Charleses, and Count Basies come from and for whom will they be able to perform? Not even for their own black people, probably.

Mine was the first fully integrated black band in the Midwest, with my precious Jewish friend Eli Wolinsky on alto sax and Jake Andrews on trumpet. It has been my policy to hire the best person available when I need a musician without regard for race or color. That integrated band of mine in 1950 was quite a novelty and a rarity in the America of that era.

Since I returned to Omaha in 1971, virtually every combo or orchestra I have led was what we refer to as "integrated." All my current groups have white drummers, white bass players, a white pianist, a white guitar player, and so on. So any implication that I am against white jazz musicians is nonsensical. Some of the very best players I have hired have been white musicians, including drummers Joe Voda and Gary Foster, bass players Dean Demeret, Ed Clatterbuck, and Mark Luebbe. Also, white guitar players such as Tom "Slim" Barnhart and Mike "Spike" Nelson have been among the white players that I have used extensively with great success and mutual admiration and respect between us. My argument with the power structure of jazz presentation is that those in charge are now excluding black musicians and singers from their employment, except for a few token cronies, while presenting a conglomeration of white "jazz" players. The power organizations anoint these players and their black cronies with totally undeserved accolades and promotion. It has become a game of personalities, not *jazz* at all. As an added insult, these black cronies often show up with all-white players except for themselves. Other black musicians in my hometown speak out and protest vehemently *in private*, but publicly they grow silent in fear of reprisals and retaliation from our city's power organizations. The fine black jazz musicians of Omaha's past would turn over in their graves or at least gasp in disbelief at the current state of jazz in the nation, especially in their once-precious Omaha.

The 1983 Countsmen tour had brought Ed Lewis and me back together after some thirty-five years of having been totally out of contact with each other. In Europe that year we rediscovered a latent friendship that blossomed even more than the one we had in the forties when we worked together with Basie. Shortly after I returned home from the Meridien Hotel engagement of 1983, Ed and I struck up an exchange of very warm and friendly letters between Omaha and Blooming Grove, New York, where Ed and Frankie had bought their home. Ed had an idea for starting an association of musicians who had played with the earliest Basie band for the purpose of starting a fund to help those older members who might fall into hard times and need financial assistance. Ed felt that those who were doing well would thus be in a position to rescue some member who was indigent or in need of stopgap aid. It is a well-known fact in musical circles that almost none of the sidemen from any of the Basie bands really received many of the financial benefits of the bands' successes. Basie did pay somewhat better wages to certain individuals in his more recent bands, but in the days of Ed Lewis, hardly anyone was ever paid a salary commensurate with their value to the band. I was shocked to learn of the pitiful salaries that my idols, the biggest stars of the first Basie bands, made during the glory years of the early Basie band.

From the time I spent in Ed Lewis's company in Europe and from his letters, I came to realize what a fine person Ed was. We had promised each other that he and Frankie and Betty and I would exchange visits with each other in Omaha and Blooming Grove. Ed was very pleased with their property in Blooming Grove and showed great pride in it. Betty and I were anxious to see their place in New York to check it out. In June 1985, when I left to go on tour with Johnny Otis, I noticed that I hadn't received a letter from Ed for some weeks, which was unlike him, but I wasn't greatly concerned. I knew that I would probably hear from him by the time I got back from Europe in July. On July 29, I arrived back in Omaha, and there was a stack of correspondence awaiting me, but no letter from Ed Lewis. I was able to catch up on my correspondence and answer the mail that had arrived while I was gone by writing at least one or two letters each day. By the end of the first week in August, I had caught up on my correspondence, including a letter to Ed Lewis telling him about the tour I had just made. About ten days after I had written the letter to Ed, I received a letter with the return address of Mrs. Frankie Lewis from Compton, California. The letter's contents left me shocked and saddened beyond words. Frankie informed me that Ed Lewis had been dead several months and that she moved back to Compton to be near her daughter and other friends and family. Frankie assumed that we had heard about Ed's death, or she would have written sooner. Within a few weeks of Ed's death, both Dicky Wells and Jo Jones were dead. I was in close contact with Jo Jones who died on September 2. Jo had called me in mid-August to inform me that he was going to get the grant for us to write his book *Me and Count Basie*. Jo even laid out his plans for coming to Omaha for the taping of the book's data. His speech was so blurred when I last talked to him that I could hardly understand what he was saying. Jo's death precipitated an exchange of calls between Johnny Otis and me. We burned up the long-distance lines between Los Angeles and Omaha. I don't think anyone on earth admired Jo Jones more than Johnny Otis and I did, nor has anyone else perceived the essence of Jo Jones as a drummer and personality more than Johnny Otis and Preston Love.

Another blow came in 1987 when Freddie Green died of a heart attack on March 1. On the occasion of Green's death I wrote a column for the

The Preston Love Orchestra at the Bistro. From left to right: Ritchie Love, Preston Love, Dean Demeret, Orville Johnson. Not pictured: Gary Foster and Portia Love.

Omaha World-Herald stating that the event eliminated any reason for the continued operation of an orchestra bearing the name Count Basie. I noted that the members of the then-current Basie band might continue to be a fine band, but Green had been the quintessential exponent of the Basie style for all of the fifty years that he played with the band. This was especially true of the late Basie bands, for with the passing of each era, these bands lost more and more of the distinctive Basie style and sound. This is not to say that these bands weren't good; they sometimes were excellent, but they didn't retain that singularly exclusive "Basie thing." Green was born in Charleston, South Carolina, on March 31, 1911. He joined Count Basie in March 1937 and played with the Basie band continuously until his death, except for a few months in 1948 when Basie operated a small combo. Green was not a stranger to adversity: each of his wives died at a relatively young age, and his youngest son died of a heart attack while only in his early forties. Green was often called Basie's left hand, which to some degree was true. I have often said that any band with Freddie Green on guitar would take on the flavor of the Count Basie style, while a band without him could never hope to get it. Even the Basie reunion band we took to Europe in 1983 immediately sounded like the "real" Count Basie band the instant Green strummed his first notes on the guitar, despite the fact that most of the members of the band had grown quite old and some were badly out of practice. Freddie was the last living member of the great Count Basie rhythm section that consisted of Basie on piano, Green on guitar, Jo Jones on drums, and Walter Page on bass. There aren't many jazz or swing critics who haven't referred to that rhythm section as the greatest in history. Green was the cohesive element and unifying force of that section. He was never a soloist, but his rhythm was the steadiest of any guitar player, and he actually produced a more powerful sound on his guitar than traditionally dominant instruments such as the drums and bass.

Green's sense of tempo was flawless, but the main thing that set him apart from other guitar players and that made it almost impossible for them to imitate him successfully was that Green changed the voicing of the chord with each beat, even if the same chord remained for several bars. This always made him and the section seem to be "walking" or moving. His touch made the strings sound as if they were singing. Green was a very quiet man, but he was not dull. He had a rather droll and quick sense of humor. We had a good friendship that I treasured. Shortly before his death, I received a telephone call from one of the members of the Count Basie band. They were spending the night at an Omaha motel before traveling on to Fremont, Nebraska, for an engagement. The caller, baritone sax player John Williams, brought me word that Freddie Green expected me to see them off at the airport the next morning since I had been unable to accompany them to Fremont. Unfortunately, I never made it to the airport that day.

Two and a half years after my article on Green's death appeared in the newspaper, the "Count Basie Band" was booked at the Omaha Orpheum Theater along with Billy Eckstine and Dizzy Gillespie. As usual, my wife and I attended the concert. We had our usual seats down front with the critics and reviewers, and as usual we went backstage to visit Johnny Williams. He and I had been friendly when I lived in Los Angeles, before he joined the Basie band in 1970. I was also quite friendly with other members of the band, including first-alto player Danny Turner and trombone player Mel Wanzo, who had been in the Basie reunion group. As Betty and I stood onstage talking to Williams and others while the band members began to assemble for the concert, I noticed a rather strange attitude toward me on the part of band members who previously had been very congenial to us whenever the orchestra came to Omaha to perform. We were standing on the left side of the stage talking with Mel Wanzo, Johnny Williams, and Danny Turner when Dizzy Gillespie walked in from the wings.

Diz and I had known each other quite well since 1943, when I was in New York temporarily taking Earle Warren's place. I was walking down Eighth Avenue en route to do my show with Basie at the Apollo Theater one day that October, and I ran into my very precious friend bassist Oscar Pettiford. I had known the entire Pettiford family when I played in Minneapolis with the Lloyd Hunter and Nat Towles bands in 1941 and 1942. In fact, Oscar's brother Alonzo joined the Nat Towles band and played trumpet with us briefly in 1942. Oscar was very happy and surprised to see me in New York, and he insisted that I take the time to stop with him at an older apartment building at 2040 Eighth Avenue. We entered the building and took the elevator to an upper floor. Pettiford knocked at one of the apartment doors, and a man answered wearing a kimono-type robe and a stocking cap to keep his hair in place. Oscar introduced him to me as Dizzy Gillespie.

Diz made us feel at home and instructed his wife to pour coffee or some other refreshment for all of us. At that time I only knew Dizzy Gillespie as the man who cut Cab Calloway's coattail when performing with Cab onstage at some theater. This had been treated sensationally in the news media a year or so before I met Diz. He was very hospitable and enjoyed a great rapport with Pettiford. As the time for our show at the Apollo approached, I left Diz and Oscar and headed for the theater for the great excitement of being onstage with that incredible band and Lester Young, who had just rejoined it after Don Byas had been fired for a verbal altercation with Basie. In the ensuing years, I saw Diz occasionally around the country. He was one of the other star attractions with the Johnny Otis Revue in 1985 at the Street Scene jazz festival in Winston-Salem, North Carolina. I was with the Otis troupe, so Diz, Johnny, and I spent quite a bit of time together at the hotel where we all stayed. Shortly after the days in Winston-Salem, Dizzy was booked at the University of Nebraska's Omaha campus. I was unable to attend as I had a gig on that night, but some of the students who were enrolled in my history of jazz course approached Diz during intermission and mentioned my name. They informed me that Diz praised me to the high heavens as a saxophone player, and when he went back out onstage he praised my name to the local audience. It became big news in our local music scene, and naturally, I was pleased and flattered. Plus, a little ego salve never hurts.

On this night at the Orpheum in 1989, however, I rushed over to greet and embrace Diz when he walked on from the wings, but he barely acknowledged me and turned to some others around him. If I had not become accustomed to expecting such things from unpredictable people, it would have been an embarrassing scene. I then turned to Johnny Williams and asked where bandleader Frank Foster and Billy Eckstine were, so I could greet and visit with them. Johnny made several awkward excuses and evasive explanations of their whereabouts, but since it was nearing time for the show to start my wife and I bade him good-bye and started to our seats. As we turned to leave, Johnny Williams called us back and embraced us both saying, "I love you both more than ever," which seemed rather strange to us. Shortly after we reached our seats, Frank Foster came onstage and went to the microphone to announce, "Ladies and gentleman, you have a critic in your town who thinks this band doesn't continue the Count Basie tradition. You are going to have to be careful who you let write for your newspaper." He then turned and brought his hand down as the band launched into a fast, rather bebop-ish and pedantic version of "Strike Up the Band." They played it with fine precision and contrived, rehearsed dynamics. It was so un-Basielike. The drummer was a Caucasian player, which naturally titillated the 90 percent Caucasian Omaha audience, most of whom have come to think of jazz as a Caucasian art form. On this fast semi-classical number, the drummer used all the histrionics at his command for the benefit of the excited "jazz" clientele. I sat there thinking, "I saw Earle Warren on that same stage five shows a day in 1943 with that great band, and I sat there myself in 1945 and 1946 for a week each year with the great Jo Jones on drums, opening shows four or five times daily with those incomparable swinging numbers always associated with the *real* Count Basie style and tradition; and now, comes this ersatz Count Basie style."

After the opening number, the audience gave a fine response, mostly for the drummer's contortions and for his being a white player. Frank Foster went to the mike and said, "And *this* is the band that your local critic wants disbanded! Eat your heart out, Preston Love." There was a smattering of approval for what Foster had said, but there was also a gasp as a strange hush descended upon the house. The Frank Foster–Count Basie Orchestra then proceeded to play an hour-long concert of music that should never have been associated with Count Basie's name. Foster's group played excellently, especially in respect to precision and ensemble playing. In fact, there is certainly no big band of today that plays any better than the Frank Foster band that I heard that night. But it certainly wasn't mindful of what I regard as the Count Basie sound, especially in its reed section. The lead saxophone player performed well enough and the section played together with more precision than the sax section in Earle's and my time because we didn't stress precision. We stressed expression, phrasing, looseness, inventiveness, and the pure Basie inflections of that incomparable Kansas City orchestra style. So far as sound and intonation is concerned, to me and to virtually all Basie purists, the Earle Warren sound is essential to the Count Basie sound. Marshall Royal became a dominant force in the Basie band of the 1950s and 1960s, and although he was far from my favorite lead sax player, I felt that the Frank Foster–Basie band's saxophone section lacked even the power and style of the Marshall Royal reed section. The brass section of the Foster-Basie band came closest to honoring the name Basie; it was very good. The rhythm section, on the other hand, was an embarrassment to the memory of Jo Jones, Freddie Green, and Walter Page, or even drummers such as Shadow Wilson, Butch Ballard, Gus Johnson, and Sonny Payne or bass players such as Rodney Richardson and Eddie Jones.

The Foster-Basie band took an intermission before Billy Eckstine was to close the show. My wife and I joined the crowd in the lobby of the Orpheum Theater at the bar where we had cocktails with friends. Numerous people crowded around me to ask what the anti–Preston Love thing was all about, and countless friends and fans began expressing their opinion that this band no longer presented the Count Basie sound even though it was nevertheless a good band and very precise. I lingered to talk with a couple of old friends after the intermission while we finished our last cocktail. By the time I got back into the theater Billy Eckstine was onstage asking "Is Preston Love in the house?" He went on to say that, "Shaw says a critic is a person who criticizes people for something he can't do himself." He then walked over to the sax section, pointed to where their lead player Danny Turner sat, and continued, "Oh yes, Preston Love sat here until Count Basie discovered he was here and fired him." Various people shouted and screamed in protest, as my wife and I became the center of attraction for all those sitting around us. They couldn't resist taking quick glances at us. It was strange and ironic that Eckstine should vilify me when only months before our return to Omaha in 1971 I had gone to Vandenberg Air Force Base in California for a three-day engagement with an all-white band except for drummer Panama Francis, me, and another black saxophone player, Charles Owens. Billy Eckstine was the star of the show at the base's NCO Club, and after the show each night Panama Francis and I would sit with Billy in Mr. B's room at our motel while he played guitar for us and we chatted and laughed about the good old days. Probably the last words Billy Eckstine said to me when we parted on the last night was something like, "Good-bye you guys, and Preston, as I told you the other night, you and Earle Warren and Scoops Carry are still my favorite first alto players ever."

It seems a local writer for the daily newspaper where my column appeared caught up with Eckstine and Foster on the road by telephone in Ontario, Canada. Eckstine said my article about Freddie Green was passed around in their chartered bus en route to Omaha, and he was chosen to attack me. He added that "Preston Love is not a *great* musician. He is just a musician, period." The young columnist from the local newpaper seemed to share this attitude when he interviewed me and when he wrote an article that rather approved of my onstage "lynching" by Foster and Eckstine. Of course, one of the main problems with so-called jazz today is that the reporters and purveyors of it are usually younger persons who haven't the slightest knowledge or perception of this great black American art form and musical idiom. Yet they insist upon writing about jazz and reviewing performances for sometimes major publications. First of all, I don't recall ever describing myself as a "great" musician, so where is the relevance of Eckstine's statement of opinion about my ability? The local writer mentioned that my name doesn't appear in certain jazz encyclopedias, which was also irrelevant, so it seems he was endorsing Eckstine's assessment. I have several so-called jazz histories in which the names Clark Terry and Sweets Edison do not appear. I remember a review of a book titled *A History of Jazz* where a major jazz authority pointed out that this four hundred and fifty-seven page book gave Glenn Miller a page and a half, but failed to mention at all Django Reinhardt, Carmen McRae, Wes Montgomery, and Elvin Jones, among others; this in a so-called jazz history! It seems our local writer was just seeking justification for Eckstine's statement about Preston Love's lack of greatness. I have always contended that it is fraudulent for bands or singing groups to continue traveling about the country and the world using the name of a deceased leader, but it was not my purpose that the touring Count Basie orchestra should be disbanded. I would have hated to see my friends in the band lose their employment, which in some cases might have been calamitous. It is simply that it is indisputable to me that the Count Basie tradition and Count Basie style died with Freddie Green and the others who followed him, including Earle Warren, so I make no apologies for the things I said in the article.

Late in the spring of 1994, Omaha saxophonist Sonny Firmature called me with devastating news. He informed me that Earle Warren had died at his Springfield, Ohio, home at the age of eighty. No one else except my wife Betty and perhaps Johnny Otis has had a greater impact on my life than Earle Warren. My love for his lead alto work with the early Count Basie band could be described fairly as idol worship or an obsession. Some young musicians and friends in my youth in Omaha even called me "Earle

Warren" to flatter me and my attempts to sound like him on the saxophone. My last correspondence with Earle had taken place a few years earlier when I wrote about him in my newspaper column. There I expressed the view that my idolizing Earle Warren was one thing in my life that bore no reexamination. Even at this late stage in my life and my career, I feel that this admiration was well deserved and that Warren was, without a doubt, the greatest first lead alto player in big-band jazz history, certainly if we are thinking of the Count Basie style of music. He was without weakness as a saxophone section leader. Arrangers built their orchestrations with Warren in mind when they wrote for the Basie band, and he enhanced their work with his lead playing, bringing something unusual to even the simplest figure in the music. He was not recognized as a great jazz soloist, but he played a number of excellent ones on Basie recordings, including the exquisite "Sent for You Yesterday," "Jumpin' at the Woodside," "Rockabye Basie," "Out the Window," and "Clap Hands, Here Comes Charlie." Throughout my career, I measured my ability against his. I still find it easy to defer completely to his genius in the context of that pure Basie thing, as should all of the first alto sax players who happened to play lead alto in later Basie bands.

CHAPTER NINE

Perspectives

✳

Somerset Maugham wrote in *Summing Up* that being engaged and in-volved in the arts does not necessarily make one an artist. Likewise, having been principally an alto saxophonist most of my life doesn't give me any special status as a critic of the instrument. I do feel, however, that it gives me some basis for a critique on the subject, and I feel that it is my duty to analyze the instrument and persons who have been recognized as the mas-ters of it. The alto sax has had two main functions in orchestras. Tradition-ally, it has been the lead melodic instrument in saxophone sections or reed sections with orchestras that use three or more saxophones. The alto sax has also been utilized prevalently as a melodic instrument for ballad solos and for ad-lib jazz improvisational solos in groups of all sizes. In most bands of modern times, reed sections have consisted of five persons with the alto sax as the lead or first part.

In only rare cases has an individual alto sax man been outstanding both at playing lead and playing ad-lib solos. Lead playing and soloing require quite different attributes and each emphasizes different qualities. A lead alto or first-alto man must have a particular sound that will stand out over the sax section. He must also be rather dominant and play with more pre-cision than is permitted soloists. Many soloists have questionable tones or sounds, but a first alto man of stature must have a beautiful tone. There have been a few cases of alto men who could play good solos and great lead, but characteristically *either* lead or soloing is usually the alto man's forte and main interest. In fact, a large percentage of lead men or first men are very limited as soloists, and conversely only a few gifted soloists can play lead in a section at all. In the heyday of big bands, many lead alto men looked upon soloing as beneath their dignity, except for an occasional short solo or a feature solo on a ballad melody. The second alto player was expected to be the jazz soloist, and many of the second alto men regarded playing lead in the section as something out of their sphere of expertise. The most notable exceptions to this rule were Willie Smith, Benny Carter, Hilton Jefferson, and Johnny Hodges. Each of them was nearly as sure-handed at playing lead as at solos. Although regarded strictly as a soloist, Charlie Parker could also play excellent lead when he could discipline himself to the restrictions and circumscription of leading the section.

For dynamism, flawless intonation and a perfect sense of rhythm, I have always regarded Earle Warren as the greatest lead alto sax man of any time. I rate Willie Smith as equal to Earle in stature when he played lead in the Jimmy Lunceford band. Outside of the particular Lunceford style, Willie's greatness as a lead man seemed to diminish considerably. When I heard him with Ellington, Charlie Spivak, and Harry James after he left Lunceford, he didn't impress me as much. Yet no one should consider their knowledge of lead-alto sax complete without hearing Willie's work on the Lunceford recordings of "Alone with You," "I Had a Premonition," "I Dream a Lot About You," and "Like a Ship at Sea." On these Willie Smith exhibits pure genius. Earle Warren was always regarded lightly as a soloist, but it is a mistake to stereotype him strictly as a lead man. His brief solos on many Basie recordings are as fine solos as were ever played by any alto sax player. They were so well conceived and perfectly fitting to the arrangements that they became integral parts of each of the arrangements. If a recognized alto soloist had been with Basie instead of Earle, Johnny Hodges would have played something warm on these arrangements; Charlie Parker or Sonny Stitt would have played something hip and progressive; Benny Carter would have played something neat, well ordered, and pedantic, but no alto player alive would have played anything better and more fitting than Earle Warren did. Warren's tone is so beautiful and sparkling that he would have been one of the most highly regarded balladeers in history if Basie had utilized him as a soloist on ballads à la Johnny Hodges with Duke Ellington.

Without getting into comparisons between the new and the old or between styles and categories of music, I would simply say that playing with R&B or soul singers today is an entirely different ball game from working with the blues and jazz singers of other eras. Playing with today's soul singers is often frustrating and unrewarding for musicians of my era, although some of the background music is fun to play. Playing backup music for current stars is only occasionally enjoyable. We instrumentalists usually feel insignificant and uninspired, even when working with the biggest names in the pop or R&B field. Soul or rock arrangements are mostly written with a type of harmony and voicing that seldom stresses lushness or prettiness. These arrangements are very simply designed as accompaniment to the singers, and R&B arrangers especially seem to avoid writing anything that will feature or highlight any section of the orchestration. A string section may occasionally have something pretty or important to play on soul recordings, but since the soul stars seldom have strings at their in-person concerts, horn sections are left with harsh and drab harmony and figures to play. With jazz and blues singers, saxophone sections were voiced beautifully and had glowing background figures to play as a prominent part of each orchestration, but in today's funk or soul arrangements, saxophone sections are almost meaningless except for the heavy bottom or foundation part played by the baritone sax. This has almost eliminated the need for the characteristic lead or first alto part in contemporary black music. Thus, lead alto players are a vanishing breed and almost nonexistent. Even a highly qualified black first alto player wouldn't get much work in the studios anyway, because first alto is entrusted almost exclusively to whites in studio work. Presuming that I have some degree of ability as a lead alto player, I seldom had the opportunity to play lead alto except on our engagements with my Motown band. In studio work, I played mostly baritone sax or tenor, but I'm positive I could've made a greater contribution on first alto, especially if I had gotten the opportunity to do it often and to keep in practice on it.

In soul or pop music, most of the orchestrations are such that every part seems to drown out the other, so lead sax or lead trumpet and lead trombone parts are no more prominent than third or fourth parts. In the din of soul concerts, the background music seems almost meaningless except for the drums and electrified guitars, keyboards, and bass. Then, too, a large number of the arrangers in this era are not really gifted or qualified in the way that big-band arrangers once had to be. A number of the current pop arrangers with big images have accomplished their successes with limited talent and ability, but they seem to have become powers in the field nevertheless. As a bandleader and contractor for a large number of the popular soul stars when I was in Los Angeles, I tried to use a balance between trumpet, trombone, and reed players who had worked with the famous big bands and younger players from the current era who understand and enjoy playing modern R&B. Admittedly, I hired considerably more black musicians than others, since I feel that R&B or so-called soul music was originally Afro-American and I am convinced that blacks still play it better and more authentically. Hiring black musicians seemed very reasonable and logical, because, after all, we were playing mostly with black singers and performers. In some areas of the country, there is a limited pool of black musicians available for backup work who can play the music with the required precision and technique. In Los Angeles, however, there are countless black musicians who can read and play the music flawlessly, who possess all of the multiple doubling instruments required, such as flute, clarinet, piccolo, and flugelhorn. So there is no honorable reason why such a large number of them should get only a small amount of the employment, especially since the black soul singers all play Los Angeles regularly. Yet as a contractor and bandleader, I ran into big trouble with some black conductors and personal managers of big-name soul stars and even sometimes with the artists themselves because I used mostly black instrumentalists to back them. No matter how well my people played the music, if they were not white or from the small clique of busy black studio musicians, their efforts were in vain.

When popular black singers are riding a crest of popularity, they are in demand at prestigious nightclubs such as the Latin Casino in Cherry Hill, New Jersey, the Coconut Grove in Los Angeles, the Americana Hotel in New York, Las Vegas casinos, or for tours of Europe. At all of these spots, black soul singers are backed by house bands or staff orchestras comprised of highly trained, virtually all-white, classical-type musicians or technicians. Until recently, the same was true of staff orchestras for the television studios, but in recent years there has been a sprinkling of more creative R&B and jazz musicians hired by the television networks. Playing at prestigious nightclubs and on national television shows represents a status situation to young black kids from humble and often impoverished backgrounds, so it is pretty easy for these soul groups to lose touch with their true heritage when suddenly they find themselves in a position of instant stardom. Without sounding trite, they lose sight of their roots. The same applies to most black conductors who travel with them and become accustomed to house band musicians and European symphony musicians backing their singers. Musicians of this type often play R&B or rock music rather blandly and insipidly in spite of their enormous overall ability, so when musicians like the ones I used played the music with guts and gusto, the newly brainwashed conductors rejected the uninhibited flavorful sound of our band. At the pre-engagement rehearsals, the conductors always tested or monitored the reading ability of any group of black players, even when I used musicians of proven ability and stature such as Cat Anderson, Bob Mitchell, Marshall Hunt, Wallace Brodis, Joe Epps, and Bill Carter. Even if our groups didn't always read the backup music as swiftly as classical musicians or studio technicians, they grasped it without much delay, and when they did get the arrangements together, they played them with many times the feeling and power of house-band musicians. I was constantly being prodded by musical directors, conductors, and personal managers to hire whites. I have even been told point-blank by black conductors and black personal managers that they felt more comfortable or safer with white musicians. One of the conductors for the Temptations told me in 1971, and I'm quoting him, "Preston, you're going to blow your thing out here on the Coast if you don't start using more white cats and fewer brothers. I know those brothers can cook when they get the shit together, but I just want the white boys."

In spite of everything, it was pleasurable most of the time when working with some of the soul stars such as Gladys Knight, Marvin Gaye, Stevie Wonder, Isaac Hayes, and others, because some of them had a few good pieces of music and some of the singers were nice people with which to work. Jackie Wilson, the Dells, Aretha Franklin, Marvin Gaye, and Curtis Mayfield were among the most enjoyable to play with, but even the nicest of soul or pop stars are quite different to work with than the jazz and blues greats of the previous era. In 1944, when I was with Lucky Millinder, we played some weeks with the great Billie Holiday and the wonderful T-Bone Walker at the Plantation Club in Watts, California. Every night Billie Holiday complimented our musicians on how well they played her music, saying that it gave her inspiration to sing better. I was only twenty-three years old. She backed up to the band during the show and said in her cool manner, "Junior, you sure are singing back there on that alto." Later in life in my Motown band, I played many dates for the singer and actress who played Billie Holiday in the movie *Lady Sings the Blues* and her group, the Supremes. I put together some of the best bands of my career with players the caliber of Joe Epps, Wallace Brodis, Bill Carter, and Tank Jernigan in my reed section. We had some of the finest sax sections I ever worked with. We received good pay, too, but hardly any compliments or encouragement of the kind the real Billie Holiday gave us.

"Daddy Bones" (T-Bone Walker) was just as complimentary as Miss Holiday, and all of this established a fine rapport between musicians and singers. "Bones" had a beautiful arrangement of a tune called "I'm Still in Love With You," and he often said to me, "Man, when I record this number, I'm going to send and get you to play first sax on it no matter where you are." I'm sorry that the number was recorded without me some years later. It is understandable how today's singers might take musicians for granted, because pop audiences pay very little attention to instrumental music and musicians as compared to their obsession with vocal music. On pop-soul concerts the orchestra isn't usually even accorded the courtesy of playing an opening band tune or overture because soul fans are so anxious and restless in anticipation of the appearance of their vocal stars. Occasionally, if there are a few moments to kill, the orchestra may be permitted to play a short opener or overture. But the band must be careful that they don't play anything that might be construed as jazz, because young soul audiences look upon jazz with scorn and even derision. The only jazz they tolerate is something along the line of Grover Washington or Ronnie Laws, who have had hit recordings that this generation regards as what jazz is all about—a strange turn of events that jazz and blues, the greatest contribution of the Afro-American to the music of the world, have become anathema to millions of young black people while other ethnic groups are embracing and promulgating jazz throughout the world.

There are those today who imply that there is no particular music that can be called black music, but how could anyone listen to any of the Afro-American geniuses of blues, jazz, and rhythm and blues and still hesitate to acknowledge that black music is a very distinct and identifiable entity? Over the past sixty years, other nationalities and races have assimilated and imitated Afro-American music so completely that the average music fan cannot separate the original creators from those who are the imitators. Furthermore, in this day of plastics and synthesis, only a few people are interested in authenticity or quality where music is concerned. Classical musicians and the real devotees of classical and symphonic music have tried zealously to maintain the integrity and quality of their art forms, and I propose that blues and jazz musicians should be as concerned about protecting the sanctity and authenticity of their music. After all, pure jazz and blues are the only serious music that America will be remembered for internationally. Yet I am disappointed in the majority of America's black youth, who are so concerned with the new and current music that they reject or ignore so many of our true giants of blues and jazz, especially when these performers are no longer young and their music no longer brand-new or in vogue. One thing that black audiences used to have, as a whole, was impeccable taste. But now the young black audiences are developing a taste for dross, the same as other audiences. Most young black audiences will accept only what they regard as music of "their generation." I have heard young blacks contemptuously make such statements as, "I can't relate to that," or "Man, that ain't real music," when referring to such black institutions as Lester Young, Coleman Hawkins, Duke Ellington, Sarah Vaughan, Jo Jones, and others. Moments later, they start snapping their fingers and shaking their heads to a poor recording by one of the lesser talented "funk" groups. Of course, I realize that the tastes of all the people of this country have been manipulated by a form of brainwashing on the part of those who control and profit from the music and entertainment business, and the mania for newness and change is an integral part of all merchandising, including the merchandising of music.

Young blacks have embraced numerous players as "jazz" stars who are very little more than rock or rhythm and blues or pop musicians with little or no jazz ability. Take the case of most so-called jazz festivals the past few years. These festivals are nothing more than pop or R&B promotions, since the pop and R&B performers outnumber the jazz stars ten to one on the rosters. It is not my intention to exalt jazz above other music, because I love the better rhythm and blues artists as much as I do jazz performers, but to describe these pop festivals as jazz festivals is to tell a lie. Would you include Duke Ellington or Charlie Parker on the roster of a rock or country-and-western festival? No, because the devotees of these music styles would not hold still for it. The biggest threat to authentic jazz and blues is commercialism, and these pop festivals (so-called jazz festivals) represent commercialism at its worst. The lineups of performers on these promotions are determined by who has had the biggest recent hit recordings and consequently has the biggest drawing power so that the "festivals" will make money.

The term "jazz" becomes more prevalent and permeates the entertainment and news media more with the passing of each day, and as this occurs it also becomes more meaningless and farcical as it is applied in most cases. Every Tom, Dick, and Harry is adopting the term "jazz" as a moniker to describe their performance. Even some who don't have the slightest ability for jazz, or any real conception of it or propensity for playing it are calling themselves jazz musicians. Most musicians now find it expedient and profitable to adopt the term "jazz musician," and they can do so without challenge, because most of the public is completely confused or unknowledgeable about what jazz really is or who really plays it. The public is fed reams of copy by newspaper and magazine columnists, radio announcers, and television people who know as little about jazz as most laymen. These media are guilty of apathy, because they are much more concerned with selling products than they are with disseminating truth and authenticity about jazz and the whole black music genre.

How could anyone who is interested in truth and authenticity associate the music of certain big-name synthetic or quasi-jazz musicians with those of the truly great, creative, black jazz players of history? How could anyone associate the singing of Elvis Presley or certain female rock singers with that of Ray Charles or Aretha Franklin, for example? Without discussing which is better or worse or which any particular individual likes better, I submit that no association can be made between Chick Corea and his highly technical electronic musical gadgetry and the improvisational gems that a Sonny Stitt or a Clark Terry plays. If the music of the Stitts and Terrys is jazz, then the music of the others is not. This might seem to be an oversimplification or evidence of narrowness on my part, but nonetheless I feel strongly about this viewpoint. If the genius of Ray Charles is valid and Aretha Franklin's singing is the wonderful art that I perceive it to be, then Presley's singing and that of the female rock stars are as lacking and horrid as I think they are. I can hardly think of anything less inspiring than Presley's "Love Me Tender," for instance. Individual taste is a delicate area to tread upon, but I can't comprehend how a supposedly informed American public could make stars of performers such as Presley and many other singers and musicians who reap bonanzas as stars in the fields of rock and jazz, or at least in music that is regarded as jazz. But then, I shouldn't protest too loudly, because I have been aware for many years that the music business must not be confused with art in this era. Music is all mixed up with entertainment and showmanship and success. Those who are able to find a gimmick or a novelty and catch the biggest hit recording prevail.

Let's take the case of Grover Washington, the saxophonist, and Herbie Hancock, the keyboard player-composer. Grover is a reasonably fair saxophonist, but he could hardly be compared with the real giants of this era or any in the past. However, he found a formula for popularizing ditties that had been recent vocal hits. Washington does creditable and pleasant saxophone versions of these tunes, which are all quite rhythm and bluesish, not jazz. To many black kids of this era, Grover Washington represents the epitome of saxophone playing, although he falls far short of the true greats of any era. The kids who hail Grover as the king of the saxophone have probably never heard of Johnny Hodges, Lester Young, James Moody, Sonny Stitt, Coleman Hawkins, Ben Webster, Charlie Parker, or even the man whose style most influenced Grover, Hank Crawford.

One day a young woman called me on my radio show and said, "Herbie Hancock's show is the most important music and jazz event to ever come to Omaha." I take into account the young lady's youth and her enthusiasm for Hancock since he is her contemporary and a popular attraction of her generation, but this same young lady would probably never have heard of Herbie Hancock if not for "Chameleon" and his other hit recordings that were more rhythm and blues than jazz. Hancock has great substance as a musician and I like "Chameleon" and some of his other works very much, but it would be heresy to describe him as the most important jazz event in the history of a city that has encountered performances by Duke Ellington, Jimmie Lunceford, Count Basie, Don Redman, Ray Charles, Fletcher Henderson, Charlie Parker, Don Byas, Dizzy Gillespie, Clark Terry, Louis Armstrong, Dicky Wells, J. J. Johnson, Fats Waller, Earl Hines, Lionel Hampton, Earle Warren, Sid Catlett, Jo Jones, Erroll Garner, Oscar Peterson, Lester Young, Jay McShann, Pha Terrell, and nearly every other important figure in music history.

Practically every village high school, junior high, and college has at least one big band that they call a stage band or a jazz band. Many of these young orchestras play excellent ensemble styles after some years of training and constant rehearsals. They have orchestrations by most of the finest arrangers in the country, but to call them jazz bands is a misnomer. In most cases the band instructors are well-trained technicians, but seldom do these musical directors have any conception of improvisational music or ad-lib soloing, which is what jazz is all about. Kids are exposed to jazz in attempts to instruct them to phrase the ensemble like the early Basie and Ellington bands. Rarely do these school "jazz" bands spawn any gifted jazz soloists, so the only recognizable jazz in school stage bands and in workshop bands is a conglomeration of exaggerated brass shakes and other phrasings à la Basie. It is all very synthetic and unspontaneous, because this is the formula approach to jazz.

For the past twenty years or more, formula jazz has been passed off as the real thing. Any player who aspires to be identified as a jazz musician can accomplish it, even if he doesn't have any innate talent for jazz or any creative ability—the essential qualities of a real jazz musician or singer. In this era, after acquiring reasonable technique and by imitating the popular jazz stars, every young musician feels he or she can turn a mental dial and play jazz. Unfortunately, the public doesn't differentiate between quasi-jazz players and those who might be gifted creative giants. Adopting my point of view, however, can get one labeled an anachronism. Most modern jazz has become too mathematical, mechanical, and technical to even be associated with the original intent of jazz. Truly meaningful jazz can only be played by those who possess a natural ear for harmonics, an innate melodic line, inventiveness, and the ability to create improvisations spontaneously. Playing jazz by some formula or preconceived mathematical process defeats its whole purpose and makes it synthetic and spurious.

Probably the only "schooled" musician whom I regard as one of the important forces in jazz is Hubert Laws. Laws reflects an equal degree of formal training and natural ability on his instrument, but the flute is that kind of instrument. It probably requires more formal study than most other instruments used extensively in jazz. I would still rate James Moody as a greater pure jazz player on flute than even Hubert Laws, however. Moody doesn't have as much "legitimate" technique as Laws, but he is a greater source of inventive jazz ideas, and he plays with more of the jazz feeling and the jazz beat. Both Laws and Moody are rather phenomenal flute players, and one might say that comparing them is like comparing apples and oranges. But I think the comparison is relevant, because I wish to stress that a naturally gifted jazz genius like James Moody accomplished his tremendous jazz virtuosity through innate ability and by his own personal devices, whereas Laws accomplished his virtuosity largely through concerted formal studies on the instrument. Some critics, however, have even denigrated Hubert's flute playing so far as it relates to jazz. I could also include trumpet great Wynton Marsalis in much of what I have said here about a "schooled" jazz player.

All of the great musicians who laid the foundation for jazz used jam sessions as their classrooms, which is probably the best way of all for the development of a jazz player. Yet there are so few places left today for meaningful jam sessions anywhere in the country. I remember when I was an aspiring young saxophonist sitting for hours at McGill's Blue Room while the great Charlie Christian, Sir Charles Thompson, Buddy Tate, Money Johnson, Doc Whidby, Debo Mills, and others played and jammed through all the difficult jazz tunes. McGill's was Omaha's jam-session center in that era of the late 1930s, and the many fine jazz musicians of the area probably got more benefit from jam sessions there than modern jazz players get from all the theory and analytical workshops combined. At least it seems so when one considers the difference between the many distinctive and individual jazz players of the past and the plastic, neurotic jazz that often prevails in this era. This is not to say that there aren't some very great jazz players and some fine jazz to be heard occasionally today as in every other era, but today's jazz is so academic in most cases. If not for the arrogance, anger, and cynicism of current jazz, it might even be an improvement over certain jazz of the past in some ways. But any musical movement that rejects charm, warmth, and sincerity cannot improve upon music that once stressed these things. The more computerized jazz becomes, the more I feel we need a better, new word to connote the art form once referred to rather generically as jazz.

In recent years, some of our main-line modern players such as Clark Terry, James Moody, and the late Cannonball Adderly felt compelled to record albums with very advanced harmonic concepts just to prove to restive young musicians and to a segment of the public that they could change with the times. In most cases, proving themselves in this way only destroyed the beauty of the styles these players had evolved and fostered. Clark Terry is one of the most versatile and distinctive trumpet stylists in history. He can rightly be described as wonderful on trumpet or flugelhorn. So why should there be any clamor for him to experiment with something potentially less worthwhile than his own beautiful style? The jazz world should be adult enough to allow all of the significant styles and concepts to coexist side by side and not feel that each concept or style must be wiped out and replaced by a newer one. After all, it is firmly established that players like Terry, Moody, and Adderly are jazz musicians of great stature and without limitations, so changing to something tasteless only proves that they are susceptible to the pressures and to the restlessness that forces them into making concessions to those who clamor for change just for the sake of change. After rising to the challenge and proving that they are virtuosos in any style of jazz, I often notice a tongue-in-cheek attitude in most of these greats toward any concept that is too wide a departure from rationality. Hence, much of today's jazz is insincere even when played by the masters.

Oh, how well I remember when all of the young drummers were belittling the four-beat bass-drum rhythm à la Jo Jones at the time when bebop was becoming the thing. Now we have a generation of young drummers who cannot keep a reasonably good rhythm, so the soloists must stagger and stumble in anticipation of what the clumsy drummers are going to do next as they wonder where the beat will go after each fill or break. No one should ask a drummer to be ancient and old-fashioned, but keeping time on the drums is as essential as playing correct notes on the horns. The rhythm is the catalyst and the inspiration for all good jazz, and to get so hip that you ignore this is to hide your head in the sand. This doesn't mean you should shackle the drummer with straight four-four rhythms and take away the freedom to play fills and embellishments. After all, who originated the fills and bombs that predated the bebop era? Jo Jones. And who was any better at these drum embellishments than Jo Jones? No one. All early Basie records bear proof of this.

I am not opposed to the idea of school jazz. In the mid-seventies grants from the Iowa Arts Council and the National Endowment for the Arts saved my family by funding me to serve as a lecturer and jazz clinician. I also did an occasional jazz residency in Nebraska. The school-jazz program in Iowa was admirable in that most of the schools there were sincerely interested in promulgating jazz. In schools such as Charles City High School and West High School in Waterloo, they had dedicated jazz-band directors, Bob Gower and Jim Young respectively, and their jazz orchestras reflected the dedication of these two men's knowledge. Charles City even had Clark Terry there as a resident jazz clinician twice, and the Charles City High School jazz bands of those years recorded albums of Clark's concert with them in their high-school gym. It might have been coincidental, but I have never heard Clark play any better than he did with the Charles City High School Jazz Band, nor have I heard any high-school jazz orchestra play any better than these kids. It must be remembered that high-school experience constitutes a very early stage of development for any musician, and especially for young kids in the hinterlands to whom jazz is still something exotic and mysterious. It is gratifying to me to see *any* interest in jazz shown by the young people of the country, especially in the Midwest. Yet in schools where the instructors and jazz-band directors are not sincerely dedicated, the so-called jazz programs are farcical. At these schools the jazz-band directors suddenly become very uncomfortable if you mention names like Snooky Young, Al Killian, Willie Smith, Clark Terry, Gene Ammons, Jimmie Lunceford, Fletcher Henderson, Coleman Hawkins, Charlie Parker, and Oscar Pettiford among others, because most of the instructors have often never heard of these jazz giants themselves. They have filled the students' heads with such names as Bix Beiderbecke, Stan Kenton, Maynard Ferguson, Buddy Rich, Chuck Mangione, and others whom I would hesitate to mention in the same breath with the others.

The school music directors also usually feel some discomfort when I set out to explain to their students that jazz phrasing cannot be confused with marching-band or concert-orchestra phrasing. In fact, it must be almost entirely different even if written the same as a marching-band or classical-music figure. It is rather difficult to explain to a group of young students (and even to many teachers) that in the beginning, very few of the nuances and phrasings were written for the great jazz bands of history. The feeling or phrasing of arrangements that they played were usually created spontaneously by the more inventive members of the group, especially by the lead men of each section. The formal arrangements brought to the bands of the real jazz era were usually mere sketches or frameworks conceived by the gifted orchestraters of that day. The phrasing and nuances were left to the discretion of the lead men, who were chosen because they were expected to have the talent and ability to decide the inflections and nuances spontaneously. Today, the orchestraters write every inflection, every staccato, every trill, every trumpet shake, every slur, and every dynamics mark, yet we still call it a "jazz" band. It is painful to have to explain to young players that these phrase marks written by arrangers are intended to imitate figures and dynamics created many years ago by musicians whom their instructors have never heard of, men with the great bands of history such as Wallace Jones, Otto Hardwicke, Sam Nanton, Johnny Hodges, Harry Carney, and Cootie Williams with Duke Ellington; Earle Warren, Dickey Wells, Benny Morton, Ed Durham, Jack Washington, Sweets Edison, and Lester Young with Count Basie; Paul Webster, Willie Smith, Trummy Young, and Joe Thomas with Jimmy Lunceford; John Jackson and Charlie Parker with Jay McShann; and all of the other jazz greats with such leaders as Don Redman, Fletcher Henderson, Earl Hines, and other big bands. Oh, how discomforting it is to stand by and watch a very mechanical band instructor try to explain to a young person how to interpret a set of grace notes or some other phrasing mark originally conceived spontaneously by some great black jazz players of the past to give the music a particular bluesy feeling or jazz inflection.

Overarranging, however, is prevalent at all levels of what is called jazz these days, as orchestraters write every phrase mark or dynamic and permit no latitude for impromptu or spontaneous creativity. In fact, studio playing discourages creativity even more than school bands, but both still call their product "jazz." The ability to read music quickly was once considered incidental in jazz, as it should be, but today a musician is judged more for reading ability than for creativity or improvisational talent. That is why fine technicians such as Doc Severinson have become even more famous than real jazz players. Back in the 1980s, I began to do a week each year in the month of June as one of the clinicians and instructors at a jazz camp held at a college located not too far from Omaha. The camp is attended by several hundred students from high schools and colleges in the general area. The instructors, numbering about twelve people, are mostly high-school and college music directors and heads of the "jazz" program at their schools. Of course, I am the only black person at a *jazz* camp, if one can possibly believe what has happened to black music in this *enlightened* era. *One black person at a* jazz *camp attended by several hundred people.* Before I was enlisted to work at it there had not been even *one* black person involved in any way at the camp.

The man who organized the jazz-camp program is a fine friend of mine going back to the days when he had the music program at an Omaha school, and he and I did an occasional gig together backing shows at the auditorium or Orpheum Theater. The week at the jazz camp at the college paid very well. We had excellent accommodations and plenty of food, and the community was very congenial to us. There were several house parties during the week, and we instructors organized a big band that played concerts at the school and downtown in the city nightly. All and all, it was a fun week. Most of the arrangements we had for the big band were Basie-type orchestrations. They brought in five or six professional musicians from the area who were friends of the camp's organizer. They completed the necessary instrumentation we required for the horn sections. I played first alto sax in the big band, and for all of us the big "Basie" orchestra was one big bash. The solos in the band were sometimes quite laughable, but all of the teachers and the guest professionals were excellent, well-trained musicians, so the ensemble played with precision and good intonation. But it must be remembered, this was supposedly a *jazz* camp, not a school for lessons in how to read music, or even to teach the finer points of intonation and ensemble perfection or precision. The first and foremost duty and purpose of the instructors should have been to bring the students some special insight and instruction in jazz improvisation, interpretation, phrasing, and expression. Aside from lecturing to the students on these aspects of jazz, the teachers should be able to *demonstrate* what they teach with their own instruments. Yet since only a couple of the instructors had the slightest natural ability for solo improvisation, the camp simply became the usual exercise of instructing the kids about reading music, annotated dynamics, and finer dexterity on their respective instruments. This camp, like most "jazz" camps, was nothing more than the usual school assembly-line approach to what they like to refer to as *jazz*. All of the teachers had taken courses in jazz at their respective universities, so naturally they felt that they were qualified to instruct jazz, but they were *not*. This was evidenced clearly by the way all of the young students sounded before and after each of the weeks, as well as by the absurd improvisational solos played by most of the instructors themselves.

Each of us teachers was assigned to conduct several workshops daily and to give private instructions to students on our respective instruments. Each day opened with a lecture or statement by one of us to an assembly of all of the camp's participants in the school's small auditorium. At the 1985 camp, I was assigned to give the lecture for the opening day's assembly. The students and instructors gathered and settled in their seats, and I was introduced by the camp's organizer with a great flourish. He seemed to be giving me preferential treatment as he pointed out that I had worked with many of the great names of jazz, R&B, and blues that they had seen in their jazz books and on the covers of the record albums in his office. He also enumerated the important jazz festivals that I had played in the United States and on my then five tours to Europe, and he listed the five European jazz festivals I would be leaving to play in in only a few days. Of course, I knew the preferential treatment thing wasn't just my imagination. It came from the fact that the organizer wanted to make me stand out since I was the *only* black person at, of all things, a jazz camp. There was, or should have been at least, some guilt in the back of his mind. Here is a "jazz" camp with only *one* black participant and with twelve white instructors, none of whom had any special qualifications for conducting workshops or clinics on jazz. Of course, I don't think they would agree with my assessment, because about four of the instructors are "big news" in the jazz scenes of their hometowns. I wonder if any of these people ever asked themselves, "How would I fare in the company of *world class* jazz players in the big cities, or what *world class* national or international credits do I have, or how big would I be in the jazz of my hometown if I weren't white, if I were a black musician and not wired into the 'politics' of my town's so-called jazz scene?"

My opening statement after the introduction was, "No one can *teach* anyone to play jazz." The students appeared to be confused and the group of teachers (clinicians) stiffened a bit. I then went on and explained that jazz is a personal expression that must spring from each individual's psyche and that it must be spontaneous. A teacher can teach an individual things to help them execute their ideas and improvisations—things such as chords, harmonics, and so on—but the individual can only play jazz as well as his or her personal talent or gift for it will permit. A teacher can help the student with technique and facility on their instruments, but even with all of these, it doesn't insure that a person will ever be able to play jazz expertly if they don't have the natural gift for it. I then said, "Jazz is unequivocally black music or black art. Others have adopted it, imitated it, and assimilated it in recent eras, but it was once considered almost exclusively black music. To answer the question no doubt in your mind, yes, there have been several great jazz players who were white." The instructors began to squirm and look around at each other. I then went on to list the great black players of each instrument who innovated and developed the various styles of jazz in each era since the early 1900s. I was kind enough to name some of the white players who became quite prominent in jazz by imitating this sax player or that trumpet or trombone player and so on. When I got to the big bands of jazz, most of my discussion was about Ellington, Basie, Jimmie Lunceford, Fletcher Henderson, Earl Hines, Don Redman, Jay McShann, Benny Moten, McKinney's Cotton Pickers, and Dizzy Gillespie's bebop-styled big band. I opined that Woody Herman, Benny Goodman, Artie Shaw, and some others had excellent swing bands, but I felt that Stan Kenton had the most significant of the white bands so far as the term "jazz" was concerned.

That was the very last speech or workshop I was assigned to give in 1985. I was scheduled to give individual instructions to several young woodwind players but nothing more except for the usual opening speech at the 1986 camp, since there is a new crop of students each year. Of course, I had the same truisms to say that year as on previous years. Since the camp administrators politely avoided having me do any clinics or workshops with the several big bands comprised of students, I sat around most of each day in one of the offices or back rooms listening to the high-school and college music directors coach the kids through Sam Nestico and others' arrangements of Basie's "One O'Clock Jump," "Jumpin' at the Woodside," Ellington's "Satin Doll" and "Take the 'A' Train," and so forth. The kids always sounded like high-school marching bands or concert bands trying to play these jazz tunes. The terms we always used for their conception of jazz were corny, ricky ticky——ta-ta-ta-ta. When the instructors would pick up their instruments to correct the students, the teachers in most cases showed as little conception of jazz as the students. It was sometimes laughable that these poor young people thought that they were getting an education in jazz. Here I was, sitting in a back room drinking coffee and reading newspapers and magazines all day, listening to· them learn "One O'clock Jump," "Jumpin' at the Woodside," and many of the other Basie things that I had played thousands of times with the original Basie band members. In fact, I played lead alto and Earle Warren's original "Woodside" solo on two later air-check recordings of Basie's band. When we played theaters, nightclubs with radio broadcasts, and so on, we would sometimes play "One O'Clock Jump" as many as twelve times in one day. Yet there I was, sitting in the back room at a "jazz camp" drinking coffee while several groups of white kids butchered these tunes in the rehearsal rooms and down on the stage of the auditorium, and never once did one of the teachers ask me to help the kids with conception, styling, or phrasing.

These are some of the reasons why I say that school jazz is mostly farcical. Except for a few of the big universities where they have great jazz players such as Kenny Barron and Larry Ridley as teachers, the school jazz concept is more harmful than it is instructive. School administrators aren't aware that a degree in music doesn't have anything whatsoever to do with making someone a jazz person. To a large extent, school jazz is fostering a total misconception of jazz. Teachers would do well to first tell their students that not everyone should play jazz. Lester Young, Jack Washington, Herschel Evans, Walter Page, Ed Lewis, Jo Jones, and Basie would have turned over in their graves if they had heard the kids and teachers messing up "Woodside," "One O'Clock Jump," and other classics. I'm sure Duke Ellington, Johnny Hodges, and Harry Carney would have rested uneasily in their graves, too, hearing the ersatz "Satin Doll" and "Take the 'A' Train" that these school musicians stumbled through while calling it *jazz*.

I once lectured to a class of approximately thirty young black children in a Waterloo, Iowa, high school, and not one of them had ever heard of Count Basie, Earl Hines, Charlie Parker, Jimmy Smith, Sarah Vaughan, or Billy Eckstine. This was a *black history* class! The young black instructor had informed the class about McCoy Tyner and some more contemporary jazz figures that he knew, but none of the students displayed much interest in the newer or older names of jazz. I was, however, agreeably surprised that one young student's parents had done their homework and had tried to make her aware of some of our great musicians like Duke Ellington.

The only reason I have any credibility and acceptability to young black audiences at schools is that I have worked with pop and R&B stars including Bobby Womack, Gladys Knight, Stevie Wonder, Marvin Gaye,

Smokey Robinson, the Temptations, Aretha Franklin, and Isaac Hayes. Otherwise, these young people would not accept my protests about their lack of knowledge about our musical past. I am always careful to take along pictures of myself with Aretha or Isaac Hayes or some other popular artist, because I have had young audiences almost demand proof from me that I have worked with "their" stars before they will listen to me. For the ones that I do not have pictures of, I am careful to take along signed contracts such as the one between myself and the Supremes, but sometimes even a contract is insufficient to quell the hostility from young audiences toward "this old man" coming in and telling them that jazz is American's greatest indigenous art form, or that some old man named Duke Ellington is America's greatest musician and composer. The young white students in each town politely tolerate this old man telling them that neither Elvis Presley nor Bill Haley created the music they know as rock and roll or rhythm and blues. They are convinced that I am prematurely senile when I say that Afro-Americans originated the blues, rhythm and blues, rock and roll, and jazz, and that blacks have been the greatest performers of this music throughout the century. How could some old "Negro" of the past named Duke Ellington have been greater than the Beatles, when their teachers have told them that the Beatles, Burt Bacharach, and Jimmy Webb were the best composers? In fact, many of the students I have encountered thought that the Beatles invented rock and roll and that Sonny and Cher invented rhythm and blues. How tedious it must become to have someone enumerate the contributions of blacks to American music and the impact of black music upon the music of the world when the listener or reader is intent upon giving the credit to someone else. But I am not motivated by narcissism. My motivation is truth.

Since the end of the 1950s, there has been a tendency to mistake musical competence for jazz ability and to confuse studiousness with the natural talent and creativity one needs to be a good improvisational musician. All the competence and training in the world cannot give a player that very special and unique thing that great jazz players possess and manifest from the very first day they begin to start playing an installment. Good jazz composers and arrangers also will usually evince that natural gift quite early in their experience. A large percentage of the best arrangers had no formal training whatsoever, yet some of these writers are responsible for the most startling of all jazz orchestrations and compositions.

The jazz solos of the truly great players would be considered simplistic by many of today's scholarly musicians, but those uncomplicated and un-pretentious solos of the jazz giants had much more meaning and purpose than the desultory solos played by many of the spurious jazz players from the jazz programs of colleges and conservatories. Undoubtedly, some formal scholastic training is helpful in today's age of technology, especially to orchestraters, but no amount of academic training can give a person a unique individual style or give them the genius of a Duke Ellington, for instance. As for the jazz instrumentalist, the scholastic approach can only give them good technical training, which I feel has no particular value in creative-expressive jazz improvisation. Let's take the piano playing of Count Basie, for instance. There was always the notion that Basie was a "one-handed" piano player with big limitations. Leonard Feather even absurdly referred to Basie as, "a capable soloist who once played good stride piano." He described Basie's piano playing as "elliptical." On the contrary, Count Basie sometimes showed amazing natural technique on his early recordings and showed enormous versatility as a pianist. While the scholars and technicians were always busy trying to put down Basie's piano playing, whenever one of them tried to duplicate or copy a Basie solo or his style, they showed how deficient they were at capturing the nuances and even the technique. The playing of even some very fine pianists became rather grotesque when they tried to capture that special Basie touch. Players like Charlie Parker and John Coltrane had very limited formal training, yet all the methodical jazz scholars will be trying for another century to emulate the dazzling technique and creative genius of such players. The so-called jazz classes at colleges today place too much emphasis upon numbers and the harmonics aspect of jazz. Therefore, most of the soloists sound like automatons. They are "mechanics," not improvisers.

Recently, an aspiring pianist in Omaha said to me that a certain internationally recognized jazz saxophonist "plays tastily, but he can't go through the changes." By this, the young would-be jazz pianist meant that the sax player had some deficiency when it came to playing the chord changes while soloing. Chord changes are an important and essential aspect of jazz improvising, but not *all* of it. Those who place too much emphasis upon the chords aspect of improvising usually sound quite mechanical and mathematical. They sound like a student practicing exercises from a method book. The sax player he was criticizing must have had a sufficient knowledge and conception of chord changes, or else how could he play "tastily"? In order to improvise meaningfully at all, you must at least play correctly, and this would require that you play the right chord changes, though not necessarily elaborate and pretentious ones. Jazz soloing should be a balanced combination of "painting a picture," "story telling," and "saying something" with expression and imagination and colorfulness. If a player doesn't have a good ear for melody and harmonics, knowing all the chord changes in the world will not help him play meaningful improvisation.

This was often said by many of the great giants of jazz history such as Coleman Hawkins, Dizzy Gillespie, Louis Armstrong, and Lester Young. Since chords are an important foundation of jazz solos, the player should have a basic and sound knowledge of chords and harmonics, but these should be filed away in the background of the player's mind and only referred to rather unconsciously as the solo or story unfolds. The indispensable thing in jazz is the natural gift for using the chord changes to tell your story and paint your picture. This is substantiated by the fact that many of the great jazz soloists had a limited academic knowledge of chords and harmonics.

While most young jazz players (and some older ones) are so concerned with what's new, modern, or hip, they miss the whole point of what creative improvisation is all about. No matter how many changes come about in music, certain things will endure and retain their validity. A solo by Lester Young, Charlie Parker, or Earl Hines will have value and validity ten eons from now. The same can be said of jazz performances by thousands of other great black creative geniuses. Some of those who put down these jazz greats as antiques or relics don't realize that they themselves have been directly or indirectly influenced by the same artists who they are trying to relegate to the past. How many thousands of new players in each generation have been influenced by or have directly copied the styles of Coleman Hawkins, Lester Young, Buck Clayton, Harry Edison, Jo Jones, and so on without being fully aware of the original? After all, there are only twelve notes in the entire musical scale, so there isn't room for a brand-new refurbishing or overhaul of music every few months, as many young people clamor for, without getting into gimmicks and commercial "bubblegum." This has happened in the pop field to appease the insatiable appetite of the commercial world for change and something new every few weeks. The clamor for change, good or bad, has opened the door for hundreds of completely untalented people to become stars in the music business and show business, jazz included. The worst tragedy in this is that many very talented people in the field are lumped together and equated with the untalented. In so many cases the completely untalented even prevail. Through promotion, press agentry, and manipulation of public taste, America has become a musical disaster area. If you disagree, then search your radio dial from end to end daily and try to find some decent music to listen to. I'm not referring just to jazz. Except in a few of the bigger cities such as Pittsburgh, Detroit, Chicago, and Los Angeles, it is as hard to find an artistic recording outside of the classical field as it is to receive free money from banks. Even in cities where there is some good music available, it is a rank minority as compared to the musical slop played on nearly every radio station. There are a few FM stations struggling to reverse this disaster, but they seem to be fighting a losing battle. The cabal of avaricious entrepreneurs, greedy and apathetic recording companies, disc jockeys, and columnists without music appreciation or knowledge have destroyed public taste to the point where it would require a whole reverse-brainwashing technique to educate the gullible consumers of the American music product.

If my anger seems excessive, consider that Elvis Presley became the biggest star in the history of show business and was referred to as the king of rock and roll while many thousands of great Afro-American folksingers and musicians with thousands of times more talent than Presley wallowed in comparative obscurity. Millions of white Americans accepted Paul Whiteman's title "The King of Jazz" without question while real jazz bands such as those of Duke Ellington, Fletcher Henderson, Claude Hopkins, Benny Moten, and Don Redman were sometimes actually struggling for recognition and survival. In the thirties and forties, America hailed Benny Goodman as the "King of Swing" while such great swing bands as Count Basie, Earl Hines, Horace Henderson, and Jay McShann existed. The *only* king of swing in the swing era was Count Basie, and after Basie there were at least fifty black orchestras that outswung Goodman by many leagues. But who ever questions fame and success? On the subject of Goodman, I never regarded his clarinet playing as creative, inspired, or great jazz at all. He is probably one of the finest technicians ever on the instrument, but his solos were always very mechanical and empty to me from a jazz standpoint. He never told a story or played inventive chord improvisations, which are essential in jazz. Lester "Prez" Young was hardly considered a clarinet player of stature by most fans, but from the standpoint of real jazz and as a fountain of ideas and imagination, Prez said more in his clarinet solos on Basie's "Blue and Sentimental" and "Texas Shuffle" than Goodman, Artie Shaw, and Woody Herman said on all of their many clarinet solos combined.

To demonstrate how even musicians whom we would expect to be knowledgeable get technique confused with innate inventiveness and creativity, I recall an incident that occurred some years ago when I was playing with Lucky Millinder. I overheard a conversation between trumpet player Joe Ludwig Jordan and several other members of the band. They were discussing how Harry James had come down to Minton's, the jam session center of Harlem, when James was playing lead trumpet with Goodman. According to Jordan and the others, at Minton's Harry James had torn into such great trumpet soloists as Roy Eldridge, Charlie Shavers, and Dizzy Gillespie. Sure, the crowd responded to a young white boy coming to Harlem and challenging black jazz greats, and along with his admiration for James, Joe Jordan was probably swayed by all this. Since I always regarded Harry James and Charlie Barnett as two of the worst instrumentalists ever to become famous as so-called jazz players, I could hardly believe my ears that a group of black musicians, supposedly in the know, could compare Harry James to the great jazz soloists of that time. Therefore I interjected, "What do you fellows think about Buck Clayton and Sweets Edison?" You would have thought I mentioned two lepers or Ku Kluxers. Jordan said, "Man, we are talking about *real* trumpet players. Don't bring up those lightweights when you're talking about trumpet men like Harry James." Let me be fair to Harry James. He is one of the finest lead trumpet men ever. When he leads a section, it has a brilliant and precise sound. But as a jazz soloist, he became ridiculous. I often referred to him and Charlie Barnett, the alto sax player, as playing spaghetti because their solos were just as conglomerate as a pot of boiled spaghetti. In contrast, Harry "Sweets" Edison is one of the most clever and tasty jazz stylists in trumpet history, and Buck Clayton was without equal for playing the perfect-fitting solo to fit any orchestration. Sweets always played with humor and levity, while Buck always played with that sweet and plaintive feeling, no matter how slow or fast the arrangement. Buck was also a master of blues solos. In light of this, it is hard for me to believe that anyone, especially another trumpet player, and a black one at that, would regard Sweets and Buck as "lightweights," especially in comparison to Harry James! Of course, neither Sweets nor Buck could challenge Harry James for technical virtuosity.

Further evidence that technique and precision are almost incidental to great jazz performance is the case of Frank Sleet. In the early 1950s, Jimmy Witherspoon recorded a blues classic "'Taint Nobody's Business." This tune is set to eight-bar minor-mode blues chords. There is a two-chorus alto sax solo on side two of this recording that ranks with the finest instrumental blues solos in history. The soloist, Frank Sleet, touches all the bases with timely and well-placed blue notes while telling a meaningful story. According to my information, Sleet had been playing sax only a matter of months and was so diffident that he was very hesitant to even play a solo on the session. I have heard the best that all of our famous alto sax men and technicians have played, but none of these could have played a more fitting solo than Frank Sleet. There is certainly nothing sacred about technique and analytical powers where authentic jazz is concerned. Although Charlie Parker was possibly the greatest jazz virtuoso in history, one negative by-product of his era is that, through technical wizardry and mathematical analysis, thousands of instrumentalists without any real innate talent have been able to pass as important jazz players by copying Parker's style but not his subtleties.

I have been accused of being racist, which is far from the truth. It's just that it is so highly unlikely that a white person, a Chinese person, or even an indigenous African who spent his life in Africa could successfully imitate indigenous black American music and capture its quintessence and purest aura. This is not to say that I don't like such players as Davey Tough, Bunny Berrigan, Mezz Mezzrow, Stan Getz, and singer Mildred Bailey. I like these artists and other nonblacks very much, but their music doesn't have the same subtleties nor the warmth of Jo Jones, Louis Armstrong, or Billie Holiday when they play or sing jazz. With all of my obsession for Earle Warren's lead and my tremendous appreciation for Willie Smith's lead, I still fully appreciate and highly rate white lead alto sax men such as Milt Yaner and Hymie Schertzer where jazz or blues is concerned. Men such as Warren and Willie Smith simply were more creative and adept and entirely different from Yaner and Schertzer. The gifts that Earle Warren, Willie Smith, and lead players such as Hilton Jefferson and Otto Hardwicke possessed are unique and novel and can't be imitated or emulated.

The big four of big-band history, the nonpareils without a doubt, are Duke Ellington, Count Basie, Jimmie Lunceford, and Fletcher Henderson during the years that their bands retained most of their original key members. The personnel of these bands at one time or another comprised the who's who of jazz greats, and nearly every other important jazz band was influenced to some degree by the styles of these big four. There were many other important big bands of jazz history, and I was fortunate to have heard all of these in person: Earl Hines, Andy Kirk, Buddy Johnson, Don Redman, Claude Hopkins, Chick Webb, Jay McShann, Erskine Hawkins, Lucky Millinder, Cab Calloway, Benny Moten, Dizzy Gillespie, Billy Eckstine, Ray Charles, Cootie Williams, Les Hite. There were a number of semi-name bands who at times had excellent personnel, and I had the good fortune of hearing these: Floyd Ray, Don Albert, Snookum Russell, King Kolax, Eli Rice, Thamon Hayes, Harlan Leonard, George E. Lee, the Sunset Royals, Nat Towles, Lloyd Hunter, Milton Larkin, the Johnny Otis big band of 1946–1947, and the Ernie Fields band of Tulsa.

Whatever these black orchestras lacked in precision and technical perfection, they more than compensated in originality, creativity, spontaneity, and raw provocativeness. White orchestras have tried to duplicate the excitement of black brass sections for many years without success, and black rhythm sections have always been known for their inspiration to the other instrumentalists and the audiences. All reed sections in the Afro-American bands of the big-band era had that moaning quality, even when they played faster tempos. Even Basie's reed section had this mournful quality in spite of Earle Warren's crystal-clear sound and bright attack. White bands such as Stan Kenton's attempted to imitate this sound of black reed sections, but at best only accomplished a synthetic imitation of it. It was probably the blues influence that inspired black reed men to that moaning quality. Unfortunately, recent black orchestras have lost sight of their tradition and have become as synthetic and technique conscious as the white bands. There are really no young black musicians left to perpetuate the tradition of Ellington, Basie, and the other great orchestras of the past, because the young musicians hardly ever understand or appreciate the greatness of their predecessors. The tragedy is that the music business is in the hands of arrogant people who often are without talent and who have no interest whatsoever in quality or in black music as an art form.

During my youth, I often wondered how the music magazines could deem Toots Mondello to be king of the alto sax, Gene Krupa to be king of the drums, Bud Freeman to be king of the tenor sax, Jess Stacy to be king of the piano, and so on. On each instrument, a white musician was named the king when there were countless black stars and even unknown black players who could play each instrument hundreds of times better than those whites. Even the white poll winners conceded as much to Lester Young, Jo Jones, Duke Ellington, Count Basie, Jimmy Blanton, Walter Page, Charlie Christian, Johnny Hodges, Dicky Wells, and others in their conversations with many people. Then it dawned on me that these magazines were nothing more than commercial periodicals and not the least bit interested in being factual or educational. But I still continued to be disappointed when their big-name columnists wrote long, flattering articles describing the greatness of some inept white players or arguing on behalf of the popular white bands as if they actually played jazz. Most of the columnists and writers for these magazines became big names as jazz authorities or the "voices of jazz" by giving the gullible public what they wanted or by playing it safe by saying unduly laudatory things that were far from true about the popular bands of that day such as those led by Tommy Dorsey, Glenn Miller, Benny Goodman, or Charlie Barnett.

Most of these so-called critics or jazz authorities would say or write anything to enrich themselves or to perpetuate their own positions as music or jazz authorities. They were guilty of one of the most heinous forms of assassination when they failed to give the great black geniuses their due recognition while eulogizing people who were in many cases totally without talent or redeeming qualities as jazz players. Yet another group of jazz historians are totally incorruptible and their lives have been dedicated totally to the study of the great black creative geniuses and to doing what they can to never let the names and history of these geniuses pass away completely from public consciousness. The most notable of these are Stanley Dance, Frank Driggs, John Miner, Harry Lim, and possibly Nat Hentoff. In Europe, there are the late Felix Steinman, Johnny Simmen, Felix Prochaska, Kurt Mohr, Norbert Hess, Tony Collins, and Hugues Panassie. These people have committed all of their energies and resources to the study of the great blues, jazz, and rhythm and blues giants of history. They would not compromise the truth about the art forms they evaluate for any price or personal considerations. Through their books and articles about great men such as Earl Hines, T-Bone Walker, Duke Ellington, and Dicky Wells, these jazz historians refuse to let America's truly great musicians and singers pass into complete obscurity. Frank Driggs alone has produced historical albums on Earl Hines, Duke Ellington, Billie Holiday, Fletcher Henderson, Ethel Waters, and Jimmie Lunceford, among others. Of course, these historians have sometimes been able to enrich themselves through their writings and record releases, but they have done so with tremendous expenditures of time and effort while doing a service to truth and justice as their main motivation. In no cases have the people I mentioned ground their own personal axes, as have most of the other self-styled jazz critics or authorities. A Stanley Dance or Frank Driggs would not corrupt the truth about jazz to benefit their best friend nor to harm their worst enemy. Their knowledge of and insight into black music and the black musician is incredible and especially inspiring to one like myself who despises all the injustice and corruption that is practiced for commercial gain.

To me, America's greatest indigenous art form is the blues, because that music represents the true expression of black American life, or at least it did before it became a commercial commodity exploited by certain parasites. Crass commercialism has reigned in the music field since the blues became known in the trades as rhythm and blues, but even in spite of this, a handful of wonderful black folksingers were able to retain some measure of authenticity with artistic blues. Among these are Joe Turner, T-Bone Walker, Jimmy Rushing, Memphis Slim, B. B. King, Aretha Franklin, Sonny Boy Williamson, Lulu Reed, Otis Redding, Arthur Crudup, Jimmy Witherspoon, Willie Mae Thornton, Charles Brown, and Ray Charles. There were hundreds of others who became known as "blues" singers with contrived quasi-blues that often became popular in spite of its worthlessness. Even a number of white kids became known as blues or rhythm and blues "artists" without the slightest talent for it. As the blues evolved into something called rhythm and blues, it became less and less artistic and was generally dominated by a procession of one-dimensional R&B stars, both vocal and instrumental. There were notable exceptions, of course, in the field. Some of the R&B greats such as Ray Charles, Stevie Wonder, Louis Jordan, Aretha Franklin, and others deserved everything they received in the way of acclaim and financial rewards.

In the earlier days of rhythm and blues during the forties and fifties, the performances of the individual singers, vocal groups, and R&B instrumentalists were usually sincere, creative, and honest. Many of the artists were gifted and innovative. By the mid-sixties, however, the R&B performers of worth had become greatly outnumbered by the one-dimensional arrogant pretenders in the field who were able to convince millions of young people that the tripe they produced had value. The trade papers began to label or categorize all black pop or R&B as "soul." Since this didn't include great, institutional Afro-American jazz giants such as Ellington, Dinah Washington, Sarah Vaughan, Sonny Stitt, James Moody, and many blues giants because of their age and the style of their music, so-called "soul" eliminated some of the greatest of Americans with real soul and included only the R&B performers of the moment, whether they had any substance or not. How unfair to categorize versatile singers such as Gladys Knight and Marvin Gaye as "soul" singers when their ability transcends all labels.

When Afro-Americans first conceived and innovated the music known as blues, inherent in this beautiful expression was an elusive and indefinable thing referred to as "the blue note." To me there is no real jazz or blues, old-fashioned or modern, if the instrumentalist doesn't capture that blue note. This requires a particular natural talent. That is why such as Benny Goodman, Harry James, Woody Herman, and so many others never played meaningful jazz or blues as compared to the better black jazz and blues players. Their playing has always demonstrated that the blue note can't be captured synthetically or through mathematics and analysis. When a player is fumbling around and striving hard to catch that blue note, it becomes discomforting and embarrassing. Technique and virtuosity *cannot* help a player capture that elusive blue note. The blue note may be a nebulous shadow, but it is so distinct and rewarding to the ear when a person has the faculty for playing it. Even many famous black jazz players have been less adept at finding that blue note than thousands of other black instrumentalists, some of whom failed to become well known or successful commercially. There was a time when nearly every locality was inhabited by African Americans who could conceive that "bluesy" feeling through jazz or blues.

In his book *Guide to Jazz*, Hugues Panassie referred to me as playing "good blues." I wish this was true, but it is far from an accurate description of my ability. I would give almost anything to be able to play blues and catch that blue note like Frank Sleet or Eddie "Cleanhead" Vinson on the alto sax, but I certainly don't possess that faculty to any large extent. Instrumental blues and rhythm and blues are the most difficult, because they require the purest essence of Afro-American feeling. Even many outstanding jazz virtuosos don't play the simple blues very well, because such things as technique and virtuosity have no special value in the blues. When I was with Basie, Jimmy Rushing, Ed Lewis, Freddie Green, Jack Washington, and several of the original Basie members often told a story about Woody Herman's band. In 1936 and 1937 when Basie's band first went east and was becoming a big-name band, they played several extended stints at the Roseland Ballroom in New York. Black orchestras of that era, especially Basie and the Kansas City bands, were adept at constructing head arrangements to the twelve-bar blues chord changes. These blues arrangements constituted a large percentage of Basie's repertoire. Some of the most delectable swing and jazz ever conceived were the blues arrangements (both head and written) of the early Basie bands. They were uncomplicated and allowed enough freedom for the exquisite solos of Basie sidemen such as Lester Young, Jack Washington, Buck Clayton, and Dicky Wells. One of Woody Herman's first bands was on the bill as the alternating band with Basie's at the Roseland in 1937. On their intermissions, the Woody Herman personnel stood transfixed before the scintillating Kansas City sound of the new Basie phenomenon. Instrumental blues was relatively new, so the Herman personnel couldn't quite fathom the structure of the many great Basie arrangements, ad-lib solos, and tunes with blues chord changes. Jimmy Rushing often told me that fellows from Herman's band approached him and other Basie members and asked them, "What is that you fellows are playing? It doesn't have a bridge or channel [middle part] or a thirty-two bar chorus or a particular form or structure." The Basie men would tell the Herman personnel, "Man, it is the *blues*, the twelve-bar blues." This confused the young white musicians with Woody Herman, because they said they thought "blues" meant vocals or songs with words sung by blues singers. Herman's arrangers began to stand around when Basie's band was on the stand and analyze the Basie instrumental blues numbers, which amused the Basie band personnel. A short time after the Roseland engagement, Woody Herman caught a big hit recording on a tune called "The Woodchoppers' Ball," which was a tasteless and very corny mishmash of ticky riffs and mechanical solos done in the framework of the twelve-bar blues changes. Soon Woody Herman adopted the moniker, "The Band That Plays the Blues." A short time later, the Herman band caught another big hit called "Blues on Parade," which also had a twelve-bar blues structure. "Blues on Parade" was even less bluesy and worse than "The Woodchoppers' Ball," but the public accepted Woody

Herman's band as a blues band, while any black territory band or non-name black orchestra could have played the blues thousands of times better and more authentically than Herman's band.

In 1943, Johnny Otis and I used to listen daily to a so-called jazz show from the radio station at Iowa State University in Ames, Iowa. Ames is 165 miles from Omaha, but the program came in clearly. The young disc jockey used Herman's "Blues on Parade" as the program's theme, and most of his selections were by bands like the Dorseys, Glenn Miller, Goodman, and the other white dance bands, but it was still called a jazz show. He played an occasional recording by Ellington, Lunceford, Basie, or one of the great black jazz orchestras, so we still tuned in and waited hungrily for a record by one of the black bands, especially because the five or six Omaha radio stations played even fewer recordings by black orchestras than the cornball program at the Iowa State station. Johnny and I finally wrote the young disc jockey at Ames and explained to him that the Bob Crosbys and Tommy Dorseys didn't compare to Ellington or Jay McShann for playing real jazz. We also expressed the opinion that Herman's "Blues on Parade" was a horrid piece of music to use to introduce a "jazz" show. The young deejay answered our letter, "I don't see anything wrong with "Blues on Parade" and after all, I do play at least *one* recording by a Negro orchestra every day." Woody Herman has had some powerful and exciting bands during the span of his career as an orchestra leader—the years when he featured trumpet player and arranger Neal Hefti (who was also from Omaha) were great for Woody Herman's band—but the bands that made "The Woodchoppers' Ball" and "Blues on Parade" were not among them. None of his bands, however, were *blues* bands.

America erects monuments to its noted statesmen, politicians, scientists, and even its famous sports figures. Some of those so honored aren't really great people. Some of the greatest individuals in American history have been black musicians and singers of jazz and blues. These are people who will be venerated throughout the universe by all nationalities, but often their deaths only rate a few lines in American newspapers or a few moments on television networks, while the deaths of Elvis Presley and John Lennon generated the biggest news of recent times. I have yet to learn of an obelisk or monument erected to one of our jazz or blues giants. I propose that America has it priorities confused, that it fails to recognize the greatness of black geniuses. It might also be that black genius in the area of creative art is taken for granted in a country where blacks were so recently enslaved. If we were to honor individuals for real greatness, America would look like a porcupine with obelisks erected to commemorate such great people as Duke Ellington and countless other black artistic giants. It is no mere coincidence that a large percentage of Afro-American musical geniuses came from the southern states, where nearly every town has monuments to General Lee, Jefferson Davis, and other Confederate soldiers and statesmen. I submit that it would be equally appropriate that Cheraw, South Carolina, have obelisks erected to John Birks "Dizzy" Gillespie and that Woodville, Mississippi, have monuments to Lester Young, their greatest contributions to posterity. There are hundreds of other such cases that I could mention: Washington, D.C., Red Bank, New Jersey, and Kansas City should be scarcely navigable with all the obelisks and shrines to Duke Ellington, Count Basie, and Charlie Parker.

In 1977, I watched with deep sadness as they demolished a building at Twenty-fourth and Franklin streets in Omaha that I passed daily en route to my job. This was the old Club Egypt, which was the first beer tavern in Omaha's black community when Prohibition was repealed in 1933. Jo Jones said he played in this club in 1934 and 1935 with a trio for a dollar and a half a night, tips, and "all of the beer he could drink." Shortly after that, he went to Kansas City where he joined Count Basie and revolutionized the popular style of drums on his way to becoming the greatest drummer in history. This dilapidated building at Twenty-fourth and Franklin should have been restored and maintained as a shrine to this great man, but it was instead obliterated. At the same time, across town, they were dedicating a multimillion-dollar monument on the site of the birthplace of former president, Gerald Ford, a clear case of mistaken priorities. I don't feel that the city of St. Joseph, Missouri, has any celebration more appropriate than an annual Coleman Hawkins Day would be. However, I doubt if St. Joe's city fathers would ever implement such a proposal to so honor a native son who was the father of tenor-saxophone jazz and maybe the greatest tenor saxophonist in history.

What hope is there for the future? I'm not very hopeful. I might be described as defeatist or a pessimist. The little deferential fan and idol worshiper who used to hang around the periphery of musicians and singers has suddenly become the record producer, the recording company executive, the promoter, the newspaper and magazine columnist, the television-show producer and director, and the "hip" disc jockey who decides which recordings will be aired on radio stations where he has become a local celebrity or star. These punks are mercenary, cynical, contemptuous of talent, arrogant, and very jealous of the stars and talented performers. They regard the buying public and fans as stupid, which isn't too far from fact in many cases, because this is the same public that gives these entrepreneurs their success story or "track record" of recording hits and successful television shows and sold-out promotions that feature bad music, bad performers, and entertainment that has no artistic value. In today's music business, very few entrepreneurs are interested in art or quality. They want dollars and a track record of producing a popular product no matter how poor the product is.

If there is any hope for the future of American music and show business, it lies in the hands of a few sincere and incorruptible individuals, some of whom I have mentioned earlier. But I am not hopeful. Middle-aged people are now dropping off their ten- and eleven-year-olds at rock concerts to hear groups of hirsute maniacs who don't have a thimble full of talent. Now a whole new generation of American youth has been polluted with garbage while making hundreds of undeserving people rich and famous. Furthermore, the music scene will continue to deteriorate and suffer so long as predatory purveyors of music control the business. These predatory animals should be driven from the business that they have destroyed artistically and raped to enrich themselves without conscience or remorse.

Take the case of Johnny Creach, the late violinist who was known as "Papa John." When we first moved to Los Angeles in 1962, I played first sax with a fine local rehearsal band in Los Angeles led by Buddy Hiles, who was a nephew of Horace and Fletcher Henderson. Buddy (Fletcher) Hiles had once played alto and baritone saxes with Earl Hines when he lived back in Chicago. He had a large repertoire of fine big-band arrangements, some of which he had written himself. After I had been with the band a few months, a violinist began to come to our rehearsals. He played through an amplifier, and I was thrilled by his beautiful solos on ballads such as "Summertime" and "Danny Boy." He appeared to be much older than his actual age because of an arthritic condition and his graying hair. Johnny Creach didn't play up-tempo jazz or blues very well, but his ballads were beautiful. He played melody excellently. After struggling around Los Angeles and getting whatever work he could, somehow, in about 1970, Johnny became friends with the members of a rock group, and they took him in as part of their organization. The group was very popular with young rock fans, and consequently he had access to big money. They took Johnny Creach on the road with them, used him on their albums, and used part of their recording budget to produce albums for Johnny under his own name, but they dubbed him "Papa" John Creach, a name no less degrading than if they had called him "Uncle" John Creach. The Papa John moniker was little more than something to identify him as a mascot or a granddaddy figure of these young rock bleaters. If this man was an artist, why couldn't he be known simply as Johnny Creach?

All of Johnny's friends were nevertheless happy for the sudden upswing in his fortunes as Johnny became fairly well known nationally and began to realize some good income. But we still chafed a little at the "Papa" nickname which young whites embraced readily. Every time one of us thought of "Papa John" with the young white rock band, we could envision "Uncle John." After appearing with the band for a year or so, Johnny Creach began to record with his own group and went on the road with it. This group was made up entirely of young rock musicians who dressed, played, and looked every bit as bad as most rock bands. Johnny Creach was as out of place with them as they were with him, but the package toured and had some successes. Johnny Creach could not play rock or rhythm and blues even creditably, and his young little band couldn't play a ballad melody meaningfully if their lives depended upon it, so they were mixing oil and water, but at least some segment of the music fandom was accepting it. I don't blame Johnny Creach, because any of us musicians would probably do the same if necessary, if we had a "lick" going for us to make some money. I blame the music trade and its consumers who force our artists to prostitute themselves and their art in order to receive any recognition and in order to earn a few dollars.

Take the case of Jimmy Smith, the organist. There have been many great organists, including Fats Waller, Count Basie, Wild Bill Davis, Milt Buckner and so on, but hardly any as fantastic as Jimmy Smith. Why should a genius like Smith have had to run a small club in Pacoima (a suburb of Los Angeles) and work in the kitchen of his club when not playing music? A genius of his stature should have been so much in demand that the National Guard would have to be assigned to keep admirers from crushing him. The same could be said of so many other Afro-American creative geniuses who are either unemployed or working for peanuts while mired down in relative obscurity. Jimmy Smith is known for his incredible virtuosity on the organ, but I think it is somewhat overlooked that he never fails to play with clever and beautiful warmth and in an infectious groove no matter how complex and technical his playing. On slow or medium tempo blues and other tunes, Jimmy Smith is the purest essence of the unique Afro-American music as we know it.

I am a great admirer of tenor saxophonist Stanley Turrentine, alto-sax player Lou Donaldson, and trumpeter Lee Morgan, all of whom did their best work on albums that were organized loosely as solo showcases for Jimmy Smith. It seems to me that the musicians on these albums were inspired to soaring heights by Jimmy Smith's organ playing. Incidentally, one of the disappointments of my career came after having the honor of recording on a Stanley Turrentine album in the early 1970s, when I was doing studio work in Los Angeles. The producer and arranger of that session, Art Freeman, listed the names of everyone at the session except my horn section on the album cover. The tenor sax and flute playing that I did on the album were insignificant, and our horns only played backup to the solos that Turrentine had recorded at an earlier date. However, the album—with a picture of Turrentine in top hat and cane on its cover—was quite successful, and naturally an admirer of Turrentine's such as I am would be proud of any association with him.

The disproportionate rewards and renown available to white musicians have been a part of jazz for a long time. I remember one night in 1946 when I was with Basie, and we were playing the Avalon Ballroom in Los Angeles. Tommy Dorsey suddenly appeared on the bandstand behind Basie, who greeted him warmly as Dorsey sat down on the piano stool beside the Count. The band was in rare form that night with its infectious groove sparked by the drumming of Jo Jones, the lead trumpet work of Snooky Young, and the reed section, which was having one of its better nights. When the band was in good form, Basie was adept at timing the program and scheduling his numbers perfectly. Dorsey was feeling very good, having had a few "nips," but he sat there in disbelief watching the Basie "machine" as the band moved from powerful things to beautiful ballads to light swing numbers to pure blues, and so on. After a while, he could take it no longer, and Dorsey asked Basie if he could take some choruses on the number that was in progress. Of course, Basie nodded his approval. Dorsey swaggered over to the trombone section, and lifted Dicky Wells's instrument from his hands. "Mr. Bones" handed over his horn good-naturedly, and Dorsey moved out to the microphone and began to take some ad-lib solos.

Tommy Dorsey was almost without equal when it came to articulating ballad melodies because of his flawless tone and smooth technique, but his jazz improvisation work was rather miserable. This night he played several choruses of ticky technical exercises that demonstrated his lip control and slide technique, but were meaningless from the standpoint of creative jazz or swing. Suddenly, Mr. Bones became irritated because Dorsey's solos seemed to kill the band's groove and inspiration. Dicky reached over and deftly lifted the trombone from Eli Robinson's hands and headed for the microphone to "get" Dorsey. Realizing that in a contest of jazz solos Dicky Wells would obliterate and embarrass Tommy Dorsey, Basie gave one of his famous signals on the piano, and when Mr. Bones looked over, Basie gave him a very faint wink and shook his head slightly. Dicky understood. He just stood there calmly for a moment watching Dorsey at the mike, and then returned quietly to his seat in the trombone section.

After playing several more choruses of sweet nothings, Dorsey proudly marched over and returned Dicky's trombone, as the audience howled with approval. How ironic that a player with one tenth of Dicky's ability as a jazz soloist had to be protected from this black genius, while the same inferior player enjoyed many times the fame, wealth, and rating in so-called jazz magazines like *Down Beat* and *Metronome*. With all of his stupendous talent and unique improvisational ability, Dicky Wells never received a fraction of the notoriety and reward that Tommy Dorsey enjoyed, and by no stretch of the imagination could anyone judge Dorsey to be Mr. Bones's equal as a jazz player.

My experiences with Dicky Wells weren't that many during the nearly three years we worked together with Basie, but I would rate him with the greatest jazz trombonists of all time. He was a special favorite of mine. In fact, it was Wells who first bestowed the nickname "Red" or "Red Love" upon me. On September 6, 1943, when I auditioned on stage at the Dreamland Ballroom in Omaha to be Earle Warren's temporary replacement, Dicky Wells and the trombone section sat right behind the reeds. After I played the first number, "As Time Goes By," Dicky Wells leaned over and touched the back of my head with his trombone slide and said, "Hey, Red, you sound just like that other red boy sitting beside you." He was referring to Earle Warren. Light-skinned black people were often referred to as "Red" in that day. From that night on, several members of the band always referred to me as "Red," especially Harry Edison and Eli Robinson. In May 1945, when I returned to replace Earle Warren permanently in the band, Dicky Wells was already gone. Basie had fired him for excessive drinking. I was most disappointed, because Dicky was such a great force in Basie's band of that day. When I learned that Dicky was playing with Willie Bryant's orchestra, I went up to catch him at the Savoy Ballroom. I was right at home at the Savoy, having played there several times with the Lucky Millinder Band in 1944 and earlier in 1945. Willie Bryant had a fine band made up entirely of players who had worked with nearly every major big-name band, but it was a big step backward for the great Dicky Wells, who fit so well with the Basie style. Most of the evening I stood in front of Dicky and chatted with him. I told him that I had talked to Basie about him and expressed my disappointment at his absence from the band. Dicky showed great interest in this, because it was obvious that he missed being with Basie. I reported to Dicky that Basie said he could have his job back anytime he would learn to control his liquor. Dicky was ecstatic, and said "all that heavy lushing" was behind him. I reported my conversation to Basie, who informed me that he had already decided secretly to rehire Dicky, but he wanted to "sweat him" a little longer so that he wouldn't go right back to the heavy drinking once he was back in the band. Much to my happiness, Dicky Wells was soon back in the Basie band, and by the time we left for Los Angeles in late June, he was back spitting out his unique trombone solos.

I was informed by various friends that after his wife Cherry's death in the mid or early 1970s, Dicky Wells became a very despondent person. The story is that he allowed some young neighbors into his apartment in New York, and they brutally assaulted him and robbed him. Wells never completely recovered from the beating. I am also told that he had become enormously obese and unkempt. This seemed quite incredible to me, since I remember Dicky Wells as one of the most dapper of all the Basie musicians. His trombone solo on Basie's "Taxi War Dance" will long be remembered as a classic of trombone jazz. If Tommy Dorsey were still alive, I am sure that he would be financially secure and treated as an American institution, but the great jazz man Dicky Wells was forced to work much of the time at things completely unrelated to jazz and to live in relative obscurity during his last years.

In this era, it seems we place a premium upon mediocrity, ineptitude, and amateurism in show business. At least a high standard of musicianship is maintained in the television and movie studios, although this musicianship is based more on acquired ability than natural talent and uniqueness. I have often wondered why such emphasis is put on the caliber of musicianship in studio work when the feature performers and big-name stars (backed by the studio orchestras) are often so mediocre or untalented. The movies and television haven't matured enough to produce shows that feature just good artistic instrumental music and vocals without any distractions or stagy gimmickry. Most of the so-called jazz shows on television are a mockery—models of crass commercialism with nonsensical choreography staged by choreographers and technically trained dancers who don't have the slightest conception of jazz. These eager "ballets" have dancers cavorting around the set supposedly doing some jazz interpretation while distracting from the instrumentalist. Then, too, how often do these "jazz" shows present the real greats of each instrument or the real jazz greats except for the obvious names that are very popular and have drawing power at the moment?

Consider, for example, the lack of recognition and acclaim accorded three men named Clifford: Clifford Jordan, Clifford Solomon, and Clifford Scott. Each of these gifted outstanding tenor saxophonists has a unique and original style of his own, yet none have received their deserved reward. If these players had come along in an earlier era when instrumentalists were venerated, I am sure they would be much more highly esteemed and famous than they are. The late Clifford Solomon is best known for having played with numerous R&B stars including Ray Charles, Ike and Tina Turner, and John Mayall, but he is also a limitless fountain of jazz ideas. He has an unusual command of his instrument and the coordination to execute many of his improvisational gems, but he remains virtually unknown to the general public. The late Clifford Jordan is someone about whom I was ignorant myself until I heard him playing on a marvelous album with the Cedar Walton Trio recorded live at Boomer's in Newark, New Jersey. Like all outstanding jazz players, Jordan plays with exquisite taste, a quality rare from someone who plays so effectively in a very modern vein. Maybe his tasteful playing is what has caused the avant-garde crowd of musicians not to embrace Jordan excitedly, since it isn't considered hip to play tastefully and melodically in this mixed-up era of jazz. Maybe, if he was more "way out," the new jazz crowd would give Jordan more of the recognition due him. Clifford Scott, known as "Scotty," did become fairly well known as a tenor saxophonist because of his memorable solo on Bill Doggett's "Honky Tonk." He also attracted some notice as a flutist for his fine solo on Doggett's recording of "Soft." Yet in proportion to his enormous talent and ability, Scotty still has never been as well known as other tenor-saxophone stars. "Honky Tonk" and "Soft" probably established Scotty as an R&B artist to most people, but he is one of the most inventive and clever improvisers of his time. While improvisational geniuses such as these wallow around in comparative obscurity, there are actually many ungifted people touring the jazz circuit and receiving acclaim from neurotic young musicians who find something appealing about the mysterious and the occult, even if it is undeniably bad music.

If each new generation of jazz musicians wasn't so preoccupied with being accused of stagnation and conservatism, there would always be instrumentalists around whom they could use as models, musicians who are modern yet who retain the essence of creative improvisation and the essence of jazz. Take alto and tenor saxophonist Sonny Stitt, for instance. He can play with incredible speed, accuracy, and originality while still retaining the warmth and beauty generated by the true giants of jazz. He shows the influence of Charlie Parker and Lester Young to a considerable extent, but this doesn't detract from his own individuality and personal genius. Some few years ago, I caught Stitt at the Parisian Room in Los Angeles. A group of free-style fanatics attended the performance and heckled him for not being "modern" enough. I later heard some of those hecklers play at a rehearsal, and they made me aware of what pure imbecility must be like. Not one of them exhibited the slightest semblance of talent for improvisation, yet they scorned Sonny Stitt for being "too melodic" and for not playing "black music" when they attended his engagement at the Parisian Room.

Recently, I rode home in the car of an aspiring young jazz musician, and for nearly one half hour I had to sit listening to his automobile's stereo as it played an album by one of the current "jazz" stars who dawdled, plunked, tinkered, and wheezed endlessly on a collection of electronic keyboard gadgets. There was no form, structure, beat, warmth, beauty, or apparent purpose to the tune he played. Finally, a soprano saxophone entered and whistled and tweedled for an indeterminate number of bars, playing a collection of nonsense that had no relationship or empathy with the keyboard and other accompanying rhythm instruments. As I sat there trying to be generous and broad-minded about this blob of nothingness, the young jazz aspirant drove along with an expression of beatitude on his face. Some nights later, I attended a performance by a band that included this young musician, and he was totally in his element, surrounded by a group of his peers whose music fully reflected the influence of the music I had heard on his car stereo. Most of the players in the group played with very bad intonation and a complete lack of harmonic rationality while their rhythm section was incredibly chaotic. Their solos were often nonsensical, except for those by the saxophonist, trumpet player, and pianist, who did show some improvisational ability. As they assaulted everything meaningful, tasteful, and rational in the name of jazz, their faces displayed expressions of complete fulfillment and satisfaction with what they were doing. Apparently, they had been advised that it might be practical to play something "conventional," so finally the group blundered through some arrangements associated with the likes of Basie and Ellington. These orchestrations really showed the inexperience and ineptness of these young players, but by they were by far the best arrangements they had in their repertoire. I sat there incredulous at this group of black players who looked bored and disgusted when they digressed from their poorly orchestrated avant-garde nonsense to play something that they probably termed traditional or conventional. I expect young players to relate to the big names of their own generation just the same as we did in my youth; this is typical of musicians of every era, but I would expect them to have enough discrimination to distinguish poor playing from good playing in *any* era. Then, too, it is not as though the greats like Ellington and Basie have become relics of the ancient past. It is not as though there is no longer any validity to the values represented by our musical institutions, even if they are older.

It was tragic to see this group of young musicians who had lost sight of real values, because there is no doubt that some of them had real talent, maybe even enormous talent. But even the talented ones will probably be carried along in the current towards musical chaos. I have also observed that in every era, but especially in current times, those with the least ability are often the ones most apt to hide behind a "genius" attitude, usually as a defense to cover up for a lack of talent or ability. I presume that inept players feel encouraged by the fact that there are so many quacks like themselves who have become highly successful in the music business today. This increases the chances for even the worst players to make it, since the best and the worst players nearly all tend to sound alike to laypeople. I have learned to avoid trying to advise young jazz aspirants in this era, although I have encouraged and assisted a number of them since I have become what they would probably call a senior citizen in music. Advice and criticism are generally looked upon as meddling or "bad-mouthing" as some put it. Bad-mouthing is unforgivable for us senior-citizen musicians, although we are usually only offering constructive criticism when we reject musical garbage. Those young would-be geniuses who attack the greats as antiques don't consider their foolish attacks as bad-mouthing, however. To them, the renunciation of Ellington or Basie is synonymous with progress or a matter of being "hip." Of course, I can't blame them entirely, because they read so many jazz critics who, for instance, describe Lester Young's classic solos as "dated" while comparing Prez with the soloists of today, many of whom are copying Lester Young as closely as possible. Certain performances by Basie's original band and *all* Lester Young solos will be valid as long as jazz is played, no matter how many newer concepts come along. Like the younger musicians, I think that jazz columnists should learn that it is not the one who plays the newest but the one who plays the "most" who is the best. We can't adjust or change the standards of ability in each era based merely on what is most modern. Chuck Mangione, for example, might be considered more modern than Clark Terry on flugelhorn by some, but I don't think that anyone would be silly enough to imagine that Mangione plays nearly as well as Clark does.

At one point a particular great drummer renounced the word "jazz" as meaningless, derogatory, and harmful to black music and the black creative musician. He announced he was writing a book entitled *I Hate Jazz*, and I suspect that this viewpoint and mine will be identical in many respects. We may soon see the day when all black musicians will disassociate themselves from this term, which hardly describes authentic black music anymore. I would like to see the term "jazz" ceded to the school music programs, to the uncomprehending writers and critics, and to the white officials who dominate the music business. A more apt term might be "black music" or

"African-American music" to identify this unique and rich art form. There hardly seems any less drastic way to preserve and protect it, because in any competition with whites—especially in the business world—black people have little chance of prevailing because whites control all of the means of informing or misinforming consumers. Then, too, there are always those few black musicians who are willing to cooperate in the theft of our art by others. It seems every town has some "Uncle Remus" types who sell out their people's indigenous music to the local white musical establishment. It is not unusual to see a local Uncle Remus leading his so-called jazz group with all or nearly all white players except himself. The fact that these groups are often playing a very mediocre or even poor grade of "jazz" is usually insignificant to the laypeople of these localities because the "white hype" syndrome comes into play. In my hometown of Omaha, of course, I have been branded as racist for pointing this out; it doesn't sit well with the local "patriotism" of the town.

The jazz musicians of my generation are probably the last cohort of musicians who will be able to bring authentic firsthand knowledge to the youth of ensuing generations. We are old enough to have lived through a large portion of the formative years of jazz, which enabled us to observe the development of this art form and to associate with many of the greatest jazz players in person. Yet we are both young enough and old enough to identify with both the very old and the very new jazz. We learned about jazz through participation and firsthand experience as opposed to learning about it from the printed word.

I don't regard myself as a reformer or a crusader, but I have always been much more concerned when those who write about music fail to give due recognition to the really significant artists in jazz history, many of whom have not received attention. Since I am not one of the most important figures in jazz history, it is no concern to me to be omitted from anyone's jazz encyclopedia. I am disturbed, however, when I read an article by Leonard Feather eulogizing a violin player/technician as a *jazz* player when this particular individual is no more a *jazz* violinist to my ears than Yehudi Menuhin is.

I think it is the duty of those entrusted with making appraisals to make very definitive statements of their opinions, even if their subjective viewpoint might disagree with that of their readers. After all, writers such as Stanley Dance, the late Leonard Feather, Frank Driggs, Whitney Balliett, and others receive handsome fees for reviewing musical performances and for writing liner notes for recordings and for other writings. I feel it is their duty to commit themselves and to attempt to instruct young music fans (and older ones, too) about the art they report on. Most of the experts and writers express very definite opinions in private conversations and off the record, but they become very cautious and vague when they write for public consumption. There is no question that the young will grow defensive and perhaps even hostile when a critic attacks their heroes and criticizes their popular music. There is no doubt that whites will be offended when you describe jazz, rhythm and blues, or blues as "black music" and point out that many of their white jazz stars are very poor players. But the music authorities say these things in private conversations with trusted friends. They say them furtively but very definitively in secret, but almost never publicly.

On a television tribute to Benny Goodman some years ago, jazz critic Whitney Balliett quickly and almost inaudibly told the host that "Duke Ellington and Count Basie were probably better than Goodman's popular band of the swing era." What Balliett should have said was, "Count Basie's was the greatest swing band in history, and Goodman's band didn't remotely compare to Basie's for swing. Duke Ellington's band was by far the greatest jazz band of big-band history. The bands of Jimmie Lunceford, Fletcher Henderson, and countless other black bandleaders could out-swing and play much more meaningful jazz than Goodman or any other white band of the big-band era." Unfortunately, Balliettt's few quick words to the television-show host probably went unnoticed by the millions of television viewers. Stanley Dance and Frank Driggs are two of the most knowledgeable persons of the jazz literati, but my two good friends become quite cautious when it comes to expressing their views and when making judgments. I would respect and probably agree with nearly everything they would have to say about jazz.

Some years ago, my five-piece group was playing at one of the small clubs in Omaha's black community. For a change, I had one of my better rhythm sections, so we were able to play a few jazz songs instead of our usual program of nearly all the latest funk hit recordings. I was therefore able to get off some of my better solos. After our second intermission, a young black fellow approached me and identified himself as a new guitar player in town who was teaching the instrument at our largest local music store. He appeared to be in his late twenties. He was interested in getting some gigs with any local "jazz" combo that was working steadily. His conversation went, "Man, I notice you guys play mostly funk and rhythm and blues. You do pretty good when you play old jazz things like 'Wave' on your flute and songs like 'Satin Doll' and 'Billie's Bounce' on your saxes." He then asked me how I liked a new "fusion" jazz group that was enjoying such popularity in the area. I could tell by his manner that he approved of them. Knowing what his reaction would be to my actual feelings about the fusion group, I became evasive and ambiguous, but the young guitar player prodded me for a definitive statement or appraisal. Time grew short as the intermission was coming to an end, so finally I told him that first of all, fusion is not my cup of tea and that, second, the new local fusion group showed me no particular ability for playing real jazz. I told him that not one of the individuals in the group had any unusual talent for jazz, although all of them were good enough *musicians.*

The guitar player looked at me as though he thought I was jesting, and said, "You mean as *improvisational* jazz?" as though it were something vulgar and unmentionable. I answered, "Is there really any *other* kind?" He then let me know that he thought that improvisational jazz was something out of date and that fusion is just about the only real jazz. I told him that I had respect for the ability of the fusion group's members as well-trained musicians so far as reading music and technique are concerned, but none of them had shown any particular talent or ability for improvisation, creativity, expression, or interpretation of the convoluted arrangements that comprised their entire repertoire. I told him that I would rather refer to them as the *con*fusion band. The guitar player replied, "But, their bass player, John Scott, is really good." "Yes, he is a fine young musician," I said, "but I am talking specifically about jazz, not just overall technical musicianship." The guitar player walked away slowly as our band returned to the bandstand, and I could just hear what he was thinking to himself, "That old narrow-minded sax player. He is out of step with what is hip now. He probably thinks Duke Ellington, Count Basie, Lester Young, and Louis Armstrong were great jazz players. Too bad he and those young guys in his group don't get modern and play some real jazz—some fusion."

So-called fusion jazz has opened the door for thousands of players with no talent whatsoever for jazz or jazz improvisation to bestow upon themselves the title of "jazz musician," since in this style of playing the general public can't distinguish between the players with the true gift for jazz and those who have none. In essence, fusion jazz has been an escape valve or a means of "copping out" for hordes of players who once would have been recognized as being devoid of the jazz gift. A number of fine, even great, jazz players have gone out and begun to play fusion because this style enjoys some popularity today. There is also a need for great players to constantly prove that they can change with the times and with each new innovation or musical fad. Unfortunately, when a real jazz player becomes involved with very bad players, the public can hardly separate them from the charlatans they surround themselves with nor differentiate between those who have the ear for improvisation and those who are playing plain nonsense on their instruments. If a player must resort to fusion, I would at least like to know if he was first capable of playing conventionally with good harmonics, good chord progressions, and ideas that indicate he has some grasp of melody. I certainly don't intend this as a put-down of the fusion style of jazz, but rather as an indictment of those who use this style as a cover-up for the lack of the true jazz gift.

Innovation for the sake of innovation is meaningless to this writer. It has its place in art and technology, but in art or music it should come about only when it happens spontaneously, as in the case of such great jazz innovators as Charlie Parker and Lester Young. Only in cases where innovation is an improvement over the past should it be regarded as worthy of replacing that which has been the standard. Then, too, the styles of each era should be able to coexist side by side without either one being considered superior to the other. In this era, great music isn't allowed to coexist with the dross of rock and some funk. Hence, all popular or commercially successful music is considered to be superior and more worthy than any other music of any other era. Popular music aimed at the youth market seldom has any artistic value or any qualities that will endure for more than the few months of its popularity. One can hardly blame the very young for the fact that they know almost nothing about their true musical heritage. This is especially true where black youths are concerned. They are constantly exposed to inane videos on the television stations and bombarded with rap music and other music, most of which insults a person's intelligence. Live music, especially jazz, has almost disappeared from the nightclubs and lounges in the black communities of most cities. Instead, the clubs feature deejays who spin recordings of the latest hits while talking jive talk and the jargon of the moment. The music is played so loud that it assaults one's hearing. To the young fans, even some in their thirties and forties, these record spinners or deejays are considered the musical authorities or musical experts of the community, although the deejays' only musical expertise is the ability to read the latest charts listing the most popular recordings of the minute, to buy these recordings, and to put them on a turntable. The young fans have even become contemptuous of their local instrumental musicians. Singers are tolerated only if they closely imitate the singers on the latest hit recordings and if they sing nothing but the latest pop, funk, or rock hits. Young fans openly declare that they *prefer* deejays and the recordings to live in-person music. Several deejays in each city become local celebrities and musical "stars" around their towns. Yet every time I see Wynton Marsalis on television or hear him being interviewed on radio, my chest swells with pride that a new young black star could be so knowledgeable and outspoken about the contribution of blacks to the music of this country. What Marsalis has to say is usually irrefutable and so well expressed. Fortunately, his genius as a player is so wonderful that he can't be discredited or ignored when he speaks out. Unfortunately, it seems as if his efforts on behalf of his black brothers are wasted on some black fans. They hardly take notice of the profound things this young genius is saying.

In 1996, at the age of seventy-five, I find my musical career at its apex, at least in the years since our return to Omaha. My musical fortunes have experienced a sudden surge largely because of an elegant restaurant–supper club in Omaha, the Bistro at the Market near the city's old market district. Starting in October 1994 my four- (and sometimes five-) piece group was engaged as the house band at this wonderful venue, which I would regard as comparable to any supper club or jazz club in the universe. Its food and its decor both compare to the best anywhere. From the very beginning, the club's management and employees have treated my musicians, my singers, and me like royalty. The size of the crowds and the degree of their acceptance of our music have both been stupendous. Because of the Bistro, our group has become possibly the busiest of Omaha's local musical groups. We have played every weekend, every holiday, and every party or banquet given at the Bistro since November 1994. Because of this venue, my group has also become virtually the official musical group for several very wealthy dignitaries and professional people in the area, and I have become friends with some of the city's most wonderful and supportive people. My music has never been as appreciated in my hometown as it has been in the past two years or so. Because of the steady playing and because of the wide variety of musical styles we are forced to play, I feel that I play all of my instruments (alto sax, tenor sax, flute, and soprano sax) better than at anytime in my career.

My employment at the *Omaha Star*, Nebraska's only black newspaper, does not interfere in the least with my musical activities, in spite of the fact that I have been the newspaper's advertising manager for seven years, as well as the author of occasional articles in both the *Star* and the local daily *Omaha World-Herald*. The presentation of "jazz" in Omaha has been mired in politics and cronyism for all of the twenty-five years that we have been back in Omaha, but it has gotten even worse during the past ten years or so. We simply can't attract or retain highly capable world-class jazz or R&B players in Omaha. My son Norman finally gave up in frustration and hopelessness and moved out to Denver and Los Angeles, where he is becoming a huge force in their jazz scenes. Norm is an immensely talented improviser on the saxophone. On the other hand, my son Ritchie, a fine rhythm and blues saxophonist, singer, and producer, has chosen to stay and fight it out with the political structure of the city's music business.

Preston Love's son Norman Love.

The presentation of jazz on the local scene is dominated by power organizations and decision makers who are young people, usually young females who were actually rock fans most of their lives, totally unknowledgeable about jazz and Omaha's once-proud history in the nation's jazz chain. They have reduced the black players to a rank minority of persons engaged for local jazz presentations. Their selections are very political and steeped in cronyism without regard for the actual ability (or lack of same) of those they favor. I have spoken out against these vehemently in my columns and on my weekly radio show, "Love Notes," so naturally the name Preston Love has become anathema to the real powers in Omaha jazz. Thank God, the Bistro has helped to make it possible for me to speak out openly without concern for the reprisals that are inevitable when one dares to tell the truth about injustice. Omaha's current jazz scene and presentation defiles the memory of those many truly great jazz players that once abounded in my beloved hometown. Having once been such a major part of the nation's black music and the jazz world because of our central location, Omaha in the past twenty years or so has completely atrophied as an important music and jazz center. In years gone by, musicians from Denver, Kansas City, and Minneapolis came to Omaha to join our local groups. They treated coming here the same as if they were joining some band in

New York or Chicago, but things have changed. Recently, I appeared in Denver as the guest lead-alto player in a big band. While I was there, I was able to observe how much greater the quality of jazz musicianship is there as compared with Omaha. Denver jazz is now world-class; Omaha's is far from it, after our once having been leagues ahead. I feel no regret at offering myself as the sacrificial lamb by speaking out openly and tenaciously against what we have allowed to happen to my city's black music.

It has been a long and sometimes emotion-filled odyssey, these sixty years since the fifteen-year-old kid played drums with Warren Webb and His Spiders on that Saturday night at the Aeroplane Inn in the village of Honey Creek, Iowa. Now, at seventy-five, I reflect upon those hundreds of towns and cities that my musical career has taken me to since 1936. All of these places became my "Honey Creek," and all the venues my Aeroplane Inn, since I owe all of it, the good and the less than good alike, to that humble beginning in that little village seventeen miles northeast of Omaha. The two-dollar pay for that evening seemed like riches to that kid from the abject poverty and privation of the Love Mansion. It would have been incredible to me to think that I would go on to earn on occasion several thousand dollars for one-night's work as an orchestra leader or music contractor, or well over a thousand dollars as a sideman for one-day's performance as a studio musician. The odyssey has come full circle, because my 1971 return to Omaha brought on certain periods during the 1970s and 1980s that I would describe as the nadir of my career, but now comes a moment that finds me at one of the high points of my life and of a career that has had many peaks and valleys.

Index

Gordy, Berry, 161
Gower, Bob, 225
Grant, Cornelius, 158
Grant, Henry, 157
Grant Music Center, Los Angeles, 157
Gray, Glenn, 8
Great Depression, 3, 7, 19
Green, Freddie, 25, 63, 68, 75, 81, 182, *199*,
    207, 209, 212, 213, 240; and Countsmen
    tour, 188, 189, 190, 192, 195; as guitar
    essence of Basie sound, 183, 184,
    208–209; and Preston Love, 185
Green, Vivien (wife of Jo Jones), 25
Green, Walter, 93, 94
Greenberg, Carl, 160, 161
Grey, Al, 182, 184
Grievious, Sam, 131
Griffith, Bill, 156
Grissom, Dan, 175
Guide to Jazz (Panassie), 196, 239
Guy, Joe, 71

Haley, Bill, 136, 231
Hall, Rene, 67
Hampton, Lionel, 94, 222
Hancock, Herbie, 222
Harding, Buster "Boot Whip," 86, 198
Hardwicke, Otto, 24, 226, 236
Harris, Wynonie "Mr. Blues," 15, 16, *33*, 73,
    74
Harry James band, 80–81
Hawkins, Coleman, 220, 222, 226, 233
Hawkins, Erskine: band, 73, 76, 183, 236
Hayes, Isaac, 166, 219, 231
Hayes, Thamon (band), 236
Hefti, Neal, 241
Henderson, Fletcher, 19, 222, 226, 229, 234,
    236, 238, 243
Henderson, Horace, 234, 243
Henry, Heywood, 183, 185, 198, *199*
Hentoff, Nat, 238
Herman, Woody, 234, 239, 240–241
Hess, Norbert, 33, 238
"High Tide," 76
Hiles, Buddy, 243
Hi Los, 171
Hines, Earl "Fatha," 8, 19, 23, 41, 222, 226,
    229, 230, 233, 234, 236, 238, 243
Hines, Frank, 145
Hite, Les, 82, 236
Hodges, Johnny, 23, 125, 216, 222, 226, 230,
    237
Holiday, Billie, 74, 158, 219, 236, 238

Holloway, Brenda, 157, 165, 167
Hollywood Bowl, 165
Holmes, Nathaniel "Georgetown," 90, 94,
    105
"Honky Tonk" (Bill Doggett), 84, 248
Hoops, Wilbur, 34, 39, 44, 48
Hopkins, Claude, 234, 236
Hotel Roswell, Roswell, New Mexico,
    139–141
Hotel Theresa, New York, 71, 75
"Hound Dog," 128
House of David basketball team, Sioux City,
    Iowa, 7
Howard White Booking Agency, 86–87, 90,
    91, 97
Humes, Helen, 25
Humphrey, Oliver, 34, 39, 40, 44
Humphrey, Paul, 175
Hunt, Marshall, 166, 219
Hunter, Lloyd, 51–53, 58, 61, 70–71, 127;
    band, 67, 88, 201, 210, 236
"Hurry, Hurry," 74

"Idaho," 86
"I Dream a Lot About You," 216
"I Found a New Baby," 63
"I Had a Premonition," 216
I Hate Jazz, 250
"I Just Can't See For Lookin'," 74
"I'll Never Smile Again," 34
"Imagination," 34
"I'm Still in Love With You," 219
Ink Spots, 69
Internal Revenue Service, 113, 124, 127, 151,
    153, 155, 156
International Sweethearts of Rhythm, 161
"In The Mood," 89, 98
Iowa Arts Council, 203, 225
"It's Sand, Man," 79, 184, 187
"I Want a Big Fat Mama," 69

Jackson, Bull Moose, 27, 74
Jackson, John, 226
Jackson, Oliver, 193
Jacksons, the, 180
Jacquet, Illinois, 60
Jacquet, Julius, 32, 33, 35, 39, 40, 43, 50
Jamerson, James, 180
James, Emmett, 63–64
James, Harry, 216, 234–235, 239
jazz: American *versus* international view of,
    220; *versus* bebop, 79; black music and,
    89–90, 229, 231; chord progressions in,

music styles, 216; accompanists and, 216; African–American, 204–206; art *versus* business, 222; bebop, 79, 225; of Count Basie, 182, 184; funk, 252; fusion jazz, 252–253; jazz, 202–203; Kansas City style, 184; manipulation of, 233–234; merchandising of, 220–221; on military bases, 135–136; pop, 202; popular, 171, 254; rhythm and blues, 202, 216, 231, 238; rhythm section and, 209; rock and roll, 231; soul, 171, 216

"Mutton Leg," 75

"My Girl," 158

"My Old Flame," 84

Nanton, Sam, 226

Nashville West Studio, Los Angeles, 166–167

Nathan, Syd, 105, 108, 110, 121

National Endowment for the Arts, 203, 225

National Orchestra Service (NOS), 131–133, 146–148, 149, 151–152

Nelson, Mike "Spike," 206

Newman, Joe, 75, 182, 185, 188, 195

New Orleans, 74

New Year's Eve gigs, 50

Nicholson, Gladys, 115, 116

Nicholson, Perkins, 115, 116

"920 Special," 184, 187, 198

NOS. *See* National Orchestra Service

Oakwood Manor, Chicago, 67, 68

Omaha, Nebraska, 32, 41, 48, 62, 255–257; black section of, 52; Central High School, 7; Dundee section, 15; Hospe's Music Store, 77; Near North Side, 2, 15; Orpheum Theater, 69, 178; Paxton Hotel, 4, 7; Pop's Buffet, 49. *See also* venues, Nebraska

Omaha Star, 184, 255

Omaha World-Herald, 62, 87, 208, 255

"One O'Clock Jump" (Basie), 22, 23, 62–63, 70, 77, 184, 191, 229, 230

Orr, Claude, 151–153, 155

Otis, Johnny, 98, 148, 153–154, *154*, 156, 213; band, 84, 124, 126–28, 158, 202, 210, 236; and Club Barrel House, 86; as composer, 109, 110, 123; and "Cry Baby," 94; in Denver, 54, 55; and George Morrison combo, 58; and King Records, 105, 121; and Lloyd Hunter band, 59, 62; at Meadowbrook, 83–84; and Peacock Records, 128; at Sloppy Joe's Tavern, 63

Otis, Phyllis, 54, 57, 58, 126–127, 130

"Out the Window," 214

Overton, Ray, 115

Owens, Charles, 212

Pacoima, California, 244

Page, Hot Lips, 81

Page, Walter, 9, 22, 25, 55, 63, 75, 76, 78, 184, 189, 209, 212, 230, 237

Panassie, Hugues, 196, 238, 239

Papillion, Nebraska, 56

Parker, Bobby, 54, 55, 58

Parker, Charlie, 76, 86, 158, 180, 216, 221–222, 226, 230, 232–233, 235, 242, 248, 254

Parker, Maxine "The Red Fox," 77

Parsons, Kansas, 13

Patterson, Alladin, 20

Patterson, Bruce, 20, 21

Patterson, Francis, 20

Patterson Brothers, 20

Patton, Mrs.: rooming house, Omaha, 126

Payne, Freda, 166

Payne, Sonny, 212

Peacock Records, 128

"People," 175

Peterson, Oscar, 222

Pettiford, Oscar, 210, 226

Phillips, Johnny "Brother," 122, 124

Phillips, Little Esther, 98, 122, 123, 126; and the Robins, 105

Pierce, Nat, 184, 185, 187, 188, 189, 192–193, 197, *199*

Pillars, Hayes, 67

Pleasants, Ed, 166

politics in local music, 178, 179

Pollard, Isadore, 34, 39, 40, 43, 44, 45

Pope, Kent, 27, 74

Powell, Jimmy, 75

Presley, Elvis, 136, 221, 222, 231, 234, 241

Preston Love Orchestra, 87, *135*, 217, *208*; bus accident and, 150–151; and bus trouble, 101–117; disbands temporarily, 124, 125; and Duffy Goodlow, 146; and Green Hornet bus, 100; at Hotel Roswell, 139–141; integration of, 206; and National Orchestra Service, 131–133, 146–148; overseas travel and, 147, 149; and Royce Stoenner, 97, 98–100, 102, 105, 110, 113, 118, 121; and Texas tour (1950), 91–97

Price, C. Q., 81, 83, 182, 183

Price, Gladys "Sumac," 132

Prima, Louis, 80–81

Prochaska, Felix, 238

UNIVERSITY PRESS OF NEW ENGLAND publishes books under its own imprint and is the publisher for Brandeis University Press, Dartmouth College, Middlebury College Press, University of New Hampshire, Tufts University, and Wesleyan University Press.

PRESTON LOVE is a distinguished musician and jazz/Motown authority. Over the course of his life he has played alto saxophone with such figures as Johnny Otis, Count Basie, Ray Charles, Aretha Franklin, and Ike and Tina Turner. He received an Honorary Doctorate of Music from Creighton University in 1992 and in 1994 received the Urban League of Nebraska's National Prominence Award.

LIBRARY OF CONGRESS CATALOGING-IN-PUBLICATION DATA
Love, Preston.
A thousand Honey Creeks later : my life in music from Basie to
Motown—and beyond / Preston Love : introduction by George Lipsitz.
    p. cm.
    Includes index.
    ISBN 0-8195-6318-8 (cloth : alk. paper). — ISBN 0-8195-6320-X (pbk. : alk. paper)
1. Love, Preston. 2. Saxophonists—United States—Biography.
I. Title
ML419.L67A3 1997
788.7'3165'092
[B]—DC21   97-14684